Interaction in Action

Reflections on the Use of Intensive Interaction

Edited by

Dave Hewett and Melanie Nind

David Fulton Publishers
London

David Fulton Publishers Ltd
The Chiswick Centre, 414 Chiswick High Road, London W4 5TF
www.fultonpublishers.co.uk

First published in Great Britain in 1998 by David Fulton Publishers

Note: The rights of Dave Hewett and Melanie Nind to be
identified as the authors of this work have been asserted by them in accordance
with the Copyright, Designs and Patents Act 1988.

David Fulton Publishers is a division of Granada Learning Limited, part of
Granada plc.

British Library Cataloguing in Publication Data
A catalogue record for this book is available from the British Library.

ISBN 1-85346-461-9

Typeset by Textype Typesetters, Cambridge
Printed and bound in Great Britain

Contents

Preface

Melanie Nind and Dave Hewett

Our aim in editing *Interaction in Action* is to follow up on the thinking and practical guidance contained in our previous work on Intensive Interaction. We hope to illustrate that Intensive Interaction is not just something that goes on in hospital schools. Here we see the approach used not only by teachers, but also by speech therapists, occupational therapists, social workers, psychologists and parents. We see the approach used in people's homes as well as in education and day centres. We see the approach used with very young children through to mature adults and with people with all kinds of complex needs. The contributors have been asked to share their insights, the way they think about Intensive Interaction as well as the way that they 'do' it. This means that the chapters contain both reflective analysis and vivid description. The contributions illustrate how Intensive Interaction has grown and developed as an educational approach and as a way of being with people, and they illustrate the impact on all those involved.

Our contribution to *Interaction in Action* has been in finding some interesting people with interesting stories to tell. There are many more practitioners of Intensive Interaction who could add their stories. We hope that the book will stimulate in these practitioners and other readers some of the fruitful dialogue and collaboration that we have enjoyed while in the process of working on it. We have also contributed commentaries on the contributors' chapters which bring together some important themes which emerge and relate this to how our thinking has been developing. We place the growing use of Intensive Interaction in the context of other recent developments in the field and we end by looking to the future and to developments and challenges which we may look forward to.

Our intention is that *Interaction in Action* will be relevant for practitioners across a range of disciplines and for parents also. With this diverse audience in mind the choice of terminology has, of course, been an issue for us. 'People with learning difficulties' and 'people with learning disabilities' are both used in this volume, reflecting not a different group of people being referred to, but the differences in language use between education and some other services. In the different contexts referred to there is the different language of children, pupils, students, clients and service-users as appropriate. At times the shorthand of students/clients has been unavoidable. We have always tried to emphasise the person first and to use language which is both helpful and respectful.

In chapter 1, we offer a description and explanation of Intensive Interaction for those readers who are less familiar with the approach and its history and principles. We discuss where, how and to what extent Intensive Interaction is being used and researched and how this book fits in with this. We review recent developments and pertinent literature and place the work in its current context. Chapters 2, 3 and 4 are accounts of Intensive Interaction in use in educational settings. In chapter 2, Chris Addis discusses the relevance of Intensive Interaction for his unit supporting pupils with multi-sensory impairment. In chapter 3, Christine Smith reflects on a single case study of using the approach with a young adult in a further education college; and in chapter 4, Carol Peters offers a detailed account of the highs and lows of working in this way with a pupil in an integrated nursery. In chapter 5, we draw out the wealth of practical guidance on doing Intensive Interaction contained within these (and other) chapters in the book.

The next three chapters focus our attention on Intensive Interaction in different settings. In chapter 6, Cath Irvine reflects on the changes in day services for adults with PMLD and the use of Intensive Interaction as part of a drive to make these more meaningful for this marginalised group. In chapter 7, Judith Samuel and Jaqui Maggs describe the introduction of the approach with a similar client group, but in their home settings, including some mini-case studies and the implications which can be drawn from them. They also provide a comprehensive overview of some of the cultural shifts in thinking about 'ordinary living' as the context for the developments. In chapter 8, Val Stothard reflects on how Intensive Interaction has gradually evolved in her special school across a five-year time-span. The institutional issues of getting Intensive Interaction established in varied settings form the focus of our second commentary in chapter 9. Here we are concerned not with 'how to do it', but how to manage the staffing and staff attitudes, how we may resolve or handle some of the conflicts with other approaches, the effect upon the workplace ethos and some controversial aspects, particularly the use of physical contact.

The next two chapters are about Intensive Interaction with children with autism and we end with parental accounts. In chapter 10, Lynne Knott and colleagues provide a vivid account of the way they used Intensive Interaction with a pupil with autism, describing the decision-making and the progress within the staff team. In chapter 11, Beth and Steve Taylor reflect on their journey to find an approach which would allow them to connect with their son who has autism, and they relate what is important about Intensive Interaction to them as parents. In chapter 12, Ian and Antonella Bruce relate a struggle to get the support they want for their daughter. They highlight some important issues for working in collaboration and describe how they interacted with their child through difficult times. In the final commentary we reflect on the relevance of Intensive Interaction for individuals whose learning difficulties are compounded by autism. We also look at the issues which arise for parents doing Intensive Interaction. In the final chapter we address the issue of how we may become better facilitators of communication development and examine some of the factors helping and hindering future progress here. We explore some thoughts about the ways in which learning experiences in interactions are structured and how we might most usefully think about and develop our thinking on such structures.

There are, of course, themes which run throughout the book and readers will find much resonance between the chapters. We found that there were both common and idiosyncratic challenges being faced by the contributors and common and idiosyncratic solutions and ways of working. We hope that reflection on these reflections will help to move us on in our understandings in a relatively new area of work, and that these case studies and narratives serve to complement the more empirical, traditionally focused research. All of us involved with the book share common goals about enhancing the quality of life, social experience and communicative competence of the people we work with and care for. This shared purpose and focus helped to make working on the book a largely heartening and definitely stimulating and enjoyable experience.

We would like to acknowledge our gratitude to Sarah Forde for her work in assisting us with the preparation of this book.

List of Contributors

Chris Addis is a teacher of pupils with multi-sensory impairment in the Multi-Sensory Support Unit of Manchester Royal School for the Deaf.

Ian and Antonella Bruce are the parents of a pre-school child who has profound developmental delay.

Cath Irvine is a specialist speech and language therapist for adults with learning difficulties and coordinator of the Six Acres (PMLD) Project with Somerset Social Services.

Lynne Knott is a teacher at MacIntyre Trust's Wingrave School.

Jaqui Maggs is Senior Occupational Therapist with the Vale Community Team for People with Learning Disability and the Multiple Disability Resource Team of the Oxfordshire Learning Disability NHS.

Carol Peters teaches pupils with a wide range of special needs in Millbrook/Fitzwaryn integrated nursery in Oxfordshire.

Judith Samuel is Consultant Clinical Psychologist and Coordinator of the Multiple Disability Resource Team of the Oxfordshire Learning Disability NHS Trust.

Christine Smith is a teacher of young people and adults with learning difficulties at Park Lane College of Further Education in Leeds.

Val Stothard is a teacher of secondary aged pupils with severe and complex learning difficulties at St Piers, Lingfield.

Beth and Steve Taylor (not their real names) are parents of a primary aged child with autism and severe learning difficulties. They also work in special education and Steve is the headteacher of an SLD school.

Chapter 1

Introduction: Recent Developments in Interactive Approaches

Dave Hewett and Melanie Nind

Introduction: the approach

Most readers of this book will already be familiar with Intensive Interaction, through reading, staff development or practice. As familiarity cannot be assumed for all readers, however, and as many may appreciate some recapping, a summary of the main features and a rationale for Intensive Interaction is given below. These are explained in full in *Access to Communication* (Nind and Hewett, 1994).

Intensive Interaction is an approach to teaching and spending time with people with learning disabilities which is aimed specifically at facilitating the development of the most fundamental social and communication abilities. Intensive Interaction is based on the model of caregiver–infant interaction and makes use of the implicit pedagogical style (Carlson and Bricker, 1982) which characterises the playful interactive process. The underlying premises are that:

- for individuals with severe and complex learning disabilities, developing these abilities to relate to others and to communicate are the primary learning needs and the priority for quality of life
- making developments here will make all subsequent teaching and learning easier and more enjoyable
- the processes fundamental to the interaction sequences which take place between caregivers and infants in the early months provide a model for how these developments are facilitated
- these processes can be applied in our work but this needs to be done with intensity, sensitivity and critical reflection.

The intention is to make use of what we know about how the rudiments of sociability and communication are ordinarily learned in infancy and to extrapolate from this a model for teaching and relating. This means taking into account what we know about normal and delayed or abnormal development, and it means using a combination of intuitive processes (we teach infants to communicate without knowing how we do it) and intelligent reflection on these processes. It does not mean an attempt to re-parent or to compensate for missed experiences, nor does it advocate treating individuals with learning disabilities as if they were babies.

Intensive Interaction is characterised by regular, frequent interactions between the practitioner (be that teacher, carer, professional from a range of disciplines) and individual with learning disabilities, in which there is no task or outcome focus, but in which the primary concern is the quality of the interaction itself. For this summary we use the term 'learner' to refer to the person with learning disabilities who is learning through the process about sociability and communication, but do not intend any assumption that this learner is only in a formal educational setting. The method can be summed up as follows:

- The practitioner of Intensive Interaction begins by subjectively getting to know the learner, getting a feel for the kinds of interactions which might be enjoyable, tentatively trying out various activities and tempos, working towards an initial connection ('accessing').
- This early work is developed into a familiar repertoire of mutually enjoyable interactive games and playful ritualised routines.
- These interactions gradually become more sophisticated and reciprocal and the learner is enabled to take a more active role.
- Throughout the interactions the practitioner modifies her/his interpersonal behaviours to make her/his facial expressions, body language, vocal and gaze behaviours interesting and meaningful. This often means joining in with or imitating aspects of the learner's behaviour and using a much simplified style of speech.
- The practitioner makes careful use of watching, waiting and timing. This may involve rhythms of activity blended with the rhythms of the learner's behaviour or dramatically timed pauses and bursts of activity.
- The practitioner responds contingently to the learner's behaviour. This creates a sense in which the activities are led by the learner who is thus given considerable control over their content and duration.

- The practitioner imputes intentionality. S/he credits the learner with thoughts, feelings and intentions. S/he attributes social meaning to actions and responds to behaviours as if they have intentional and communicative significance, long before this is so. This intentionality is clear in the responsive behaviour of the practitioner to the learner.

These features of the approach clearly have a basis in what the psychological literature has highlighted as significant processes in caregiver–infant interaction. The repertoire of playful routines provides the safe and stimulating context for exploring the effects of one's behaviour (McConkey, 1989) and for learning the conversational rules of joint reference and turn-taking (Field, 1979). The absence of task means that one's efforts are not judged against concepts of 'rightness' or 'wrongness' but that learning takes place in an overriding positive context. The practitioner has a role in 'scaffolding' the experiences so that there is an optimum balance of the known and the challenging (Bruner, 1983). The modified interpersonal behaviours are like those which infants elicit from their caregivers which are most helpful to development at their particular stage (Stern, 1974; Pawlby, 1977). The simplified linguistic code is like the 'motherese' which Snow (1977) found to be important in supporting language development. The emphasis on timing comes from the role this plays in infant development in creating turn-taking (Kaye, 1977), and maintaining optimum levels of arousal (Beebe, 1985). The contingent responding was found by Goldberg (1977) to create the all important sense of efficacy for the infant. The significance of imputing intentionality for facilitating the transition to truly intentional communication behaviour can be seen in the work of Schaffer (1977) and Newson (1979).

The premise which underlies Intensive Interaction is that learning to communicate and to be social is not like learning a basic skill which can be task-analysed and its constituent sub-skills taught separately in a structured programme. Learning to communicate involves learning about oneself and others, it involves learning that we can have an effect on others and that we can share meaning. To be effective communicators we have to want to communicate, to have a concept of what communication is all about, and simultaneously to apply many complex and inter-related skills. The only model we have for teaching all this is in caregiver–infant interaction.

When practitioners apply principles from caregiver–infant interaction to work with older children and adults with learning disabilities in Intensive Interaction, they are faced with all kinds of challenges and dilemmas. Some of these are practical and some are philosophical. Successful practitioners of Intensive Interaction manage to combine spontaneous, intuitive responding with extreme sensitivity to the idiosyncratic needs and behaviours of the individual and an intellectualisation of the developmental principles being applied. They develop an interactive 'style' which permeates their whole way of being with the learner(s), creating an optimal environment for communication to develop. The challenges they face are not just with the learners themselves, however, but with how others see their role. Controversial issues such as age appropriateness, which arise with the use of this method, are discussed in our earlier work (see for example, Nind and Hewett, 1996), and are included here in the reflections of the various contributors to this volume.

Where are we now – in practice?

There is clearly a well-established and still growing interest in Intensive interaction and interactive techniques in general in work with people with severe learning difficulties. Travelling around the country, it is easy to meet professionals everywhere in education, social services, health and the voluntary sector who know about interactive approaches or who are keen to know more. In many schools, day centres and residential establishments, it is possible to see staff employing the techniques. Interactive techniques are included on courses for special needs teaching and books on these matters can be found in the libraries of universities where teacher education takes place. A large county social services authority has set up a long-term evaluation project on Intensive Interaction and ensures that all staff who work with people with learning difficulties have at least initial training in the approach. Other social services authorities have adopted similar service-wide training commitments. Virtually all of the speech and communication therapists one meets seem at least academically conversant with the issues.

There continues to be a healthy debate in special education about the relative worth and the conflicts between objectives-driven curricula and process-orientated ones. Interactive approaches are referred to by both 'camps' in the debate and the work given to the implementation of the National Curriculum in special schools does not seem to have dulled it.

From our point of view as advocates of interactive approaches and of one interactive approach in particular, we could be beguiled into believing that something akin to a general adoption of what we are interested in has taken place. We might be misled into thinking that Intensive Interaction is well established in the armoury of practitioners in our field. We do not believe this to be the case.

It is our perception that with the approach for which we are responsible, we are well into a period of establishing the adoption of it. However, we are most assuredly still within the period of establishing its general use. It may even be a fragile period for the work that we advocate. We estimate that there are still so many more professionals everywhere who are not versed in the ideas, have not even heard the ideas, than those who have familiarity or are already integrating them into their practice.

As part of a research project to find where and why Intensive Interaction is used (Nind, 1996-98, Oxford Brookes University) data have been gathered which give a more informed picture of the extent of take-up of interactive approaches generally and Intensive Interaction in particular. Questionnaires were sent to 118 special schools, units and resource bases across the four counties of Berkshire, Buckinghamshire, Hertfordshire and Oxfordshire with approximately half (58) returned. Of these returned about 70 per cent (40) use interactive approaches and about 20 per cent (11) use Intensive Interaction. Removal of the schools where one would not regard Intensive Interaction as appropriate (providers for pupils who are hearing impaired, in hospital education, have moderate learning difficulties, have specific learning difficulties, have emotional and behavioural difficulties, and who do not have additional severe or complex learning disabilities) gives a more accurate indication of the take up. This leaves 32 respondents, a third of whom indicate that Intensive Interaction is used by them or their school. Of those who indicate that Intensive Interaction is used, half (5) indicate that it is used 'occasionally' and half (6) indicate that it is 'part' of their curriculum, used alongside other approaches. None of this sample indicated that Intensive Interaction was 'central to' their curriculum, though some said they would like it to be!

Early analysis of the data indicates that the major factor which encourages teachers to use Intensive Interaction is being faced with learners who do not know how to communicate, who 'don't join in' and whose needs were not being met. One teacher highlighted the trigger of having 'one particular child who seemed stuck' and another summed it up as 'desperation'. The data on what discourages these teachers from using the approach, or what challenges its use presents, indicate that they are being held back by practical factors (staffing levels, time factors) or factors related to a conflict with the whole school ethos (lack of management support, lack of confidence, lack of wider commitment, age-appropriateness issues, accountability, 'feeling okay in the face of OFSTED').

For those teachers who indicated that they did not use Intensive Interaction, lack of knowledge about, or lack of experience of using the approach, dominated the responses. Understandably perhaps, none of the respondents working in provision for pupils with moderate learning difficulties, hearing impaired pupils or pupils with specific learning difficulties had heard of Intensive Interaction. Some of those working with the appropriate pupil group with severe and complex learning difficulties were also unfamiliar (4). For those who were familiar with the approach, through reading or staff development, reasons for not employing it were mostly voiced in terms of practical factors (high staff turnover or newness of the provision). One response gave the reason of other initiatives currently in use. The questionnaire included a question about 'what teaching approach or approaches are primarily used?' This has yielded interesting data about other approaches used alongside or instead of Intensive Interaction. Whilst many respondents indicate that a variety of approaches are used, TEACCH[1] is the most commonly cited specific approach (8 schools/units), with approaches based on Waldon[2] (3 schools), gentle teaching, conductive education and EDY[3] also mentioned. Interestingly, with the exception of conductive

---

[1]An approach which creates an ongoing structured environment for people with autism, Treatment and Education of Autistic and Related Communication-Handicapped Children (Olley, 1986)

[2]An approach based on the work of Geoffrey Waldon for developing general understanding without language which involves activities undertaken *asocially*

[3]A behavioural programme, Education of the Developmentally Young (McBrian *et al.*, 1992)

education, these approaches co-exist in schools alongside Intensive Interaction, although the staff and pupil groups may of course differ.

We do not in any way feel depressed or daunted by a state of affairs where we are still apparently some distance from a general take-up of Intensive Interaction in service provision. We accept it as being simply an obvious and understandable reality. The general 'noise' about interactive techniques really only commenced in the mid to late eighties. Collis and Lacey (1996) cite the 1987 Westhill College, Birmingham, Conference on interactive approaches in special education as a particular milestone. We concur with that view, meeting still other teachers who were present and who still refer to it. Ten to fifteen years is not a long time for what amounts to a transformation in thought, philosophy and practice to take place. It almost seems appropriate that progress toward the adoption of large-scale alternative or additional approaches to what went before is slow. In addition, we make the point later in this chapter, and in the final chapter, that even those of us who research, write and work constantly with the topics are probably still at early stages of understanding the full ramifications.

Nonetheless, we do maintain that for people who are still in the earliest stages of learning, who are pre-verbal, not making rich, fulfilling contact with other people, there are now some articulately described methodologies for staff to help them relate better and know more about communication. We do look forward to a situation where there is a pervasive adoption of these approaches and to the flexible, imaginative thinking and staff behaviour which goes with them becoming general – the 'norm' everywhere. We look forward also to the available literature continuing to grow, with further vital contributions by academic researchers, but also vitally, a healthy growth in the number of ordinary teachers, care staff and other professionals who take it upon themselves to reflect upon and write about their work.

Interaction in action

Intensive Interaction has been the subject of doctoral research (Nind, 1993; Hewett 1995) and the subject of various evaluations (Watson and Knight, 1991; Nind, 1996; Watson and Fisher, 1997). These studies have incorporated elements of quasi-experimental design and have brought together elements of action research with traditional research rigour. Most of the contributors to this volume, however, would probably not see themselves as researchers at all. They are people going about their daily work of teaching, speech therapy, clinical psychology, occupational therapy, social work and parenting. These practitioners, however, are truly reflective practitioners in the tradition of the style of action research advocated by Lawrence Stenhouse (1975). They are teacher-researchers (or therapist-researchers etc.) researching their own practice, identifying problems and working collaboratively, systematically and creatively to find solutions. We do not want to get into a discussion here about when reflections like those included here stop being just good practice and start being research. By contributing to this book, however, these reflective practitioners are bringing their practice into the public domain, often for the first time in any formal sense. They are actively engaging in sharing their insights, and enjoying collaborating in a project to explore interactive approaches to facilitating communication development in people with complex needs.

In some way then, *Interaction in Action* is about action research. It is about bringing together people working in related fields on similar aims. It is about sharing good practice and maintaining a dialogue about the application of Intensive Interaction. There are no claims here for 'scientific' truth; *Interaction in Action* is not about research in a positivist sense. We have not sought objectivity, but rather encouraged a subjective involvement with the subject matter and a subjective element of relating what it feels like to be involved with this developmental work. Of course there is a place for more experimental accounts, and we are pleased that the efficacy study at Harperbury (Nind, 1996) will be replicated in a study of the efficacy of Intensive Interaction in use with children in a special school setting in the community (Griffin, Oxford Brookes University, pending). We also see a place, though, for an exchange of information emerging from the agenda of practitioners themselves. People tell us that yes, they want to know that an approach claiming to be effective has been systematically evaluated, but they also want to know who is using it, in what ways, and with what benefits and challenges. There is a richness in the individual stories here which we hope will help to answer some of the questions people have about the approach and which will encourage others to engage in similar exploratory and reflective practitioner–researcher work.

In some senses, *Interaction in Action* is a series of case studies. In some of the chapters the case or focal point is the learner/client/child, and in others the focal point is the school or service and its work to develop effective practice in communication and social interaction with the learner/client/child. In the style of good case studies we are enabled to learn from the particular. The fact that we bring together a series of case studies means that we can begin to form a wider picture. Again, however, we emphasise that our concern is less with universal truths than with individual practitioners, institutions and services finding what works as good interactive practice for them.

Finally, we would like to think of this book as having some allegiance with emancipatory research. The disability movement has highlighted the way in which much disability research has served to oppress disabled people, by doing research *on* them rather than *with* them. In a recent exploration of this challenge to academic researchers (BERA conference 1997) Sheila Riddell showed how difficult all this becomes when our research subjects have severe learning difficulties. While we inevitably cannot involve as co-researchers people whose intellectual, social and communicative abilities are greatly impaired, we can still involve as co-researchers those working most closely with them and we can attempt to tackle that which oppresses and disempowers them .

In Barton and Clough's (1995) terms, the contributors to this book are not researchers operating as 'reporters' of 'facts', nor do they distance themselves from the subjects of their research. They are more often taking the role of change agent, teacher (that is, 'persuader, . . . explorer, . . . raiser of consciousness' p. 146), learner, and critical friend of those they research. In the book we aim to give a voice to practitioners and parents who are engaged in reflective practice and research which seeks, in turn, to 'hear' people with severe and complex learning difficulties. The spirit of Intensive Interaction and *Interaction in Action* is about enabling people to be the best communicators and social interactors that they can. We cannot claim to represent the truth of the people with extensive support needs who are the subjects of our research, but we can claim to *try* to understand their lives from their perspective, and we can disassociate from research and practice which in effect silences them.

Recent literature

Since we last wrote a review of literature pertinent to the field in which we work (Nind and Hewett, 1994), there have been a number of interesting publications on topics which might conceivably fall within areas of thought related to Intensive Interaction, as well as work which looks at the wider uses of interactive techniques.

Educating Children with Profound and Multiple Learning Difficulties (Ware, 1994a) has several chapters which should be mentioned as relevant to the topics of this book. It is worth making the point, to those professionals reading this who are not working with children, that this book contains a great deal of technical advice and provocative thinking which should be usable to some extent by all, despite use of terms such as 'child' and 'curriculum'.

The first chapter (Ware and Healey, 1994) is particularly thought-provoking. Ware and Healey set out an eloquent philosophical and technical critique of just what it is we all expect when we are looking for 'progress' from people with profound and multiple learning disabilities. Their argument is related to present and historical arguments as to what constitutes 'quality of life' in our society and the relationship between visible, measurable progress in individuals and the concept of educability. In particular, they make the crucial philosophical point that quality of life is 'relative to more than one set of criteria' – not just to what our society deems desirable, but relative also to the 'needs and desires of the individual'. This issue is then studiously related to our ideas of what we teach and why, the difficulties of assessing people with PMLD by formal assessment procedures, and whether formal, step by step assessment and teaching sequences are pertinent to the reality of the learning of people with PMLD. This argument resolves to the statement:

> This phenomenon suggests that an important feature of effective methods of assessing progress in children with PMLDs is the extent to which *they* sensitize *us* [our emphases] to positive changes in the child. Additionally this sensitization can help us target our teaching effectively by starting precisely where the child is and thus facilitate further progress. (p. 13)

In the same volume, Juliet Goldbart (1994a) describes her 'observational tool', the Observational Assessment of Early Interactions (Goldbart and

Rigby, 1989) aimed at helping staff to respond to potentially communicative behaviours. This can be used in addition to the Affective Communication Assessment (Coupe *et al.*, 1988) as a means for 'teachers to identify the idiosyncratic patterns of responses which might be shown by pupils with PMLD'. The use of these instruments is linked to her argument that many people with PMLD fail to benefit from our attempts to teach communication due to 'unnecessarily restricted' definitions of what communication is.

Also in the same volume, Jean Ware (Ware, 1994b) links a review of communication development in infancy to the deployment of teacher sensitivity and responsiveness in all aspects of classroom life. She reports on the findings of the Contingency-sensitive Environments Research Project, which forms a major aspect of her more recent book *Creating a Responsive Environment* (Ware, 1996) which will be described below. Watson (1994) gives two case studies in use of an Intensive Interaction approach. The case studies arise from an earlier report of a curriculum evaluation project at Gogarburn School (Knight and Watson, 1990).

Another book published in 1994, *Taking Control: Enabling People with Learning Difficulties* (Coupe O'Kane and Smith, 1994), contains papers which explore the theme of what services may or should be doing (and sometimes are not doing) to ensure that people with severe learning difficulties exercise more power and control in their lives. John Harris (Harris, 1994) emphasises the crucial role of the development of communication abilities for people with learning difficulties as a fundamental to the exercising of personal powers. He catalogues his view of the adult's role in the development of a child's personal powers in communication development, citing such matters as: creating the conditions whereby the child's actions can be treated as socially significant; responding to the actions as if they are expressions of intention; helping the child to conceptualise alternative outcomes; showing the child that other people have personal powers; helping the child to compromise and negotiate. These items are linked to the crucial role of the adult in early interactions, even more crucial for infants with profound and multiple disabilities, where 'if unable to "connect" with adults and actively participate in the world of social experience, instead of developing personal powers, children with learning disabilities are likely to become increasingly vulnerable and powerless' (p. 41).

John Harris moves his argument on with a warning developed out of this perspective. In schools, many of the accepted practices may, unless we exercise thought and care in these practices, work against the development of communication and personal powers. Many skills training approaches for children with severe learning difficulties may have obvious visible benefits, but tend to be teacher-led and teacher-controlled, thereby 'reducing the range of permissible social interactions' (p. 47). Reversing this situation implies also creating 'situations where adult power can be relinquished and shared'.

The developmental value of play is emphasised by Juliet Goldbart (1994b). She reviews the importance of play in the development of language and communication, in cognition, and the development of symbolic play. She goes on to describe the potential for a parent, teacher or therapist to use play as a 'vehicle for intervention in the areas of cognition and language and communication' (p. 13). Goldbart uses some concepts from research which are rapidly developing in familiarity in literature on learning difficulties, in order to describe the nature of such play interventions: 'social transaction rather than solo performance' (Bruner, 1985), 'scaffolding' (Bruner, 1983, 1985), and Vygotsky's (1978) 'zone of proximal development' as well as the use of 'joint action routines' (Snyder-McLean et al., 1984) as an approach to planning play situations. Goldbart also utilises Garvey's five characteristics of play (Garvey, 1991 – a short, but invaluable guide to the developmental significance of play) to stress that play, whilst having characteristics such as being apparently pleasurable, spontaneous and without goals, is nonetheless central to the development of communication and cognition.

Reflection Through Interaction (Watson, 1996) is a book concerned with current research and the state of current approaches to fostering reflective learning, thinking and reasoning abilities in work with pupils with learning difficulties. The role of the teacher in developing reflective abilities within pupils of all abilities is technically examined and related to a research project carried out in a school for pupils with moderate learning difficulties. The teacher's role as an effective interactor is emphasised and related to some of the same concepts of teacher or caregiver activity cited by Goldbart, such as: 'scaffolding' (Bruner, 1983), the 'zone of proximal development' (Vygotsky, 1978), 'apprenticeship' (Miller, 1977; Bruner 1983), 'apprenticeship in thinking' (Rogoff, 1990) and 'mediated' or 'assisted performance' (Tharp and Gallimore, 1988). We deliberately reference Judith Watson's perspective in this way (as she does) because of

12

the relevance of her arguments to the subject matter of this book, and because any of the just-given references are, in our view, good reading for practitioners becoming involved in any formal study of their practice related to communication.

The intriguingly titled *What Teachers Do: Developments in Special Education* (Garner, Hinchcliffe and Sandow, 1995) contains a chapter devoted to the relationship between behavioural and interactive methods of teaching. The history of what they term 'interactive-process approaches' is described and referenced, together with accounts of personal experiences by serving teachers. In their conclusion to this topic, they emphasise eclecticism, noting that behavioural and process approaches should not be seen as mutually exclusive. They quote the experiences of a teacher who maintained 'it is possible to be interactive when using behavioural approaches and utilise behavioural principles when working within an interactive model' (p. 88).

A practical report of her methods, aimed at helping staff to adopt interactive methods for working with people with learning disabilities and 'extensive support needs', is given by Phoebe Caldwell in *Getting in Touch* (Caldwell, 1996). There are many accounts of the development of attention-getting and turn-taking with people who are difficult to reach, and this book should be accessible, interesting and helpful to staff in all disciplines. Phoebe Caldwell is known for the way in which she also fabricates 'personalised equipment' incorporating the 'particular stimulus to which the person responds'. Her approach to the use of any objects which come to hand to further foster shared activity is imaginative and often ingenious. She stresses, though, that such equipment is not 'an end in itself. Its power to engage attention and facilitate interaction is lost if it is allowed to become a solitary occupation' (p. 16).

For some time we have been likely to mention the benefits of using 'Sherborne Developmental Movement' (SDM). In our view the use of this approach can enhance the development of communication for people with severe learning difficulties and particularly address issues of giving them warm, supportive, communicative physical contact in a structured setting that many staff would find to be 'safe'. Cindy Hill (Hill, 1996) describes her views on how SDM can assist with access to the National Curriculum. She also focuses on the central role that these activities can play in the development of communication, particularly with regard to 'co-active movement' and 'meeting people where they are'.

We have mentioned Jean Ware's recent work earlier, but *Creating a Responsive Environment: For People with Profound and Multiple Learning Difficulties* (Ware, 1996) merits further description. The book is written from the point of view that it is intended to be used by all staff, not just teachers and teachers' assistants, but residential and day-centre staff or nurses in adult services. It is devoted to helping staff develop the nature of the social environment provided by staff to service users, throughout all activities at all times. The book is illustrated with the experiences from a research project in two schools. Coherent practical/technical advice is progressively set out and the chapter headings (The Importance of a Responsive Environment; Getting Started, Making Sense of Children's Behaviour; Responding to People's Behaviour; Starting a Conversation, Giving the Child a Chance to Reply; Sharing Control; Moving On; Keeping the Responsive Environment Going) illustrate this coherence and the relevance for practitioners interested in interactive approaches.

Staff groups are advised by Ware to work through the materials together chapter by chapter during meetings, because 'an important aspect of creating a responsive environment is the sharing of information between staff' (p.v). The materials are well-organised for this purpose and the whole book embodies a satisfying blend of theoretical/technical underpinnings and clear, practical advice about becoming a good, sensitive responder and interactor. The problems staff may have are not glossed over. 'Sharing control' is recognised as a skill we may have to learn in our work: 'difficult for teachers but vital for children' (p. 68). Ways of relaxing control and promoting interaction are discussed through employment of means such as use of pause, waiting for the other person to start, use of imitation – this can 'decrease the extent to which the more competent interactive partner dominates the interaction' (p. 70) – and being sensitive to the other person's need to stop the interaction.

In our final chapter, we give some thoughts for the future with regard to where work on such approaches might be taking all of us in our work with people with severe learning difficulties. In Ware's work here, there is the sense of a significant signpost. One of our hopes is that more such volumes will become progressively available to staff. They will embody substantial theoretical knowledge derived from recent research on communication and sociability, together with realistic description and advice about techniques; realistic both about the manner in which staff may best be helped to take on new approaches and skills and realistic too about the nature of the services in which they work.

A similarly significant signpost is provided by Mark Collis and Penny Lacey (1996) in *Interactive Approaches to Teaching: A Framework for INSET*. This book serves both as an authoritative text on interactive approaches and as materials for staff development. The chapters are structured as ten sessions which staff groups can facilitate amongst themselves. Once again, though educationists, the authors stress their desire for the materials to be used by practitioners from other disciplines and attempt a use of terminology accordingly. The book aims to present a summary of interactive approaches to teaching and learning, to enable teachers to re-evaluate their basic teaching methods in the light of interactive approaches and to provide a means by which teachers of students with learning difficulties can investigate and experiment with interactive approaches. They caution too that the interactive approaches are not to be looked upon merely as a set of 'techniques' or a 'recipe' to be followed, 'rather they are presented to readers as a series of ideas that are intended to cause them to question how they teach' (p. 3).

The content ranges across conceptualisations and definitions of interactive approaches, the history of the development of interactive teaching methods, the nuts and bolts of interactive teaching techniques (Hewett, 1996, in the appendix, also describes the practicalities of starting Intensive Interaction), assessment, planning and record keeping, curriculum design and development, including using interactive techniques in broader areas of the curriculum beyond communication. In their thoughts on curriculum design, Collis and Lacey support a resolution between behavioural/objectives approaches, interactive-process approaches and the apparent strictures of the National Curriculum, a viewpoint enthusiastically advocated elsewhere (for example Byers, 1994; Garner, Hinchcliffe and Sandow, 1995).

The evolving literature on interactive approaches also includes two noteworthy journal articles reporting research findings on the effectiveness of Intensive Interaction. 'Efficacy of Intensive Interaction' (Nind, 1996) reports the findings of a twelve-month intervention study in which the effects of using Intensive Interaction with six students with various disabilities were observed in considerable depth. 'Evaluating the Effectiveness of Intensive Interaction Teaching' (Watson and Fisher, 1997) provides further data on the effectiveness of Intensive Interaction with a report of two projects. In one project already written-up elsewhere

(Knight and Watson, 1990; Watson and Knight, 1991) the authors focus mainly on comparing pupils' typical communication performance in the classroom (measured using the 'Pre-Verbal Communication Schedule', Kiernan and Reid, 1987) with their performance in Intensive Interaction sessions (measured using subjective recordings and video observation). They found that communication abilities often occurred in the Intensive Interaction context which had not previously shown on PVCS recordings, and they conclude that the Intensive Interaction context especially facilitates communication.

In the second study reported by Watson and Fisher, five pupils with profound and complex learning difficulties were studied over a period of one school year in two contrasting teaching contexts. One context was teacher directed movement and music group sessions and the other Intensive Interaction sessions. They found evidence of progress during both approaches, but that this was 'much less obvious' during group time:

> During Intensive Interaction all pupils demonstrated higher levels of active participation and enjoyment. Initially eye contact was engaged and maintained; there was evidence of more movement; turn-taking sequences developed and gradually pupils learned how to initiate, set the timing and pace of interactions and conclude sessions with their helper. (p. 87)

The work on interactive approaches in the United States, based upon knowledge arising out of parent–infant interaction research, is catalogued by Siegel-Causey and Bashinski (1997). These authors offer a review and historical account of the development of communication strategies for people with 'severe disabilities' (see also Siegel-Causey and Guess, 1989). Their account focuses particularly on the development of approaches since the early 1980s where the thinking shifted away from 'sole remediation of the learner's repertoire' to 'enhancement of the communicative behaviour of *both* learner and partner within natural interactions' (p. 107). In these 'interventions' the focus was on naturalistic 'partner strategies' incorporating such elements as joint action routines and focusing on learners' interests and following their lead. They note that:

> The fields of psychology and infant development have provided increasingly valuable information concerning the relationships

between cognition and language, as well as the social aspects of language and communication. (p. 108)

In their recent work, Siegel-Causey and Bashinski have conceptualised an intervention model they term the 'Tri-Focus Framework'. The framework has three primary components which are inter-related in the development of communication for the learner – the learner, the partner and the environmental context. They offer practical advice on staff technique and processes within the three components of the Tri-Focus Framework. The framework should indeed be a helpful tool for staff and its use will, we think, enable staff to arrive at a state of affairs where they are carrying out interactive work which would look familiar to us. It is difficult, however, to gain a perspective on the extent to which the influence of work such as that by Siegel-Causey and Bashinski has become visible in the daily practices of staff working in education or care in the United States. The authors do not describe the extent to which the approach has been taken up by services or to which the average professional in services in their country is conversant with the style of work they advocate.

Overview

The works reviewed here share clear themes. Firstly, and perhaps most significantly, is the theme of the growing recognition of the importance of work on communication and relationship in and throughout any developmental work with people who have severe and complex, or profound and multiple, learning difficulties. This may seem a strange thing to write as it would surely always have been the case that communication would receive urgent, priority attention from staff as the most vital aspect of the lives of people with such learning difficulties. However, the work of the authors here underlines the reality that, for most of us in the work, this situation has always been the aspiration, but it is only recently that we have started developing the knowledge and the techniques for achieving it. Indeed, we dare say that all of the authors and researchers we have mentioned would agree with us that we are still at the beginnings of developing such approaches. However, we now have a small wealth of good, well-founded knowledge that is accessible to staff everywhere and has the potential to enable them to enhance the lives of their service-users.

Secondly, there is the theme or perhaps trend, notably from Ware (1996), Collis and Lacey (1996), Caldwell (1996) and to some extent Siegel-Causey and Bashinski (1997), to provide the detail of their work in a manner which gives direct advice to staff on the practical aspects of 'how to do it'. The authors display a pleasing blend of the academic knowledge gained from recent psychological research transformed into down-to-earth particulars about practice and technique. Their work is also infused with empathy – a perspective on what the world may be like for people with learning difficulties – with the recipients of our practices. Our experience is that staff want the approaches they use in their work to be of this nature – well founded and underpinned, rational and realistic in their outlook, humane and human, practical and methodically thought-through.

Thirdly, radiant, then, in all of these contributions to the development of early communication abilities, is the central theme of the role of the more experienced person in the learning of the less experienced one. The terminology associated with conceptualising this role is derived mainly from the parent-infant interaction research, but is arising frequently enough in the literature on work with people with learning difficulties, to make some of them almost common coinage. These are terms such as 'scaffolding', 'partnership', 'zone of proximal development', 'apprenticeship', 'assisted performance'. If there is a feeling of 'breakthrough' in the development of interactive approaches during the last fifteen years, we suggest it arises particularly from these conceptualisations. It has always been logically obvious that the fundamentals of communication development arise in inter-personal situations, but we now have a range of authoritative literature which describes in great detail the style of behaviour to be adopted by the more experienced interactive partner in facilitating such development. This is not to say that there will not be further developments in our knowledge on this, but it is possible to state now that we have well-developed teaching methodologies which guide the teacher behaviour style.

The writers reviewed above are also looking to break down barriers between the professions. They are attempting to make their work accessible to and usable by staff in all disciplines. They recognise that work on communication is crucially not the sole preserve of the teacher or of the speech and communication therapist. Staff who work in residential establishments, for instance, are ideally placed to carry out work on relating and communicating. They tend to be 'in contact' for extended periods, in a home situation – a (hopefully) relaxed, naturalistic environment full of everyday occurrences.

This trend to 'naturalism' can be seen as a fourth theme. The work on interactive approaches has brought with it a recognition that communication learning, at least, best occurs in regularly recurring natural situations. There is also a recognition that for learners at early stages, sitting on the opposite side of a table from the teacher, in order to carry out a formal, teacher-directed communication/language session, can be less than ideal. Ware makes this point eloquently throughout her work, with her insistence on the development of the whole fabric of a responsive social environment, throughout any given day. This has implications for our traditions in classrooms, but not ones that are insuperable. In any event, our work has shown to us that staff who become competent at promoting incidental interactions with a person are also more likely to become competent at achieving scheduled sessions with that person where necessary.

Lastly, the writers here all share to some degree a desire not to throw out the baby with the bath-water. We have already cited Garner, Hinchcliffe and Sandow (1995) for making the point that interactive or behavioural or other approaches need not be mutually exclusive. Ware suggests that all other activities 'can be done in a way which is consistent with providing a highly responsive environment' (p. 98). Collis and Lacey (1996) maintain that any critical examination of traditional approaches in the light of interactive ones 'may equally lead to identification of positives that we should retain within our battery of techniques' (p. 11).

The body of literature available in the late 1990s, then, contains a balance of emphasis on the behavioural and the interactive. We have literature which guides practice in a practical way, but also in a way that seeks to empower practitioners to make their own careful decisions about which approaches might best fit their purpose. There is recognition of the importance of the natural, social learning environment and there is recognition of the skill and talent of practitioners. Furthermore, there is a sense of optimism about further improving our ability to teach communication.

It is useful to see *Interaction in Action* in the light of these recent developments in the literature, and particularly in the light of the themes we have highlighted as these provide a context for the chapters which follow. In this book we too seek to provide practical guidance in a format which is accessible across disciplines. We intend that this book will complement the texts we have mentioned here, add to the picture of where we are now in terms of using interactive approaches to teach early communication, and stimulate further developments.

References

Barton, L. and Clough, P. (1995) 'Conclusion: Many urgent voices'. In: Clough, L. and Barton, P. (eds) *Making Difficulties: Research and the Construction of SEN*. London: Paul Chapman.

Beebe, B. (1985) 'Interpersonal timing: the application of an adult dialogue model to mother-infant vocal and kinesic interactions'. In: Field, T.M. and Fox, N.A. (eds) *Social Perception in Infants*. Norwood: Ablex.

Bruner, J. (1983) *Child's Talk: Learning to Use Language*. New York: Oxford University Press.

Bruner, J. (1985) 'Vygotsky: A Historical and Conceptual Perspective'. In: Wertsch, J. (ed.) *Culture, Communication and Cognition*. Cambridge: Cambridge University Press.

Byers, R. (1994) 'Teaching As Dialogue: Teaching Approaches and Learning Styles in Schools for Pupils with Learning Difficulties'. In: Coupe O'Kane, J. and Smith, B. (eds) (1994) *Taking Control: Enabling People with Learning Difficulties*. London: David Fulton.

Caldwell, P. (1996) *Getting in Touch: Ways of Working with People with Severe Learning Disabilities and Extensive Support Needs*. Brighton: Pavilion Publishing/Joseph Rowntree Foundation.

Carlson, L. and Bricker, D.D. (1982) 'Dyadic and Contingent Aspects of Early Communicative Intervention'. In: Bricker, D.D. (ed.) *Interventions with At-Risk and Handicapped Infants*. Baltimore: University Park Press.

Collis, M. and Lacey, P. (1996) *Interactive Approaches to Teaching: A Framework for INSET*. London: David Fulton.

Coupe, J., Barber, M. and Murphy, D. (1988) 'Affective Communication'. In: Coupe, J. and Goldbart, J. (eds) (1988) *Communication Before Speech: Normal Development and Impaired Communication*. London: Croom Helm.

Coupe O'Kane, J. and Smith, B. (eds) (1994) *Taking Control: Enabling People with Learning Difficulties*. London: David Fulton.

Field, T.M. (1979) 'Games parents play with normal and high-risk infants', *Child Psychiatry and Human Development*, **10**, 41–48.

Garner, P., Hinchcliffe, V. and Sandow, S. (1995) *What Teachers Do: Developments in Special Education*. London: Paul Chapman.

Garvey, C. (1991, 2nd edition) *Play*. London: Fontana.

Goldbart, J. and Rigby, J. (1989) 'Establishing Relationships with People with PMLD'. Paper presented to University of Manchester Department of Child and

Adolescent Psychiatry Regional Study Day, 10 April 1989.

Goldbart, J. (1994a) 'Opening the Communication Curriculum to Students with PMLDs'. In: Ware. J. (ed.) (1994) *Educating Children with Profound and Multiple Learning Difficulties*. London: David Fulton.

Goldbart, J. (1994b) 'Playing in the Zone: Communication and Cognition in the Classroom', *BILD: SLD Experience*, **10**, Autumn 1994, 12–15.

Goldberg, S. (1977) 'Social competence in infancy: a model of parent-infant interaction', *Merrill-Palmer Quarterly*, **23**, 163–77.

Harris, J. (1994) 'Language, Communication and Personal Power: A Developmental Perspective'. In: Coupe O'Kane, J. and Smith, B. (eds) (1994) *Taking Control: Enabling People with Learning Difficulties*. London: David Fulton.

Hewett, D. (1995) Understanding and Writing a Methodology of Intensive Interaction – Teaching Pre-Speech Communication Abilities to Learners with Severe Learning Difficulties: A Naturalistic Inquiry Using Qualitative Evaluation Methods. Unpublished Ph.D Thesis, Cambridge Institute of Education.

Hewett, D. (1996) 'How to Start Doing Intensive Interaction'. In: Collis, M. and Lacey, P. (1996) *Interactive Approaches to Teaching: A Framework for INSET*. London: David Fulton.

Hill, C. (1996) 'Sherborne Developmental Movement: Accessing the National Curriculum', *The SLD Experience*, **15**, Summer 1997 p. 9–11.

Kaye, K. (1977) 'Toward the origin of dialogue'. In: Schaffer, H.R. (ed.) *Studies in Mother-Infant Interaction*. London: Academic Press.

Kiernan, C. and Reid, B. (1987) *Pre-Verbal Communication Schedule*. Windsor: NFER-Nelson.

Knight, C. and Watson, J. (1990) *Intensive Interaction Teaching at Gogarburn School*. Edinburgh: Moray House College.

McBrian, J., Farrell, P. and Foxen, T. (1992) *EDY: Teaching People with Severe Learning Difficulties Trainee Workbook*. Manchester: Manchester University Press.

McConkey, R. (1989) 'Interaction: the name of the game'. In: Smith, B. (ed.) *Interactive Approaches to the Education of Children with Severe Learning Difficulties*. Birmingham: Westhill College.

Miller, G. (1977) *Spontaneous Apprentices*. New York: Seabury Press.

Newson, J. (1979) 'The growth of shared understandings between infant and caregiver'. In: Bullowa, M. (ed.) *Before Speech*. Cambridge: Cambridge University Press.

Nind, M. (1993) Access to Communication: Efficacy of Intensive Interaction Teaching for People with Severe Developmental Disabilities Who Demonstrate Ritualistic Behaviours. Unpublished Ph.D Thesis, Cambridge Institute of Education.

Nind, M. (1996) 'Efficacy of Intensive Interaction: Developing Sociability and Communication in People with Severe and Complex Learning Difficulties

Using An Approach Based on Caregiver-Infant Interaction', *European Journal of Special Needs Education*, **11**, 48–66.

Nind, M. and Hewett, D. (1994) *Access to Communication: Developing the Basics of Communication with People with Severe Learning Difficulties Through Intensive Interaction*. London: David Fulton.

Nind, M. and Hewett, D. (1996) 'When age-appropriateness isn't appropriate'. In: Coupe O'Kane, J. and Goldbart, J. (eds) (1996) *Whose Choice? Controversial issues for those working with people with learning difficulties*. London: David Fulton.

Olley, J.G. (1986) 'The TEACCH Curriculum for teaching Social Behaviour to Children with Autism'. In: Schopler, E. and Mesibov, G.B. (eds) *Social Behaviour in Autism*. New York: Plenum.

Pawlby, S.J. (1977) 'Imitative Interaction'. In: Schaffer, H.R. (ed.) *Studies in Mother-Infant Interaction*. London: Academic Press.

Rogoff, B. (1990) *Apprenticeship in Thinking. Cognitive Development in Social Context*. New York: Oxford University Press.

Schaffer, H.R. (1977) 'Early interactive development'. In: Schaffer, H.R. (ed.) *Studies in Mother-Infant Interaction*. London: Academic Press.

Siegel-Causey, E. and Guess, D. (1989) *Enhancing Nonsymbolic Communication Interactions Among Learners with Severe Disabilities*. Baltimore: Paul H. Brookes.

Siegel-Causey, E. and Bashinski, S.M. (1997) 'Enhancing Initial Communication and Responsiveness of Learners with Multiple Disabilities: A Tri-Focus Framework for Partners', *Focus on Autism and Other Developmental Disabilities*, **12** (2), 105–120.

Snow, C.E. (1977) 'The development of conversation between mothers and babies', *Journal of Child Language*, **4** 1–22.

Snyder-McLean, L., Solomon, B., McLean, J. and Sacks, S. (1984) *Structuring Joint Action Routines: A Strategy for Facilitating Communication and Language Development in the Classroom*. Seminars in Speech and Language 5. New York: Thime-Stratton.

Stenhouse, L. (1975) *An Introduction to Curriculum Research and Development*. London: Heinemann Educational.

Stern, D.N. (1974) 'Mother and infant at play: the dyadic interaction involving facial, vocal, and gaze behaviours'. In: Lewis, M. and Rosenblum, L.A. (eds) *The Effect of the Infant on its Caregiver*. New York: Wiley.

Tharp, R.G. and Gallimore, R. (1988) *Rousing Minds to Life: Teaching, Learning, and Schooling in Social Context*. Cambridge: Cambridge University Press.

Vygotsky, L.S. (1978) *Mind in Society: The Development of Higher Psychological Processes*. Cambridge MA: Harvard University Press.

Ware. J (ed.) (1994a) *Educating Children with Profound and Multiple Learning Difficulties*. London: David Fulton.

Ware, J. (1994b) 'Using interaction in the education of pupils with PMLDs (1) Creating contingency-sensitive environments'. In: Ware, J. (ed.) (1994)

Educating Children with Profound and Multiple Learning Difficulties. London: David Fulton.

Ware, J. and Healey, I. (1994) 'Conceptualizing Progress in Children with Profound and Multiple Learning Difficulties'. In: Ware, J, (ed.) (1994) *Educating Children with Profound and Multiple Learning Difficulties.* London: David Fulton.

Ware, J. (1996) *Creating a Responsive Environment: For People with Profound and Multiple Learning Difficulties.* London: David Fulton.

Watson, J. and Knight, C. (1991) 'An Evaluation of Intensive Interaction Teaching with Pupils with Very Severe Learning Difficulties', *Child Language Teaching and Therapy,* **7** (3), 310–325.

Watson, J. (1994) 'Using Intensive Interaction in the Education of Pupils with PMLDs (ii) Intensive Interaction: Two Case Studies'. In Ware, J. (ed.) (1994) *Educating Children with Profound and Multiple Learning Difficulties.* London: David Fulton.

Watson, J. (1996) *Reflection Through Interaction: The Classroom Experience of Pupils with Learning Difficulties.* London: Falmer Press.

Watson, J. and Fisher, A. (1997) 'Evaluating the Effectiveness of Intensive Interaction Teaching with Pupils with Profound and Complex Learning Difficulties', *British Journal of Special Education,* **24** (2), 80–87.

Chapter 2

Using Intensive Interaction with Pupils who have Multi-Sensory Impairment

Chris Addis

Very few people can be described as being totally without sight and totally without hearing. There are a number of working definitions of multi-sensory impairment – a condition often referred to as 'deaf/blind.' One which describes all the children in our Unit is this:

> a heterogeneous group of children who may suffer from varying degrees of visual and hearing impairment, perhaps combined with learning difficulties and physical difficulties, which can cause severe communication, developmental and educational problems. (Department of Education and Science, 1989)

We cannot and should not make any generalisations about children with MSI. The pupils in our Unit are as different from one another as are any group of individuals. And yet we are able to declare that Intensive Interaction has been an ideal device for all of us, a benefit to both children and staff. I think we need to look at the overall organisation of the Unit to understand why the Intensive Interaction philosophy is so appropriate and practical.

What features, then, might be unique to a Unit whose pupils all have some degree of vision and hearing impairment, and most have additional physical disabilities? (The pupils in our charge do all have learning difficulties which add further hindrance to their attempts to act independently and express needs and choices.)

- The staff ratio is one adult to one pupil.
- The issue of 'touching' and physical contact has already been addressed as School Policy.
- Timetabling and daily activities are 100 per cent child-based and are

24

extremely flexible. A new idea can be slotted into the curriculum without difficulty . . . bearing in mind that any sudden change in routine for a deaf/blind child will be somewhat bewildering.

- Staff are able to share experiences on a daily basis.
- All celebrations of child interaction and progress are shared with parents daily.
- The objectives of staff and carers are the same as those of any other caring or educational establishment. We strive to let the students know that they are welcomed and loved and respected and heard, and that they are fun to be with. We offer them as much opportunity as possible to express choice, and we use as many means as possible to elicit communication.

The Unit, then, is clearly a friendly environment for Intensive Interaction, welcoming it as a useful power tool in the task of eliciting and identifying communications. Intensive Interaction can be explained easily and can be incorporated into the curriculum without having to call in the contractors or redesign classrooms. In our case, as we embraced Intensive Interaction, we needed to make some big changes to our philosophy and some little ones to the timetable.

Our unit in particular

For those who have not yet visited the MSS Unit (Multi-Sensory Support Unit) at the Royal School for the Deaf at Manchester – and you are most welcome to do so – a brief description here would be appropriate. We are a part of a very large School for the Deaf where all pupils have some degree of hearing loss and all have some learning or behavioural disadvantage. Recent admission figures show an increasing number of physical difficulties. A large proportion of the school population is residential, and ages range from four to 23, with new residential building projects for young adults actually at the plastering and painting stage. We are well off for space – spare classrooms, darkrooms, audiorooms and Snoezelen Rooms are available for individual work with children.

Our Unit is a part of the whole establishment. Unit staff, who will have worked in other areas of the school, are teachers, classroom assistants, and intervenors. There are at present nine children aged between five and 12 in the primary department of the MSSU and five in the secondary department. In the primary unit one member of staff is named for each pupil and the ratio is one-to-one. For obvious reasons we timetable things such that all staff work with and know all the children in the Unit, but it will usually be the named member of staff who shares daily information with the child's parent and perhaps exchanges telephone calls with them in the evening.

This rather brief pencil sketch of the Unit layout should make it clear that we were in a good position to incorporate the Intensive Interaction approach into the scheme of things.

Baseline and Intensive Interaction

All professional teachers of all disciplines will need to know something about where their students are starting from. Some will call this 'baseline information', others may never have heard the term. Within a group of pupils with MSI, 'baseline' is much, much more than another bit of jargon. It is genuinely not possible to embark upon any useful interaction with our young people unless we have a working knowledge of:

- how much they can hear
- how much they can see
- their present repertoire of communications
- what they like and dislike.

This baseline information can be extremely difficult to obtain. If a young girl has severe learning difficulties you cannot ask her to read the bottom line of an optician's chart, nor can you expect her to signal to the audiologist the moment she can hear a pure tone presented at threshold level. I am sure that you have come across students whose hearing turns out to be much better than was first thought: the reason that they had not been responding to incidental sounds was that they had come to learn that such sounds never promised anything interesting for them. If the telephone is never for you, you cease to hear it!

The specialist can tell us that an individual can probably see in black and white, or probably suffers a severe hearing loss. We can help to make that assessment more precise. We learn best about a student's level of vision and hearing if we combine the information provided by the clinician with observational evidence, even anecdotal evidence. If John's mother noticed that he responded when Dad called out from the garden, that piece of knowledge is new and important.

Clearly, because sessions of Intensive Interaction are so successful in producing motivation, they are ideal for gleaning information about a pupil's functional use of his or her senses.

Communication

Again, the baseline repertoires of communication offered by our pupils with MSI are essential to, and can by aided by, Intensive Interaction sessions. This is really what it is all about. If we claim that we love and respect our students – if we have promised their parents that we will rejoice with their children in shared interaction – then we must do our utmost to know what the children are saying and to know what they mean. If we are not trying our hardest to do that, then the love we profess is rather one-sided and patronising. We are adoring them in their disadvantaged state, but we are not listening!

Identifying meaningful communications is not easy. Take an example. Tom is nearly toilet-trained, in the urine-passing sense. Sat upon a special toilet seat five times a day, at exact times, he will perform appropriately and his trainer pants are rarely wet. Occasionally, either because he is early or we are late, he wets himself. Now, I am convinced that, at the moment Tom is about to empty his aching bladder into his pants, something in his body-language must be shouting out, 'Hey, you lot! Get me to the toilet!' We have not found it yet, but the important thing is that we are looking. That is our job.

And this is where Intensive Interaction comes into its own. We note down and share anything new we have discovered about the children's communications, received or expressed, during the interaction.

Communication audit

I like to call this planned collecting of communications a Communication Audit; Repertoire of Communications or Dictionary of Communications will do. It is of course something we do instinctively with pupils and with

27

our own tiny babies. Let's think about Sue, the mother used as an example by Nind and Hewett (1994) in *Access to Communication*. Inside Sue's head as she has her fun with Thomas, her nine-month-old, will be a growing list of Thomas's expressed or understood communications, rather like a programme on a computer screen. She is probably not consciously aware of the fact, but her language will be appropriately tuned in to Thomas.

If she also has a five-year-old, she will instinctively re-adjust her language level. This starts at day one. When my 18-month-old son was at last uttering some words, I remember a visitor, who had no children of her own, saying, 'It must be wonderful now he is talking – you'll be able to know what he wants.' This was miles out. Ask any parent. The arrival of words is only a marker in a history of useful communications which began at birth, perhaps even before. The communication can be as subtle as a movement of an eyebrow which says, 'This breast has finished. It's time to move across', or the fractional widening of the eye which says, 'Don't I know you?'

These are the minute expressions which should be finding their way onto the Communication Audit list, certainly with some of the multi-sensorily disadvantaged children we work with in the Unit. It can be the most exciting, and again the most frustrating and disappointing, part of our work. The assembly of the Audit is one of the more important 'tasks' expected of the adult during a 'taskless' session of Intensive Interaction ... to confirm, or reject, the latest bits of body language and facial communication which we think we have identified.

It can be as difficult as that. We have a Tom. Our Tom has a number of chest-tapping and ear-lobe tapping mannerisms which seem to be related to environmental incidents. I had hoped that his Communication Audit would look something like a page out of Hugo's *Useful Phrases for the Tourist in Greece*. Shoulder-shrug equals 'toilet please'; slow-head-roll-to-left equals 'I think I like that music but I'm not sure'. That sort of thing. It was never destined to be as clear-cut as that, of course. These are the disappointments. We have been able to pin down quite a few gestures which have exact meaning, but there are as many again which seem to occur regardless of what is going on around Tom. Possibly he is thinking, or remembering, and his actions are responses to his inner thoughts.

We are attempting to 'listen' to Tom, and to answer him. His joy at being a part of an Intensive Interaction session is a pleasure to see. He is clearly happy – of course he is! It is natural and human to enjoy taking an active part in conversation. (It is worth noting here that Tom's parents are far better at this than we are. They have done the Sue/Thomas thing with him for all of his seven years, seven difficult years of surgery, illness and set-backs.)

What the children like best – 'reward assessment'

The adult embarking upon an Intensive Interaction session should, then, be armed with some useful knowledge of the student's functional vision and hearing ability, and an idea of the communications the student is already attempting. Actually, you will need to know these things before you go anywhere near the child. If you are changing her after five minutes on the potty, if you are helping her to hold a spoon, you will not be much use to her if you do not know how much she can see or what she is trying to tell you.

A further knowledge of the student as an individual is, of course, the acquired information about what she likes. What particularly gets her motivated? What will she work for? We need to spend no more time on this here because it is so obvious, and because anybody working with anyone who has learning difficulties must have done this already. In Behaviour Modification jargon it is called 'reward assessment', but whatever you call it, it is the business of doing your best to find out the things your pupil likes. As with the Communication Audit, the information will not just come to you in a vision. Your job is to lie in bed at night thinking of new ideas, or new extensions to the activities you have already discovered.

With children with MSI the task is the same as with other children with learning difficulties. It could be suggested that many children with MSI need several goes at an activity before they demonstrate clearly their enjoyment of it. Also, where there is limited sight and vision the staff have to be especially imaginative in offering new activities. There are things that vibrate and spin, hanging balls and pat-a-cake games. Again, the Intensive Interaction session is the ideal experience for adult and child to have fun sharing what they like doing best.

'What Jenny likes best is to be left alone'

I think that a paragraph here is well dedicated to a discussion of statements such as this. It is true that many children with MSI and many people with profound learning difficulties do give the impression that they want no interaction with anybody else. They want to be left to that internal entertainment they have developed over days and years of being 'left alone'.

We have to start with the belief that no human being really wants to be left alone. Prisoners and lonely old-folk and medieval torturers all agree on this one point, that being left alone in a soundless dark world is not pleasant. We have to know that if Jenny is communicating to us that she wants to be left alone, then it is up to us to discover the means of access to Jenny. (We do have such a 'Jenny', and she does reject approaches with biting, scratching and head-butts.) What amazes me is that I have heard people making the above statement about children, and these are children whose level of understanding is that of a very young child. Are these people actually suggesting that there are young children on the planet who really enjoy being ignored?

Access to Jenny is really only possible through Intensive Interaction. Intensive Interaction with a member of staff who is able to try to imagine what it is like to be Jenny. Jenny's world stops at the reach of her arms. It is a dark, silent world. Jenny does not know anything about the world beyond, except that it frightens her. Of course she will fight against it and react in ways that seem to work. To say that Jenny has 'chosen' to be left alone is to imply that Jenny has been offered all the options and has made her choice. It is our job to offer her those options.

How did Intensive Interaction make a difference to our unit?

Our Unit consists of a small number of students, all of whom experience some degree of multi-sensory impairment. They are all quite different from one another in what they can see, hear, understand or enjoy. Some cannot walk. With a trained staff team working at a ratio of one-to-one, 'intensive interaction' – without the capital letters – is of course taking place with every pupil throughout every day, with the express intention of eliciting communication. We have had some glorious results

And yet I would be the last person to have said, 'Oh, yes, Nind and Hewett, Intensive Interaction, we are doing that already.' Because there are certain features unique to Intensive Interaction, both as a practice and as a philosophy. When you share some special time with a child, however valuable that time may be, if those certain features are missing then your intensive interaction is not Intensive Interaction. What are those features? They are laid out lucidly in *Access to Communication* (Nind and Hewett, 1994), but here I can explain what needed to be new or different before we in our Unit could say that Intensive Interaction was in place. Perhaps I can break this into two parts, the philosophical and the practical.

Presenting the philosophy to staff

The philosophy of Intensive Interaction is sound and logical. It is easy to present it to staff. Almost every member of our team has personal experience of parenting very young children, and we could commend those pleasant memories to them. We only had to look at the Sue/Thomas example of adult/infant interaction. 'Wasn't that exactly how you did it with your own children? You actually taught another human being to speak English. Just think, thirteen-month-old French babies can speak fluent French. How did they do that? It is all there in the Sue/Thomas examples and there is nothing at all in that summary of interactions which you yourselves did not do with your own children.'

There are, obviously, some massive limitations with our children with MSI against Sue's style in the book, because of their inability to hear, see, imitate and so on, but this in no way changes the fact that this is the level our children are at and this is the appropriate natural approach.

We were, and perhaps still are, very 'task' orientated. It is built into our mental software to think in terms of short- and long-term targets, distant aims reached through a series of learnable objectives. These ideals are not bad in themselves, but with our particular population perhaps sometimes it has led us to ask the wrong questions at the right times. Let us look at an example. We set up a vibrating footspa for Tony, and fill it with jelly. This is good – we have discovered already that he likes this sort of thing: he oozes positive body language. But we feel obliged to select a 'short-term learnable target' for the session, an 'outcome', which could be predicted at the beginning of the session on the record sheet and ticked off as 'achieved' at tidying up time thirty minutes later. Or we might use the session to reduce Tony's inappropriate behaviour: we switch off the vibration every time Tony rocks, and log the decline in undesirable rockings.

I think Intensive Interaction philosophy would encourage us to rethink the object of the session, not the activity itself. We could make fewer demands upon Tony, and rewrite the session record sheet. We could celebrate with Tony the fact we have discovered an activity he loves, and that we have been able to 'hear' his communication that he likes it. We could try to remember the fun we had with our own children in that tiny plastic bath with those bubbles and giggles and all that talc. When the session is over the teacher records and shares with her colleagues anything she has learned amidst the tickling and the splashing.

'When the session is over' – think hard about this. In our Unit we are lucky to have a timetable which is flexible enough to be as student-based as possible. Tony did not write the timetable, and he may express his opinion that he wants a bit more time in the bubbles or the jelly. Of course you will have to end the session at some stage, but do be aware of what you are saying to each other:

Tony: (Speaking clearly in body-language. We don't yet understand many of his body-language 'words', but this is certainly one that we do understand.) I am enjoying this session. We have had fun together. Can I stay here a bit longer please?
You: (Tidying up) No. (or perháps) Sorry, Tony. I don't understand you.

Behaviour modification techniques and multi-sensory impairment

Everyone who has to consider the education of children with dual-sensory impairment and additional learning difficulties will have been introduced to Behaviour Modification. This is the business of breaking down a task into minute stages and rewarding success at each stage. The principle is that all human beings will tend to act in a certain way if reward – 'reinforcement' – is applied regularly and then intermittently.

I have to include a mention of this for a number of reasons:

1. Like Intensive Interaction, reward training is a 'whole way of thinking'. Without sounding too dramatic we in the world of MSI do have to ask ourselves the question, 'Can these two ideologies live together?'
2. Our own staff use Behaviour Modification techniques and needed to know if they were to change their approach during Intensive Interaction.
3. As a trained Instructor I myself taught the EDY Behaviour Modification method to teachers for a number of years.

There are good things about Behaviour Modification, and there are bad things. There are features which cannot by definition occupy the same space as Intensive Interaction, and there are some which complement Intensive Interaction. I shall run through these briefly as they relate to deaf/blind education, the opinions expressed being very personal ones.

The 'good things' about Behaviour Modification are very good things. Its basic principles are sound psychology and they do indeed work throughout humankind. It is usually possible to identify the causes of bad behaviour in a child by identifying reinforcers. This is what behavioural psychologists do, and it is good stuff. The toddler who refuses to eat is probably being reinforced by knowing that his problem is the main subject of conversation between his parents, and that is a stronger reinforcer than eating. This is the 'behavioural' way of thinking, and I believe that it should be known by every parent, teacher, manager, army officer – by everybody, in fact. One fundamental of Behaviour Modification is that incidents of praise must outnumber incidents of criticism. The high school teacher and the team leader of a good Intensive Interaction regime will only succeed if they know this.

The psychology of Behaviour Modification is, then, good common sense in principle. Its other particularly useful features in special education are these. It does work in specific instances – it is an ideal way to teach a child to, say, load a spoon. Physical prompt from wrist, then from elbow: reward with cuddles and cheers. That sort of thing. Further (and this is where Behaviour Modification *can* share the same space and even the same bed as Intensive Interaction!), it does emphasise the importance of reward assessment, over-the-top praise and celebration. Moreover, like Intensive Interaction, it is 'professional', in that staff are at pains to know exactly what stage a child has reached. There is also no sense of failure.

The Intensive Interaction practitioner will not be able to avoid the principle of reinforcement. An example might be offered where, during a session, a student wants to delve into some antisocial orifice or produce socially unacceptable behaviour. Those of us who have been presented with this have found it not too difficult to sidestep by getting the pupil to invent a pat-a-cake game with the hand in question, say, and moving on from there. 'Hey, Mary's patting her knee! She's patting my knee! It's a patting game!' We can celebrate the patting. The psychologist in us knows that we avoided celebrating the other behaviour because to do so would have been to reward it and make it more likely to happen again. Of course we know it is going to happen again, but my point is that, even here in a 'taskless' interactive session, we are 'bending' the direction of the proceedings out of respect to the child by avoiding the reinforcement of difficult behaviour.

We are all behaviouralists at heart, and we can feel the glow emanating from a motivated child during Intensive Interaction. It is good, it is rewarding, and the student is likely to want to do the same sort of thing again. It is rewarding for us too, of course, and we are encouraged to continue the sessions because they are successful!

Those are the positives, what of the negatives? At its very worst the worship of Behaviour Modification can become an obsession, although hopefully those days are now a part of recent history. I have met head teachers and practitioners who seemed to have forgotten that they lived on the planet Earth. At a Birmingham Unit for profoundly handicapped youngsters in the late 1970s, an edict was pinned to the notice board with the instruction: 'From now on children are to be picked up or cuddled only as a positive reinforcement for specific appropriate behaviour'. A Midlands head teacher I visited regretted that his wonderful Friday afternoon country dancing session for teenagers with learning difficulties was not yet committed to the Curriculum in exact behavioural terms. Such daftness was around a decade ago, and served to give Behaviour Modification a bad name and lose the goodwill of school teachers and workers. I will admit, too, to other negative features of reward training. One practical fault is that it requires in its purest form a mass of paperwork, every possible developmental skill being broken down into dozens of stages. Such a requirement is certain to stop any project dead in the water.

Then there are the aspects of Behaviour Modification which are diametrically opposed to the philosophy and practice of Intensive Interaction. Firstly, it does rather view the student as a piece of wood set on a lathe, ready for shaping. Secondly, there is no opportunity for adult and student to have genuine fun together in equal portions. Thirdly, and most importantly, it is totally prescriptive. The adult decides what task is to be learned and every teaching session is absolutely dedicated to achieving short-term learnable objectives with that task as the ultimate goal. Finally, it is not an access to communication. We do agree with the maxim: 'Approaches involving the setting of tasks and objectives can be fine for all sorts of learning, but not, we think, for the fundamentals of communication' (Nind and Hewett, 1994, p.188).

Interestingly, there will be direct behavioural benefits resulting from Intensive Interaction, but the important point is that the adult should not be setting himself or herself toward those targets. We will see later that Peter's self-injurious behaviour reduced considerably. Probably, with hindsight, a psychologist could identify some of the behavioural antecedents and reinforcers which produced that happier disposition, but Peter is so developmentally young that a 'let's take Peter through a detailed behaviour changing programme' could not possibly work. It is not the approach that Peter needs.

So, as a way of thinking, Intensive Interaction does require the intervenor or teacher to view her interaction with the child from a different standpoint. Here she is not the 'trainer' who anticipates an encouraging series of ticks on a task analysis form. (Again, I am not decrying the use of such forms in their place – with pupils who are multi-sensorily impaired they do represent a way ahead and an indicator of progress. But a 'teaching' session of any sort does involve the adult sitting at her files and deciding what it is that the pupil should do – and therefore that some responses will be 'better' than others. Confess – have we not all at some time boasted that a child remained 'on task'.) Intensive Interaction is not about keeping the student 'on task'.

Differences in practice

Above I have laid out some of the changes in philosophical approach, or policy, needed by someone who wants to use Intensive Interaction. How, in practice, do we change, or continue, present good practice so that we can describe it as genuine Intensive Interaction? As I have argued, much of what goes on in a Unit for pupils with MSI could be called 'intensive interaction' – without the capital letters. Massage, aromatherapy, physical education, sensory sound, light and vibration experiences, and unsighted mobility training are examples. The list is very long, and the majority of our pupils need a considerable daily input of physiotherapy and mobility programmes co-ordinated by the physiotherapist. Those severely physically disabled need to operate from a number of different standing, seated and lying positions, often strapped into complicated equipment. Toilet training is important, and successful because it is offered five times in the school day. The nature of the children's disabilities means that most of what they do throughout the day must take place with an adult in close proximity, and these activities have always been so devised that they are joyful and rewarding for the adult and the intervenor.

Clearly, these daily events should not be changed for something else. So could we adapt them a little so that they can be seen as Intensive Interaction in Action? If we look again at Nind and Hewett's (1994) criteria for a good session, the answer will often have to be 'no'.

Multi-sensory Unit daily activities cannot be Intensive Interaction if:

- there is an element of a teaching target in them, or they take place in a noisy room that intereferes with the signalling between the two people; or
- they are specifically directed by the adult (we do several such sessions – exciting events which are repeated unchanged over a period of half a term, with the intention of eliciting recognition and anticipation); or
- they are the enactment of an ideology. Conductive education and aromatherapy might be examples. There is nothing wrong with these, but the fact that the intervenor might be constrained by specific methods, training or expectations means that they cannot be part of Intensive Interaction; or
- they have a non-negotiable fixed ending time; or
- they are likely to be seriously interrupted (we do try to avoid all interruptions).

A true Intensive Interaction session, then, must be *planned for* in space and time. Just as a good parent will consciously, not incidentally, ensure that each of his or her children is getting some 'special time', so will our students sense that Intensive Interaction sessions are theirs alone, for as long as they want.

The limitations upon Intensive Interaction where a student is dual-sensory impaired

It would be all too easy for any of us to scan the summary of Sue's style in *Access to Communication* and comment, 'I won't be able to do that, because Peter can't see,' or, 'we won't bother with that, because he is deaf.' It does not actually work like that. From the adult's point of view there are, in fact, very few features of Sue's style which cannot be applied to a deaf/blind child. In *Access to Communication* Nind and Hewett (1994) observe Sue's style and then suggest how this natural approach can be used to aid communication progress with the most disadvantaged of students. Few, or none, of the Statemented population will be able to satisfy all of the Sue/Thomas criteria, and deaf/blind children are no exception to this. Indeed, the whole ethos of the Intensive Interaction approach is that an interaction which works so well between parent and normally developing baby is the ideal means of communication where comprehension is limited, feedback is low, and stereotypical behaviours interfere. These are the students Intensive Interaction is for. Whilst in our Unit we are doing our best to overcome the limitations of deafness and blindness, other carers in other places may be struggling with the problems of serious challenging behaviour or epilepsy.

When you know a child very well, when you are close to that child in a fun situation, her deafness or blindness is not the tremendous problem it might appear to be. Of course we have difficulty with eye contact and imitation, and our student will not be able to celebrate with us in mutual eyebrow raising – the difficulties are so obvious that we need not dwell upon them. It is very likely that our children with MSI do not understand yet that they are of the same species as we are – that what they feel is what we feel. Certainly they cannot know that we have sensory abilities which they lack. Might we instead take the positive view? Could we not look again at Nind and Hewett's model of Sue and Thomas, and look this time at what Thomas has learned from the session? Could Peter, who is profoundly deaf and blind, learn the same things?

After a re-reading of that section of chapter 3 of Nind and Hewett's book, we can certainly answer 'yes' to that question:

- He can know that what he does is worthwhile, that his noises have meaning and, hopefully, are responded to by his play-partner in an increasingly consistent way.
- Words may come to have meaning if Peter is gaining much from his powerful hearing amplification – we cannot be sure what he is hearing so hands-on signing is used in addition, consistently and respectfully. It may be years, if ever, before Peter demonstrates better understanding of words or signs, but progress will certainly not be possible if words or signs are not used, or only occasionally used, or used inappropriately. This is in fact exactly the position Sue's Thomas found himself in. When he was four hours old surely none of the words spoken to him had any meaning for him at all, and yet his mother used them and repeated them so that within fifteen-or-so months he will be communicating in English with a beautiful and breathtakingly complicated syntax.

    Peter may not get that far. But he is entitled to as much Intensive Interaction as Sue gives Thomas and he might surprise us. We are all aware that a forlorn prediction of failure will always come to pass, not because the prediction was accurate, but because people cease to apply the sort of interaction which might have produced success. This is the phenomenon of the self-fulfilling prophecy.
- Communication is fun – if we make it so.
- Peter will discover that he has power. Every movement of his body is noticed and made into part of a game and he is in control.
- He will know that he is good to be with. This is the most important piece of information which any teacher in any area of education can pass on to his or her pupils.
- People are fun to be with. Peter lives in a world which stops at the farthest reach of his arms. A loving session of fun has got to be good.
- Objects and their properties. With his knowledge of Peter's preferences his teacher will introduce objects and toys to the sessions – but it is up to Peter what is to be done with them! Peter thrusts away a light metal tube which is placed near his hands, and it rings noisily on the hard floor, sending the readout of auditory trainer up into the red. 'Peter dropped the tube! Did you hear that tube go! Feel my

hands, Peter. I'll drop the tube. We're playing a tube-dropping game!'

Peter has these massive disadvantages, then, and yet from Nind and Hewett's list of 'What is Thomas learning?' Peter is only denied the one feature, the understanding of eye-contact. All the other aspects of learning are available to him through Intensive Interaction.

That list is a very important one. I find it useful to return to it myself frequently to make sure that I have all of it loaded, as it were, into my own mental software. There are perhaps a dozen ideas there, and they should influence my actions as I interact with Peter.

What the adult should bring to a 'taskless' interactive session

Throughout this chapter I have suggested that, while the student who is multi-sensorily impaired comes to the session with no expectations imposed upon her, there are a number of demands which must be made upon us, her intervenors, before we go in there. We should perhaps draw these together.

Before commencing the session the adult should be aware of the following points:

- how much the pupil can see and hear
- the present known levels of communication
- that hearing aids and spectacles are in place
- that seating position is correct and safe
- what the pupil likes and dislikes
- where to look for new communications – smile, eyebrows, body movements, reduction of undesirable behaviours
- the limitations of multi-sensory impairment
- possible dangers – does the child hurt herself or others?
- the appropriateness of the setting – quiet and uninterrupted, correct lighting etc.
- the school policy on conducting intimate interactions
- that the adult should bring well-thought-out equipment to the session, so as to repeat and extend the fun of previous sessions
- the notes written after the previous session

- and that it really does help to have a regular look at the 'What is Thomas learning?' section of *Access to Communication*, chapter 3.

During the interaction the adult will be looking for:

- new fragments of body-language and facial expression
- evidence of fun
- evidence of anticipation
- evidence that the student remembers what happened in the previous session
- any sort of pattern.

After the session the adult should:

1. Get something down on paper immediately – not even ten minutes later. It is amazing how quickly we can forget the best bits when other crises distract us. This means a bit of sensible teamwork. A lovely quarter hour of Intensive Interaction will be quite spoiled for both parties if the student is left somehow abandoned while the notes are being written up. Audio and video recorders are useful pieces of equipment here.
2. Ensure that a system is in place to share any new discoveries with colleagues.

I will try to illustrate the above with some stories of what typical interactions may be like for both the pupil and the teacher.

Peter

Suffice to say that Peter is eight, he cannot walk, but is learning to bear his weight with assistance. He has no functional vision. A combination of clinical assessment, observation, and anecdotal evidence point to a profound hearing loss.

He will wear Auditory Headphones or post-aural hearing aids. He will take them off after fifteen minutes or so – earlier if the input setting is reduced. We are working with the School Audiologist to devise cunning means by which we can deduce his hearing loss with more accuracy.

Peter will bang his head on the handles of his wheelchair, and if thwarted in this he will slap his own face. As we get to know him better we are learning how to identify this as a communication, and often we can change some feature of his environment to reduce the probabilities of the undesirable behaviour occurring. The phenomenon of Self-Injurious Behaviour is not as easy as that, of course, and we are a long way from eliminating it from Peter's repertoire. There is no doubt, however, that it has reduced dramatically since the advent of Intensive Interaction. I think that the reason for this can be found not only in the sessions themselves, but in the whole ethos of Intensive Interaction. Throughout the day Peter is spoken to appropriately and without pressure or expectation. He is one of the gang and he knows we like him. We don't baby-talk him, and we don't patronise him. We do everything that we can to 'hear' him, and we remember what he has said so that next time we meet him we can play the same games.

To go into a more detailed profile of Peter will not be interesting. More illuminating might be a script of an interactive session with him:

The scene: Peter is sitting strapped in his special chair in his classroom. The door to the corridor is open. In his lap is a large red beaded plastic percussion shaker.

Addis: Hey, Peter, it's Game Time! (Taps his palm up Peter's leg, towards his knee. This is the signal of reference for Intensive Interaction.)

Peter: (Wiggles his knees in and out.)

Addis: (Helping him wiggle his knees, exaggerating the action for him.) Oh, yes. It's the knee game. We're wiggling knees.

Peter: (Stops. Pause.)

Addis: (Nudges the shaker so that it touches Peter's hand.)

Peter: (Reaches for the shaker and chews it.)

Addis: Chewing the shaker. Peter is chewing his shaker. (Addis puts his own hand on Peter's, his other hand and then Peter's other hand.) Hands. We're holding hands.

Peter: (Wiggles knees in and out.)

Addis: (Takes the shaker, and the pile of hands, and uses them to exaggerate the knee movements. This lasts twenty seconds.)

Peter: (Stops. Pause. An elbow flaps.)

Addis: (Taking a hand from the pile and flapping the elbow harder.) The elbow! Yes!

Peter: (Giggles.)

Addis:	(Repeats the elbow flapping assistance.)
Peter:	(Giggles.)
Addis:	(Repeats.)
Peter:	(Smiles, then stops.)
Peter:	(Waves hands at head level, and sings.)
Addis:	(Listens for five seconds, then joins in, trying to match the pitch.) Singing. We're singing. Peter is singing. (Pause.)
Addis:	(Puts a hand on his, on the shaker, and Peter's other on top. Peter does not remove it.)
Peter:	(The legs start again.)
Addis:	It's the legs. It's the wiggling legs game. I like this.

And so on. Some points worth noting:

This is a real session, recorded above exactly as it happened. With hindsight an observer might note a dozen faults in my responses to Peter, but I was there, thinking on my feet, and that is really how Intensive Interaction works in the real world. Two real people interacting. The same applies to mums and dads everywhere – their responses are genuine and honest and probably reflect their own weaknesses. If we were to attempt to make our own responses perfect, then the whole point is lost. Nind and Hewett (1994) emphasise that Sue does not flaunt her sophistication and experience. Nevertheless, our special task in the field of multi-sensory impairment is to embrace, during a natural session, the sensory disadvantages of the student, and with practice you do get better at that.

The activities Peter chose were very basic – he is developmentally young. They were, actually, quite fun. I did not have to pretend to enjoy the session. The classroom door was open and my session was within the hearing of the other staff in the Unit. Obviously in our field of work this is quite unnecessary, but in these sad suspicious days it is probably best to adhere to such a policy. Intensive Interaction is an intimate one-to-one activity.

What did I learn?

1. I found a means to extend vocabulary. There was a pattern there, a cycle of actions which at the next session I developed a little. (With a hot-water-bottle 'Ow, it's hot!', and with a dangling microphone to amplify his voice.)
2. The elbow movement was perhaps unintentional, and did not occur

in later sessions. In the session above I assumed intentionality, for Peter is entitled to that.

3. I learned how to make Peter laugh.
4. I had begun the process of tuning in to Peter, of understanding which approaches to Peter are received with enthusiasm, which with neutrality.

What did Peter learn?

1. We are not logging short-term learnable targets here, of course, but as we continue the sessions Peter will learn that every action of his, voluntary or not, will be responded to.
2. To date Peter has always been happy during the sessions. He has never slapped his face during a session.
3. He recognised the rules of the game he invented. In later sessions – we always begin with the shaker – he always wiggled his legs and left his hands in place on the shaker. He usually sings at some point.
4. This is the basis of communication. He is telling us what he likes and he is discovering that he is heard.
5. I did actually really enjoy the session, and hopefully, through human transmissions we do not yet understand, Peter sensed this. It is very important.

John

In spite of right-side hemiplegia, John manages to walk. He is blind, and wears powerful hearing aids. If he is tired or upset he will pinch, bite or head-butt his intervenor. His fist comes up regularly to hit his own chin. It would be all too easy for an adult who did not know him to conclude that these behaviours mean, 'stop it', 'leave me alone', or 'I don't like this activity'. Those of us who do know him have long understood that John works on a different communication system. Intensive Interaction confirms this. We found it more useful first to admit that we have not yet fathomed the meaning of these gross, apparently negative communications, and then to put them aside and look for smaller signals which might tell us something.

During Intensive Interaction:

- John gripped the edge of the chair on which he was sitting. Intervenor gripped the same spot over his hand. John forced Intervenor's hand away by the thumb.
- After a few goes at this, John would tap his lip with two fingers.
- During the sessions he head-butted the Intervenor a few times, and struck his own chin.
- Towards the end of each session, John sang and 'conducted' with his hand high in the air.

So there were a few communications in these sessions to which we could respond.

The chair-gripping and lip-tapping were behaviours which John used only during the Interactions. They proved that John remembers what happened in previous sessions, he enjoyed it and wants it to happen again. This also proves that John recognises the Interactive sessions as a separate 'special' time. The conducting and singing came as a bonus, a communication already known to mean, 'I like this'. The Intervenor ignored the head-butting as best he could, but decided to 'notice' the chin rapping, because it was quite gentle and happened so frequently. 'You are hitting your chin. Does it hurt? Hey, feel your chin – feel mine. I've got a chin.'

The undesirable behaviours continue during the sessions. It would have been ludicrous to have expected them to stop. But hopefully we have transmitted to John that these gross movements, which may be beyond his control, are okay by us – we can still have fun together.

A late report on the head-butting is that it now occurs very rarely during Intensive Interaction sessions, *but it would not have mattered even if it had continued in strength*. We as staff have agreed that we must avoid:

- hoping that the sessions will reduce the self-injurious behaviour
- expecting that the behaviours would reduce
- feeling failure if the behaviours continue
- taking it personally if, at the end of a pleasant session, John feels for the Intervenor's wrist and pinches it hard. (He does do this.)

Intensive Interaction as we see it is not about predicting improvement in behaviour. That would be a 'demand' upon John which he might sense. How much better if we can convey to him the joy we genuinely feel at the number of positive communications he has allowed us during the sessions.

References

Department of Education and Science (1989) *Educational Provision for Deaf-Blind Children*. London: DES.

Nind, M. and Hewett, D. (1988) 'Interaction as curriculum: A process method in a school for pupils with severe learning difficulties', *British Journal of Special Education*, **15**, 55–7.

Nind, M. and Hewett, D. (1994) *Access to Communication: Developing the Basics of Communication with People with Severe Learning Difficulties Through Intensive Interaction*. London: David Fulton.

Chapter 3

Jamie's Story: Intensive Interaction in a College of Further Education

Christine Smith

Jamie and the challenge he gave us

Jamie was referred to us by his social worker. He had been in residential care since birth and had no family contact. At the time of referral he was 22. All the other residents were accessing school, college or day centre placements and Jamie had spent the previous 12 months as the only resident left at home without a day time placement He was described as having 'challenging behaviour' and becoming 'increasingly isolated and depressed'.

Our first assessments of Jamie described him as 'pre-verbal', using no actual words but having a large repertoire of noises, sounds, almost songs. These sounds sometimes became very rhythmic, and there was a feeling he may have some understanding of verbal language. We sensed he was capable of understanding but chose not to show it, and he chose not to interact with anyone. He was very socially withdrawn and exhibited autistic type behaviours. He had a range of obsessive behaviours such as staring for long periods at his thumbs, twiddling string, towels, clothes – anything he could get his hands on. He would constantly tear up paper, paper towels etc. and be fascinated by watching the pieces slowly fall to the ground. He would also pick up bits of earth, stones, grass from the ground and either drop them and watch them fall or eat them. At other times he would stand in the centre of the room, apparently oblivious to other people, and stare with great intensity at the light, head on one side, repeating the same sound again and again. He was fascinated by peeling off wallpaper and eating it along with plaster, effectively making a series of little holes in the classroom wall. He would frequently make for the toilets. If he decided that was where he was going he would hurl himself towards the door, not looking at anybody. If anyone was in his way they would be shoved aside. Whenever he was confronted at these times he would appear annoyed and sometimes hit out in order to get his way. There seemed to be nothing personal about this aggression. It didn't seem to matter 'who' he was hitting, we were all just objects in his way. Once in the toilets he would rush to press the flusher and then stick his head down into the bowl and drink the flowing water. After using the toilet he would sometimes pick up his faeces and either eat it or smear it over the toilet walls. All this was done at high speed and with such single-mindedness that we were having to use a great deal of force to even attempt to stop him.

All these 'behaviours' excluded other people but appeared to provide Jamie with some sort of self-fulfilment or stimulation which he was unable to get from being with people. Jamie occasionally made eye contact but in a very remote way and he did not keep still in one place long enough to really notice anyone. In fact, he was so active staff would describe him as being comparable to a whirlwind. Early recording sheets show that within the first five minutes of the first day he had wet himself, eaten a plant, semi-stripped, and nicked everyone's mugs of tea.

We all initially found him very unapproachable. He seldom looked at us and when he did it was because he wanted something, usually for us to open the door to let him escape from the room. He appeared to be very unselfconscious and this gave him a certain air of innocence. One staff member questioned whether he had any awareness of his own being. There was a simple childlike quality about him. He gave the impression of having little if any reflective thought. When he wanted something he instinctively reached out to get it. He seemed bemused by his own body, as if he didn't fully recognise it as his. There was an air of 'aloneness' about him. It was very difficult to find a level of approach that would get through to him. He would ignore our usual forms of 'hellos', 'handshakes', and signing.

At best we were coping, and we were simply containing him. On arrival in the morning he would charge into the room, apparently not noticing anyone, and with his great strides he would head for the furthest, emptiest point. He would usually drape himself over the biggest radiator, with his head facing the wall. He seemed to like the heat and the comfort. Over the first two months we tried out any activity or approach we had in our experience. The most we achieved was a quick attempt at an inset puzzle.

The fact that he could easily complete the puzzle made us all the more sure of his potential. However, in order to get him to sit at the table to do it involved using an amount of physical compulsion we were uneasy with. In any case the activity itself seemed to have little value in our eyes, and he gave the impression he was just doing it so that afterwards we might leave him alone again.

We were becoming exhausted from chasing around after Jamie. We had to be constantly on the alert in case he made a dash for the door etc. and I was starting to feel more like a guard than a teacher. We were also depressed that we were not getting anywhere. We are an educational establishment and we needed to find a way of progressing with Jamie. We didn't want to continue to be simply containing him, and his disruptiveness was affecting the rest of the group. I had begun my 'career' teaching Art and English in mainstream high school, moved into special schools and finally spent eight years in FE. I had made a particular choice to work with those students with the most profound and complex needs. It was a challenge and it is an area which I find very important and very interesting. I had put a lot of effort into researching and planning my work. We were all used to working with challenging people with a varying degree of success. This time we had to admit we just didn't know what to do to enable him to learn.

I work at Park Lane College of FE in Leeds. It is a large college, set in the city centre, and it offers a huge variety of courses. Many people with learning difficulties attend the college. Most attend inclusive courses with learning support, while others are discrete. A number of us work on the group of discrete courses for people with severe and profound learning difficulties. The majority of students are school leavers, others are referred later in life as a result of hospital closure, regression at home or years in a day centre. We work in a former school building, shared with mainstream students, adjacent to the large main college site. I am a lecturer and I work closely with two learning support staff, Mick and Debbie. I work on the courses for people with profound learning and/or emotional difficulties. Group sizes are small, and we have a high staffing ratio. The curriculum includes life skills, communication, art, music, baking, sensory, community experience etc. These courses are all part-time. Jamie was attending for two days a week over a two-year period.

We found we had very little success with Jamie. He was so speedy we were unable to take him out into the community. He would be reluctant to link arms or to walk 'with' us. As we are based in the city centre, going out and learning to use local facilities is an important part of our curriculum. Not being able to do these things had implications for the rest of the group. Table-top or skills based activities were almost impossible. Jamie would sit only for very brief periods. He would eat all the art materials. He preferred to roam around the room, apparently oblivious to both peers and staff, constantly searching for some form of stimulation such as paper to tear, inset puzzles to repeatedly pick up and drop onto the floor, essentially causing chaos. I felt I was constantly getting 'on to' him and saying 'no don't do that'. As I have stated, I have to admit that I used an amount of physical compulsion – coaxing and arm pulling and directing in attempting to get Jamie to 'do' something. This was all very fruitless. Jamie was clearly well used to people saying no to him. He would totally ignore our pleas, and he appeared even more determined to cause havoc. If we took hold of his arm to redirect him from his destructive path he would firmly pull away from us and to stop him involved using a considerable level of force and arm pulling.

Finding a way

Eventually, one afternoon after a number of unsuccessful attempts I 'gave up' with the feeling that I was unable to teach Jamie successfully and perhaps I had better change my job. I lay down on a bean bag in a corner in a state of exhaustion. This was actually where the turning point came; instead of 'being in control' I had totally relaxed. Jamie continued to stalk around the room. I closed my eyes and soon became aware that he had come and sat near me on the mat. I reached out to touch him and he was off again. I remained where I was and he later came back and sat near me again for a few seconds. I realised that for the first time Jamie was making an initiative, and that by completely relaxing I had made myself approachable. It dawned on me there was something seriously wrong with both 'what' and 'how' I was working with Jamie. We started to rethink our whole approach, and started to focus on him as he actually is and not how we wanted him to be. Jamie was so self-absorbed and so determined there was no way we were going to be able to stop his behaviours. They seemed to provide him with a source of comfort and retreat. We needed to respect that and to totally accept him, behaviours and all, as a whole person. We decided we would change our attitude to the behaviours and hoped that by showing Jamie an acceptance of the behaviours we would be creating a starting point to get through to him.

We began by making the classroom less easy to destroy by locking things up in cupboards. We wanted to feel we didn't have to be saying no to him all the time. It was actually very hard not to say no to someone who was so chaotic. It is an instinctive reaction to prevent someone from tearing paper, emptying out cupboards, picking up piles of books to cascade around the room. Yes, we needed to adapt the environment so that it was less easy to damage, but that was just the beginning.

Around this time we all had a training day in Intensive Interaction. This had made us more optimistic and confident about changing our approach. We had the feeling this is it, this is just what we need for Jamie, essentially to begin at an earlier baseline. We spent time in staff meetings discussing the approach and the best practical way of introducing it into our particular set up. Our previous learning programme was discarded. We wrote a new set of learning outcomes for Jamie all based on the skills of getting on with another person, skills like making eye contact, sharing space, turn-taking. We time-tabled an hour each day when we were able to have one-to-one staffing and could take it in turns to work with Jamie. Where possible, we would video these sessions. We realised the necessity for detailed written recording of not only Jamie's initiations but also of our responses to his behaviours. This was one of the most difficult areas initially. We had all worked in this area for years and thought of ourselves as 'experts' so it was sometimes painful to 'question our practice' and to admit that maybe we were not responding in the best way. In place of our previous discussions around Jamie's behaviour we were now focusing on our responses to him, as being crucial for success. We decided to use a recording sheet which would include (a) a general description of interaction, (b) any new or significant occurrences, and (c) an evaluation of 'our' staff performances including anything which was successful/ unsuccessful and our feelings about the session.

We all have different personalities and it was interesting how our relationships with Jamie developed in different ways. I am quite a still person. I had found chasing around after Jamie very uncomfortable. By deciding to relinquish some control and give him the time to take a lead I found myself immediately beginning to feel more relaxed. I would always start the day by showing Jamie I was pleased to see him, by putting my face near to him, smiling, stroking his arm. I would approach him on his own terms. If he was kneeling on the floor tearing up paper towels or dropping inset pieces I would sit next to him and also tear paper etc. At first he would go away quite quickly to another part of the room. I would stay where I was and continue the activity he had started. I would give him time. I soon found that he would return quite quickly to where I was and we would resume the activity again and it would be repeated until he stayed next to me for longer times. This became one of our 'games'. Another game developed when I made a game out of grabbing/trying to pull the other end of the towel he was twiddling. I would create a sort of jokey atmosphere; 'I'm going to get your towel'. Jamie would begin to laugh and an exaggerated tug of war would develop. If he pulled it really hard I would let go and fall on the floor as if to show him I'd fallen because of his pulling. I wanted him to realise that his actions had some effect.

We began to find Jamie has a brilliant sense of humour and we could build on this. Some days were more successful than others. It could be hard to judge when to push on and when to leave it when nothing seemed to be happening. Jamie would make it clear when he didn't like something by shaking his fist or grimacing. We respected these signs and would stop the activity. We had to tread a fine line between trying to sensitively push the interaction forward without taking over control again. If Jamie had really had enough we needed to respect that and wait until he was ready.

After a few weeks Jamie started to show us when he was ready. I found that after an initial grimace from him, I would stop the interaction but I would remain nearby and 'available'. This might still be the end of the interaction and Jamie would move away wanting to be on his own. Sometimes after a few minutes Jamie would return and make eye contact or reach out to briefly touch us. Again it was important to give him time. A change of tempo or tactic could also work. One particular day Jamie refused to let me join in his game of dropping inset pieces on to the floor, and so I introduced a ball, bouncing it round his head very light heartedly, he began to laugh and grabbed the ball and this became a chase which ended with him lying on the mat and offering his foot to massage, smiling.

Sometimes I found the time-tabled sessions difficult. As the teacher I felt I needed to manage the whole group. We only had one room to work in and I would sometimes find I would be distracted by keeping an ear out for what was going on elsewhere in the room. I found some of my best interactions would occur in the lunch break, after Jamie had eaten his sandwiches with the others and chosen to return to the empty classroom. At these times I would sit in the room with him without pressure, I was more relaxed and Jamie clearly found me more approachable. It was interesting that Jamie appeared to make initiations towards me more frequently when I was sitting down on a chair or even the floor, as if this gave him a feeling of being more in control. Control and the negotiation of control became a central issue for us. Although I am not naturally a big controller it was still difficult to shake off the traditional teacher role of 'being in control' and also of being 'seen to be in control'.

Although we kept to these time-tabled sessions for intensive interaction we quickly found that our new approach permeated throughout the days and that we needed to remain constantly receptive and ready to seize any opportunity to interact as it arose. I soon found too that the minibus was a good place for interaction. Jamie really enjoyed travelling in the bus. I would sit next to him and either offer him a hand for a clapping game or blow gently on his neck. Sometimes this would work well, other times he would make it clear I was crowding him. I learnt from those experiences not to push it and would quickly stop the activity. Most times after this Jamie would reach out after several minutes of sitting quietly and take my hand, wrapping his fingers between mine. It was as if . . . yes, he did want to make contact, but on his own terms.

Swimming sessions were also successful. Jamie liked swimming. He would head for the deepest point and jump up and down in the water, using his toes to spring up from the bottom. I would follow him and do the same facing him until we got a pattern of synchronised jumping going. It was good fun and a lot of eye contact would develop. One day he reached out with his foot under the water and briefly touched my leg. I became aware that he was looking at me more often. One lunchtime, I was sitting in the corner of the busy dining area. Jamie was at the far side of the room totally self involved in staring at his thumbs. He caught my eye from across the room, I tapped my legs and he came and very briefly sat on my knee and was gone again.

Debbie's personality is very direct and outgoing. She has a fairly boisterous sense of humour. She developed a unique set of 'games' with Jamie. She has a small child of her own which was possibly reflected in her approach. She would sometimes use a teasing, 'telling off' mother/child type tone: 'what do you think you are doing? . . . I'm coming to get you ... give me that'. She would often plunge in with a good humoured physical tussle, pretending to try to steal the ball, object etc. from Jamie and it would turn into a game which might involve chasing, tickling, throwing cushions, shouting in an exaggerated way. Jamie became very responsive to this approach and would often laugh out loud. This type of physically active sequence would often develop into a quieter, easy interaction with Jamie being very happy to share Debbie's company and close proximity, eventually starting to put his own cheek next to hers.

One of Debbie's recording sheets reads:

> I sat next to Jamie on a beanbag. Jamie sat for some time completely engrossed in looking at his thumbs so after a while I showed him mine ... do you like mine? ... he took hold of both my hands, brought them round in front of him and held my hands looking at my thumbs in the same position he looks at his. This has never happened before. He seems to be completely in his own world but he brought me into it and was very relaxed about it. I felt good he wanted me to share his private space and be so close. It lasted 10–15 seconds.

Debbie is musical and unafraid of 'making a fool of herself' and was the most successful of anyone of echoing Jamie's sounds. She would echo his sounds and also his movements, often in an exaggerated manner. Jamie was surprised by this at first and would stop and look before repeating his sounds. This would be repeated until Jamie changed the pattern of sounds, and then Debbie would change also. This could go on for some time and develop into a sound conversation. If Debbie paused Jamie would look to her in anticipation. Debbie and Jamie both liked the Jacuzzi which was next to the swimming pool. Jamie would visibly relax in the warm water and sink down until only part of his face was above water level. He would start a particular pattern of sounds, Debbie would respond and a sort of singing conversation would develop which echoed amazingly around the swimming complex.

Mick's approach was much quieter. He treated Jamie very much as an equal, as a 'mate'. Sometimes Jamie would clap his hands loudly. Mick would use this to begin and develop a clapping game, which would become a pattern of claps, sometimes with pauses, Mick's face close to Jamie's, looking into his eyes. Mick also used massage as a starting point, especially in view of Jamie's activeness. He would begin with a foot massage on the mat, which is something Jamie enjoyed. He would quietly stroke his feet and softly echo his sounds, ensuring that he was sitting fairly close to Jamie's face. A feeling of trust and a relaxed, together atmosphere would develop. Jamie sometimes would reach out and stroke Mick's beard. At first Mick would simply carry on with his feet stroking afraid to spoil this interaction by trying to push it further.

Recording our sessions became very important. We experimented with a number of recording sheets. We found the two shown here to be the most useful. Sheet no. 1 (figure 3.1) was particularly successful for reflecting upon and developing our observation skills, observation of Jamie's smallest signals and our own responses to those signals. Sheet no. 2 (figure 3.2) became the most popular. The descriptive section was fairly straight forward. We all found the most difficult section to write was the evaluation of our own performance. We got better at this as time went on, and it made us realise how important our role was in the success of the work. We found that if we left it to the end of a busy day to write up our sessions we would often have forgotten details. Whenever possible after an interaction staff would go straight to the adjoining staffroom to write up their sheet. Naturally, good, flexible teamwork was necessary to make this possible at all, and it was not possible all of the time. Video use was sporadic. We had practical problems with our video camera breaking down, then being stolen. I would sometimes observe a session between Jamie and a staff member. I would make notes to write up later and discuss, and this worked well.

In the early days there had been an embarrassment factor. It took a while to stop feeling self-conscious when working with Jamie in front of others but we soon got used to it and we found the approach began to come naturally. The atmosphere of the sessions started to be much more light hearted. When a new member of staff joined us for a session we would be a bit inhibited but this did not usually last for long.

One thing common to us all was finding how difficult it was to judge when to carry on trying to develop an interaction, and when enough was enough. It was a sensitive judgement that we all had to make of our own intuition, and much of it we learned by trial and error. Whenever a particularly interesting interaction occurred with Jamie making new initiatives with one of us, we seemed to all sense it and there would be a sort of hushed atmosphere where no one wanted to spoil what was going on, for example, when Jamie first stroked Mick's beard. After moments such as this we would be elated and feel a sense of achievement we had

---

'STEP BY STEP'
INTERACTIVE COMMUNICATION SESSIONS

Name of staff: Christine   Name/s of student: Jamie   Date: 22/9/96

1. Did the student enjoy the session?

   I would say he was certainly interested and appeared to enjoy parts of it, some of it not so much.

2. If not, when and why?

   Several times he showed annoyance in the first part of the session. I think it was because I was not sensitive enough to his signals of wanting to be left alone, of having had enough.

3. Was the signalling effective today?

   Jamie did signal to me that he'd had enough by moving away. I was too pushy, too eager for something to develop. Once I did back off, he actually came over after a while and things started to happen.

4. Did I miss some signals or clues?

   Probably – especially at first.

5. Did something new happen?

   Towards the end of session he took hold of my face with both hands and there was a definite but brief eye contact.

6. Why did it happen?

   It happened after I'd relaxed and stopped 'pushing' him. We'd shared some humour and I'd chased him around the room, I had laughed and sat down.

7. What was the student's mood and did it affect performance?
   OK.

8. What was my mood?

   I had begun by feeling rather wound up. This made me less easy to be with and I was too intent to push forward.

9. How good was the session?

   It became good, after a faltering beginning.

10. What have I learned?

    How important it is I relax and sensitise myself to Jamie and his signals so that it really is a 'negotiation' and not just me controlling the interaction.

Figure 3.1 Recording sheet no.1

INTERACTION DAILY RECORD

Student: Jamie   Date: 5/10/95   Time: 1:45-2.30   Place: Room 9   Staff: Mick

Description – what happened and why:

Clapping games – Student and I played clapping games and other hand games. Gave good eye contact and followed my hands. Took the lead himself and smiled a lot when doing the game.

Catch & chase – Jamie gave me clear sign he was bored with the hand game, so I tried to tickle him, he ran away laughing so I chased him and tickled him when I caught him. He enjoyed this for a while and gave clear signs when he had had enough.

Jamie looked at my face and stroked my beard then got me to rub ears, smiled and instigated some hand games.

Please try and evaluate your performance. What did you do that was successful/unsuccessful. How did you feel and why:

Successful: I tried to keep good eye contact all the time, this was successful for short periods. Getting the student to take the lead and enjoy the games and contact.

Unsuccessful: Jamie would not copy my clapping. Tried to make games last too long. When playing chase game, did not read the signs at first when Jamie had had enough.

I enjoyed Jamie's company and felt he enjoyed me being there. Though maybe I could have been more verbal and encouraged Jamie to take the lead more. I still say 'no' when I shouldn't.

Figure 3.2 Recording sheet no. 2

not felt before. Also, it took us some weeks to get the negotiation right, to actually be sharing control and we would occasionally slip back into the 'no' syndrome, particularly if we were feeling tired ourselves. It was important that we got that issue right. We were allowing Jamie to feel some empowerment by responding to his communications in a meaningful way, and by doing this we were convinced we were teaching him the basics of self-advocacy. Developing the very basics of Jamie's communication was actually developing the very basics of self-advocacy. This must surely be at the heart of any FE curriculum.

We experienced one moment of panic when another student in the group suddenly sat down on the floor and began to desperately tear paper and stuff it in her mouth, the whole time keeping her eyes fixed on us. It was particularly alarming because she was a student who was actually able to communicate quite well, she was the high flyer in the group, and we certainly didn't want her to regress in any way. Immediately we turned our full attention to her, she happily got up and returned to her work at the table. We realised that Jamie had taken up a large part of our time over the week and that this 'copying' behaviour was simply a way of drawing that to our attention. We redressed our balance of support and we had no re-occurrences. In fact that particular student had been making enormous progress, in her own way, over the months we were working with Jamie and she has now moved on to another group.

The use of physical contact had become an important part of our work and we were aware that it can be an area of concern. Mainstream schools are very wary about the use of any form of physical contact. Obviously there are students who need to be taught not to hug and kiss strangers. However, at this pre-verbal level touch becomes inevitable and essential. Previously our main use of physical contact with Jamie had been in restraint and compulsion. Now we were using it as a means of giving and receiving communication. Although Jamie is a sexual being who sometimes displayed sexual behaviours, the timing and frequency of any sexual arousal bore no relationship to our new use of touch. Most of his sexual behaviour seemed to occur when he was alone and bored.

A comment over age appropriateness was raised during a review/inspection which took place well into our work with Jamie. We were very disappointed and surprised. By this time we had put a great deal of time and thought into our work and it was well documented. The whole point of our use of Intensive Interaction was to more effectively address Jamie's needs, to address what had been a deficit in our previous programme, and to now work at a 'stage' appropriate level. The concern seemed to have been mostly around the use of a large ball for passing back and forth as a means of establishing communication, and also our style of beginning where Jamie was at, which mostly involved having to sit down on the floor with him. My experience is that all people of all ages and abilities like balls, and so I find them an extremely useful tool. Uppermost in our priorities is the promotion of student dignity. We believed that by using an Intensive Interaction approach with Jamie we were accessing him and promoting self-advocacy, which must surely allow him dignity and is essential for adulthood. Using the approach was also allowing him to increase his life opportunities, and to enjoy his life more. He was now active in his own learning, and we felt he was beginning to feel a certain empowerment as a result of our new responsiveness and 'negotiation' of control. Previously we had been having to use some force with Jamie. Physically directing him to a table had not seemed to us to be an age appropriate way of treating a 22-year-old.

I was aware of how much responsibility the approach put on support staff. They were essentially themselves teaching rather than just supporting me. They were having to make decisions, using their own judgements, without there being time for consultation. In fact this worked well and allowed our distinctly individual relationships with Jamie to develop. We would spend a lot of time after sessions talking through what had happened. We became a close team. Their contribution was crucial and valuable. They spent more time with Jamie than I did and sometimes they were developing interactions more frequently and easily than I can. All the support staff commented that they enjoyed the opportunity of utilising their own personal skills, and developing their own individual work with Jamie. Although much of the interactive approach is based on intuition it also provides a practical framework and structure within which to work, and staff commented that they felt clear about how, why and what they were doing. I was reassured by this comment as many times staff have said that they don't enjoy working with students with such profound difficulties because they are unsure about 'how' to work with them. There was enormous enthusiasm and they would give unpaid time to come to meetings.

After only a few months interaction was occurring more and more frequently both during our time-tabled sessions and also throughout the whole day. Jamie was becoming noticeably calmer. We felt calmer too. There was less of the desperate speed about his movements. A new atmosphere of ease had developed between us. He appeared more aware of other people and was making eye contact. He clearly recognised the signals to begin the different sequences or games we had developed with him. He had begun to quickly and easily respond to the signals. Above all he was enjoying the sessions and our company generally. As his relationships with us developed so, it appeared, did his feeling of self esteem. This inevitably had a spiralling effect. I am convinced that the development of self esteem forms the roots of all learning, and that this is true at any level of education.

Jamie's attainments – and ours

After a year of using Intensive Interaction Jamie had developed in many areas. He was easily accepting our physical proximity for minutes at a time, sometimes for as long as 15 minutes. We could not only sit together but could share an activity that he enjoyed such as spinning circular wooden pieces or bouncing a ball and this would develop into a turn-taking activity. He had learned a variety of ways of interacting and could recognise the different patterns. Jamie was now clearly initiating interactions himself through clear signalling, usually with eye contact or physically touching our hands and sometimes our faces. He was also making choices about whom he wished to interact with, and how that interaction was going to develop. He never made a particular favourite, but on certain days it was clear he would prefer to relate to a certain person according to his mood.

In general he was less destructive. He was no longer smearing, hitting, eating away the walls. There was a great diminishment in his intensity to eat dirt and grass. He still maintained most of his self-involved characteristics in particular the twiddling, staring at his thumbs and staring at the ceiling light, but he had become so receptive that we could approach him and he would easily break out of himself to join in an interaction. Within the regular classroom sessions Jamie had started to join us at the table, staying for minutes at a time, even managing a few strokes of painting. Particular progress was made within our circle games. Jamie would remain sitting in the circle for increasing lengths of time. He was much more aware of others in the group and understood the turn-taking nature of the games.

The boundaries of Jamie's life were widening out. We were now able to include him in our kitchen sessions without him grabbing everything and causing chaos. We could now go out as a group and Jamie would link our arms. He was even able to access a busy supermarket where we would walk around with him and instead of forcibly holding his arm we would touch hands and play a finger tapping game. The rest of the group were also benefiting. We were now able to work together. There was a calmness and in fact a whole new atmosphere in the classroom. One which was constantly expectant of and receptive to communication.

We believed that Jamie had achieved the set of learning outcomes we had aimed for:

1. His social skills had improved:
   - He had shown an increased desire and ability to be with another person, in fact to be with a group of people.
   - He seemed more at ease with other people's proximity.
   - He was initiating social interaction. He appeared to understand feelings of emotional empathy.
2. His communication skills had developed:
   - He was using and understanding eye contact meaningfully.
   - He was taking turns in exchanges of behaviour with another person.
   - He was exchanging signals with another person.
   - He had developed his production of sounds.
3. His cognitive abilities had developed:
   - He had become interested in communication, as shown by the increase in his initiations.
   - He appeared to have an understanding of his ability to affect the behaviour of others.
4. His emotional well-being had developed:
   - His self esteem had increased. We felt this to be true because he was clearly more relaxed, smiled more and demonstrated his destructive behaviours less frequently.
   - He had learned that communicating effectively with another human being was pleasurable.

He was beginning to transfer the skills he had learned into new situations. He started to initiate more with staff who were not directly working with him. He then began to make initiations towards another student in our group. He would approach her and bend himself down to her level much as we had been doing with him, and would look intently into her eyes. Unfortunately her response was not particularly friendly but he repeated this several times. He also developed a relationship with a student in another group. One day he held out his hand to her in the same way that Mick had done to him many times to signal the initiation of a 'clapping game'. She clapped his hand boisterously and there was a feeling of good humour. This interaction became a regular event when the pair met at lunchtimes.

Progress had been a two-way thing. As staff we had improved our skills of observation and response, and this had had the knock on effect of improving Jamie's communications. We had learned a set of skills which we found we could successfully transfer to using with other students in other groups. After our initial successes with Jamie we had begun to use Intensive Interaction with some students we taught at a local day centre. Despite only seeing them for two hours each week we soon developed a set of individual interactions which were very different from those with Jamie, yet similar in that they allowed each person to have an active part in their development. There was a great deal of satisfaction for us in seeing different relationships develop and new students starting to initiate contact. We had all become much more reflective and sensitive to observing small signals. We were all a lot happier in our work.

Problems

A student's years in FE are often a time when they might make the transition from either family home or children's residential establishment into adult care. Jamie was moved very suddenly from his children's home into an adult residential care establishment. He found this move very difficult and there were a great deal of staff changes in his new home. Over the first three months after his move there was a gradual deterioration in Jamie's behaviours. We were no longer making progress. The description 'whirlwind' reappeared in our notes. He started to retreat into the old and also some new behaviours. With so many changes going on in his life it was impossible for us to maintain the level of development we had achieved, particularly as we were restricted to only two days a week. Over the other three days Jamie attended a day centre. His relationships here broke down completely so that he lost his placement. We felt that our placement too may have broken down had we not firmly established our approach. Even on his most chaotic days he remembered our patterns of relating. The end of his final year with us arrived before he had really come to terms with his transition. We didn't make any further progress but all three of us maintained our individual relationships with him. Should a future situation arise with another student we hope we will have the opportunity to work more closely with care staff, to be able to together share and develop our methods of working and our successes, and hopefully to make transition easier. Intensive Interaction could become a useful tool with which to bridge the gap between education and care.

Conclusion

Intensive Interaction is now firmly established in our curriculum. We have found it invaluable for those students who are at the earliest stages of communication. In some ways its use is particularly relevant to FE in that it develops self-advocacy at its earliest levels. In other ways FE is not such an easy setting to do this work in. There is a continuing national debate which questions both the presence of such students in colleges and also the issue of what is care and what is education? I see my present job as being no less important educationally and in many ways no less different than teaching GCSE English. It can be difficult to measure progress and steps are often so small that this can be a stumbling block. Some form of external accreditation is now essential in FE. We are currently writing up an accreditation of some elements of Intensive Interaction such as sharing of space, achievement of eye-contact, turn-taking and giving and receiving of physical contact, which will hopefully be accepted to form part of an externally accredited communication package. This might make the use of Intensive Interaction more acceptable .

Since the 1992 Further and Higher Education Act all colleges have been forced to essentially become business-like institutions. The business ethos can sometimes seem at odds with the needs of students with very severe learning difficulties. However I firmly believe that students with profound and complex difficulties should be part of all colleges and that this is beneficial not only for those students but equally for the mainstream students and the colleges as a whole.

Our college has a belief in equal opportunities which includes a strong commitment to such students, and we are also fortunate to receive (non-

Schedule 2) funding from Leeds City Council Department of Community Benefits and Rights, which gives us the flexibility to devise programmes which really meet the needs of individual students, and we do not have to directly link our programmes to vocation as under Further Education Funding Council criteria.

In 1996 the report *Inclusive Learning* was published following a three year review by the Tomlinson Committee. Colleges are now having to work towards inclusivity. Although this is clearly a good thing, I hope that by being more inclusive generally, colleges do not feel they have to exclude certain students for whom it is a major step simply to access a discrete college course. Inclusion is not the same as integration. The Tomlinson Report itself acknowledges that people with profound and multiple learning difficulties continue to have scant access to further education. If positive learning opportunities are to be meaningfully available to such people with such highly individualised needs we have to design programmes that are specific to their needs. We need to be wary of 'inclusive' working being taken to mean that we need to virtually close down discrete classes and include people into mainsteam provision, as this is really missing the point of what the *Inclusive Learning* report proposes. The 'normalisation' theory is still often banded around in this area of work. In my view it is not a question of our students becoming more normalised, but of mainstream staff and students becoming more accepting. There has lately been a lot of discussion around widening participation in colleges of FE and I hope this will make for an easier climate.

References

Tomlinson Committee (1996) *Inclusive Learning*. London: FEFC.

Chapter 4

Sabrina's Story: Curriculum in the Early Years

Carol Peters

Background

Sabrina was born in the summer of 1991 and there were soon concerns that she was 'failing to thrive'. She was later diagnosed as having microcephaly and was also operated on to correct a 'club foot'. At six months of age she was visually alert and smiling but because she did not always respond to sounds there was some concern over her hearing; she was given grommets at eighteen months. She generally seemed a 'contented', but rather passive, baby. Before Sabrina's first birthday a Pre-School Teacher Counsellor began to visit weekly to support her family and work on the development of basic skills.

Sabrina and her family were introduced to me when they came to look around our school shortly before her second birthday. Our school is a special school which takes children with profound and multiple, severe or moderate learning difficulties from the age of two to sixteen. At this stage Sabrina was a little scrap of a thing who gave little eye contact, but nevertheless seemed aware of and mildly interested in her surroundings. She was just beginning to sit briefly without support. She tolerated a little contact with me and at first sight I felt there were some encouraging signs of awareness and readiness to learn. Sabrina came from a rather unsettled home background and, over the next few years, was to have to come to terms with many major changes in her life.

Sabrina started attending our school for two full days a week the month after her second birthday. Whole rather than half days were chosen as she had quite a long distance to travel to the school. Over the next two years she made slow but steady physical progress, gradually sitting upright unsupported for longer periods of time, beginning to tolerate standing upright briefly with support, later walking with the aid of a walking frame, 'cruising' along holding onto furniture or walking holding an adult's hand and finally walking (insecurely) unsupported shortly after her fourth birthday.

However, there was very little, if any, progress in other areas. I worked on 'Waldon' style[1] activities (see Waldon, 1983) involving many concrete experiences of handling and organising objects as well as the usual classroom activities involving sand, water, paint, dough, television, music, PE, computer. The only activity in which Sabrina showed any interest at all was music: she would sit, rocking gently with her fingers stuffed into her mouth and a fixed gaze showing total concentration. We were unable, though, to persuade her to make any attempt at controlling the music (for example using a Pethna box or switch-operated tape recorder); when the music stopped she merely lost interest and moved away.

As Sabrina only made a very restricted range of sounds (mainly just happy or distressed noises) we tried hard, without success, to get her to use basic signs. After one term at school I wrote a report in which I described Sabrina's reluctance to comply with adult wishes or guidance: she resisted strongly if she was physically prompted to do something, crying, withdrawing her hands, extending backwards, 'falling' slowly back if she was being encouraged to sit upright, lifting up her legs or going completely limp if encouraged to bear some weight on her legs. I described her at this point as a 'contented little girl when she is engaged in activities of her own choosing'; she responded briefly in play with an adult and showed slight interest in toys presented to her but resisted as soon as a physical response was expected from her. By the summer of the following year (that is, after three terms at the school) my Annual Report on Sabrina described her as:

---

[1] Dr Geoffrey Waldon's techniques are based on the idea that there are two sorts of understanding about the world: 'general', which is the knowledge any child in any country is exposed to; and 'particular', which is knowledge specific to groups and cultures. Controversially, Waldon believed that although particular understanding is necessarily learned through language, general understanding can (and in the case of individuals with significant learning difficulties should) be developed initially without language. Lessons run along Waldon lines involve the adult in little or no use of spoken language and social interaction is avoided.

... [showing displeasure] by crying angrily and stiffening her body and pleasure by smiling, clapping or clasping her hands and making 'eeh' sounds. She responds well to attention from an adult and will give eye contact, smile and hold out her arms when she knows she is about to be picked up.

Her responses to objects were to mouthe or delicately stroke and manipulate them with the tips of her fingers.

Over the next year Sabrina's general behaviour changed very little except for the developments in physical skills mentioned above. I accepted that she was making slow progress in all areas except motor development and continued working in the same ways. Over time, however, I began to become increasingly frustrated with working with Sabrina – school life seemed to be nothing but a constant battle to stop her grabbing at things and eating them. What was sand but something to crunch between her teeth? Would she like to ride a specially adapted tricycle? – well the foam handlebars were certainly tasty! Isn't paint made to drink, glue to lick, dough to swallow? What is the use of bricks except to put in your mouth? The more mobile Sabrina became, the more problems we experienced in keeping her from eating everything that was not nailed down (meal times themselves were a nightmare as she fought to grab everything and shove it into her mouth). These behaviours were especially difficult to cope with now as the special school class Sabrina had entered at the age of two had been closed and children and staff moved to join another 'mainstream' teacher and Nursery Nurse at a newly opened integrated Nursery nearby; this move took place a few months after Sabrina's third birthday.

Change in approach

Over the Easter holidays following the opening of the Nursery (when Sabrina was nearly four) – those blessed times when you can actually stop and think – I began to mull over my ideas for the new term and for the children's individual education programmes (IEPs). As I thought of Sabrina it began to dawn on me that all of her experiences with us adults, and ours with her, were negative. We were in a constant battle trying to stop her from doing the very thing she most wanted to do – EAT!

However, even when food was present and allowable, she was still not in what could be described as a relaxed mood which might be conducive to learning. I began to question the purpose of the activities I had been asking Sabrina to tackle. This was a child who, for whatever reason (and we could all take a few educated guesses about this), was 'obsessed' with the idea of food and seemed to find nothing else meaningful in her life. What possible motive could she have for wishing to move bricks from one container to another, press a switch attached to a computer or put paintbrush to paper?

As my mind began wandering along these lines I came more and more to the idea of 'Intensive Interaction' – could I find a way of helping Sabrina to find pleasure in interacting with another human being, pleasure that could compete with the urge to acquire food? No wonder she hadn't wanted to look us in the eyes or be close to us until now. We were simply the creatures who were constantly preventing her from indulging in the activities she found most meaningful; the creatures who were continually talking in cross or frustrated voices and who were offering her nothing to replace the pleasurable experiences we were removing. I had spent Sabrina's first term in my class assessing her needs and abilities and I had included interactive games on her individual programme, but only paid occasional lip service to this approach. Not until now had I really considered making it the centre of her individual programme.

Sabrina began the new term with an IEP which highlighted motor development and interactive skills as the two main areas of focus. I always discuss the children's termly aims with my Nursery Nurse and, as she shared my frustration over Sabrina's slow progress and 'challenging' behaviours, she was in total agreement about a change of approach. A copy of the aims was also sent home to Sabrina's foster parents. I hoped that over time we might begin to see some slight changes in the way she interacted with us but imagine my feelings when changes began to appear almost immediately after we started our new regime: a mixture of elation that I had finally found the right approach and that Sabrina was responding so well and horror that I had wasted so much of her short life putting her through a lot of meaningless activities and experiences. It wasn't that Sabrina couldn't learn, just that I had been unaware of the best way to help her learn. My Annual Report at the end of the term described Sabrina in this way:

Sabrina communicates through eye contact, body language and sounds. Since we decided to stress interactive play in Sabrina's individual curriculum in May [three months earlier] her behaviour has changed quite markedly: she gives eye contact more consistently and regularly seeks to interact with adults, communicating (through physical movements) both when she wants to interact and when she has had enough; she requests physical contact by attempting to climb on an adult's lap or by moving their hand to make them stroke her hair; she has begun to 'lead' adults in the direction she wants to walk. These changes are all very positive and extremely encouraging.

Progress

My experience of using Intensive Interaction in a conscious, planned and 'intense' way rather than in an ad hoc, rather superficial manner was that, basically – it works! I had noticed some significant changes in Sabrina in a very short space of time after having worked with her with little 'light dawning' (for either her or me) for a comparatively long time.

Within the first month of using the Intensive Interaction approach (and then not as often and 'intensely' as I would have liked due to the usual pressures of time, space, staff etc.) I had noticed some remarkable changes in Sabrina. I was not the only one to see these developments as the speech therapist and occupational therapist who worked with her on a weekly basis commented on the changes, and even staff who only saw her once a week in passing in the hall or playground commented on how much more aware and alert she seemed. She began to give eye contact more willingly (usually only when she was receiving one-to-one attention, however briefly, from an adult). It seemed that she began to realise that she could influence our behaviour and through us influence her own experiences; for example, she began to realise that we were responding consistently and, if she pulled us by the hand, we would follow where she wanted to lead us (we spent much time going on 'guided tours' of the Nursery and Sabrina seemed particularly fascinated by the office where she was not normally taken!). She would pull our hair (ouch!) to get our mouths nearer to her ear when we were making a noise which interested her. She would watch the expressions on our faces and smile back with an accompanying 'Eeeh' sound, which we had previously recognised as a pleasure sound. She would continue a physical action which was part of an interactive game, for example I would hold her hand, move it up and say 'Uuup' with a rising intonation, then drop it with a quick 'Down' with a falling intonation. She would then continue to pull my hand up and down and gaze at me expectantly, waiting for the appropriate noises. She began to 'request' both beginnings and endings to interactive sessions by pulling at (and pinching) our upper arms to indicate she wanted to be picked up, and turning her feet round towards the floor and leaning away to indicate she had had enough. Part of these changes may well have been that we became more aware of Sabrina's attempts to communicate rather than that she was producing new behaviours, but this does not detract from the importance and quality of these interactions.

Around this time routine tests revealed that Sabrina was long-sighted and that she was likely also to need another operation to insert grommets as she was again suffering from glue ear. It was amazing to think that she had made such progress in interactive play sessions when she could neither see nor hear us very clearly. Sabrina was prescribed glasses and the Nursery Nurse and I waited in fear and trepidation for their arrival, as Sabrina's favourite activity of the moment was what has been politely described as 'casting', that is hurling objects across the Nursery narrowly missing the heads of other vulnerable young children! However, as it turned out, we were amazed to see that Sabrina neither 'cast' nor even sucked (well, only on rare occasions) her glasses. This would seem to indicate that Sabrina was really appreciating the ability to see more clearly and the glasses certainly must have helped her to focus on our faces as we played with her.

Gradually over the next term the rate of progress slowed but Sabrina gradually (and thankfully) seemed to be moving on from pulling our hair to request 'more' to just reaching towards us. Perhaps she was starting to realise that a symbolic gesture is enough. I was now beginning to feel more hopeful that Sabrina might one day learn to use a few signs since she now clearly recognised the value of communication, was beginning to appreciate how she could get her message across and (most importantly) wanted to relate to familiar adults.

Content of Intensive Interaction sessions

Having originally decided that Intensive Interaction would be an appropriate method to use to meet Sabrina's needs, full of enthusiasm that I was 'on the right track' at last, I then had to decide on the content of the sessions – or did I? The central element of Intensive Interaction is that the child/student should experience pleasure in the activities and the hope is that he or she will also become an active partner in the games. Imposing the content, therefore, was unlikely to achieve these aims, particularly in the case of Sabrina, who had had years of negative experiences where her curriculum had been decided solely by her (misguided) teacher. My aim, therefore, was to let Sabrina decide the content as much as possible. Clearly I would have to offer her ideas, but it was then up to her whether or not she accepted my 'suggestions'. Generally I just followed my instincts and interacted with her at a level I felt to be appropriate, dropping any games she did not take up and continuing with those she clearly enjoyed. We soon developed a small repertoire of games which gave us mutual pleasure, but I also continued trying to introduce new games or variations of old games in order to prevent the situation (and more especially myself) from becoming stale and ineffective.

Video recording interaction sessions

In order to become more aware of Sabrina's attempts to communicate, and to acquire a means of illustrating clearly the differences in her behaviour when in an interactive session as opposed to her usual behaviour, I made a video of her. Firstly I videoed her usual behaviour in two different settings: in a small room along with two other children with significant special needs (in a separate withdrawal room at the Integrated Nursery) and in a sandpit along with many children with and without special needs. In both settings I found that Sabrina showed very little facial expression, only a very occasional smile, for no obvious reason, or a wince when noises were too close for comfort. She used very little vocalisation, only frequent 'Mmm' sounds in the withdrawal room (usually monotone sounds and only once with a rising intonation) and she made no sounds at all in the sandpit. The video gave me further evidence that her 'Eeeh' sound, which she often made at other times, was a pleasure sound and also revealed that her 'Mmm' sound indicated that she was concentrating, for example when she was practising her walking skills. During the videoing Sabrina paid very little attention to other children or adults. In the little room she looked at another child only once out of the corner of her eye when he made a loud noise close to her. In the sandpit she did look across at groups of children briefly on occasions but she did not change her facial expression or make eye contact. In both settings she occasionally looked towards me (or at the camera?). Her play was very limited, consisting almost solely of holding small objects (such as toy buttons) between the middle and ring fingers and the thumb of either hand (in what has been referred to by an occupational therapist as an 'idiosyncratic grip'!); she often swopped the objects from hand to hand and either tapped the objects gently on her lips or rubbed them from side to side over her teeth.

After making this video I was faced with the problem of finding the space, time and staffing to enable a video to be made of me interacting with Sabrina. I solved the problem of staffing by asking my headteacher to video me as part of the Teacher Appraisal process and found a time when I could work one-to-one with Sabrina in our little 'quiet room'. After making the video I analysed it, comparing it with my 'control' video. The Interaction session was not one of our best, mainly due to the fact that I had had to plan a particular time for the session (when the room, the video camera and the headteacher were available) rather than picking a time when Sabrina indicated she was feeling responsive or wanted to play. Also, as someone who hates having my photograph taken, I was certainly not at my most relaxed either! Even so I did notice some marked differences between Sabrina's behaviour in this video as compared with the earlier ones. There were many incidents of eye contact between us (often quite prolonged – for example when she was anticipating the conclusion of a tickling game). Sabrina frequently used physical actions to request more, such as pulling my hands towards her face so that I would tickle her neck. There were many meaningful smiles and quite a few hearty 'belly laughs' during our games as well as frequent 'Gee' sounds (and repeated 'Gee-gee-gee' noises). There were frequent short pauses where Sabrina retreated into her usual self-stimulating behaviours such as hand gazing or mouthing buttons, but she was generally much more 'with me', alert, interested and responsive than in the other video (or than she was in general).

What I noticed most on looking through the video and focusing on my behaviour as well as Sabrina's (especially for the purposes of my Appraisal) was how intimate the interaction was. Sabrina and I were physically close (actually touching) throughout the session and there were lots of incidents of even closer contact such as me blowing raspberries on her hand, making noises directly into her ear, bouncing her on my lap and bringing my face very close to hers. Clearly in the 'current climate' there may be concerns among staff about interacting with a child in such an intimate manner. I feel very confident that this is the right approach for Sabrina and, given her age, chronologically and, even more relevantly, intellectually, most people would accept that these behaviours are actually entirely 'normal' and appropriate within a close relationship, for example parent/child. Some people may feel that these behaviours have no relevance to the teacher/pupil relationship, but I had found that more 'usual' teacher-like behaviours had had no effect on Sabrina's development – and what was my role as a teacher if not to help my pupils develop? However, I can see that such concerns will be heightened considerably when the pupil concerned is older, particularly when they are of the opposite sex to the teacher.

Whatever one's views about this sort of interaction (which is, after all, the sort of interaction which is used naturally by parents and which does clearly have positive effects on their child's development), there was quite a significant change in Sabrina's behaviour over this time and these changes continued to be evident whenever Sabrina interacted with a familiar adult. Her frantic eating of non-food substances also lessened slightly: she still brought everything to her mouth, but only actually ate more fluid-like substances such as glue and paint (her eating of sand also lessened quite significantly).

Intensive Interaction techniques did not bring about miraculous changes in Sabrina and some of the changes which occurred in her in the latter months of this history are undoubtedly affected by her move to a loving and stable foster family. However, there were clear and positive changes in Sabrina's behaviour before this and, whatever the cause or causes, her experiences of school life and of interactions were significantly altered for the better. There is certainly no doubt, therefore, in my mind of the benefits of using Intensive Interaction techniques with children such as Sabrina, but what of the practical implications?

Timetabling Intensive Interaction sessions

The main problems facing someone who wants to try Intensive Interaction within a school (or any other situation) are likely to be questions of 'where?', 'when?' and 'with whom?', that is, the practical 'nuts and bolts' of working with a child in what has to be such a highly individualised way. As mentioned above, I did not find that pre-planned sessions were the most effective, rather that it was better to grab (literally) Sabrina for a few minutes at that point in time when she was at her most responsive – especially if she herself was indicating a desire to interact. I found story times were often a good time for a brief interactive session. This may sound crazy as there were then twenty-five other children trying to concentrate on another teacher reading a story, but at that time I tried to confine our play to relatively quiet and not too physically boisterous games. Sabrina was not at the stage of development where she could be expected to listen to a story, but she would sometimes gain pleasure from the other children singing or acting out a story so I did not want to withdraw her from these sessions totally. Also, my choosing to segregate her on a given occasion would not necessarily lead to a successful interaction session for the reasons mentioned earlier, and 'whipping her out' of the story because she seemed in the mood to interact would probably have distracted her and destroyed the very mood I was trying to encourage. Instead I used the moments where she was less 'involved' in the group's activities to play our interaction games.

Another time when I found frequent opportunities for Intensive Interaction was at playtime. There are always two adults outside at playtimes so, as long as none of my other pupils were climbing the fences or causing any other disturbances, I could concentrate on Sabrina for a few minutes. Sabrina was not yet confident enough to move around independently outside, so she often used to play in or on the edge of the sandpit and sometimes appeared to watch other children playing. I made regular use of these times to sit beside and play with her.

Although I took the lead in suggesting Intensive Interaction for Sabrina and initiating the first games, my Nursery Nurse is happily also skilled in interacting with young or developmentally delayed children and soon became involved also. It is noticeable that not all adults feel comfortable about interacting with children in this way (particularly once the children are beyond the physical stage of appearing to need it). I have observed adults reacting very strongly (understandably in one sense), pushing Sabrina away when she pinched their arms, not recognising this as an attempt to climb on their laps. Some adults may even disagree with the theory behind Intensive Interaction and feel it is not in the interests of 'age appropriateness' to interact with the child in this way. However, fortunately my Nursery Nurse was comfortable with this approach and even, like myself, gained pleasure from interacting with a child in this way. I feel that the adult's experience of pleasure is important as Intensive Interaction is intensive for both the child and the adult, and I often finished a session before Sabrina was ready to stop because I felt drained, or did not even start a session because I was not really 'in the mood'. This may sound selfish or maybe even unprofessional, but I do not believe the child will have a truly positive experience if the adult is not properly prepared emotionally.

Recording

This is another area of concern for many teachers – how can I offer 'proof' of both 'lesson content' and 'outcome'? This was especially relevant for me as we approached our first OFSTED inspection. I tried to consider both the elements of interactive play which were important and a way in which progress over time might be measurable. At the same time I realised (like all teachers) that it was important the recording should not take up too much valuable time or I would not be able to keep it up. Over time I came up with a sheet which was easy to understand and quick to complete so that anyone working with the children could pick it up and use it successfully without seeing it as too much of a burden (see figure 4.1).

Skills recorded

Eye contact: Sabrina rarely looks directly at people and, when on her own, spends much time staring into space or watching her own hands. During interactive play sessions she can sometimes give some startlingly intense eye gazes and seems aware that eye gaze can be used as a means of communicating (usually meaning 'more' or 'again'), whereas looking away can mean 'I've had enough' or 'I need a brief rest but then I'd like to

DATE:

SESSION: MORNING/AFTERNOON:

AIMS:

To give the child a pleasurable experience of interacting with an adult. To help the child to realise that they are a person with whom the adult wants to interact – that is, that they are important; also that they can influence and affect the world around them – that is, they can affect the adult's behaviour in a positive way. To stimulate and develop the skills set out in the 'COMMENTS' section.

RESOURCES:
The adult and any toys/objects the adult or child choose to introduce.

COMMENTS: (ring appropriate response)

EYE CONTACT	poor/fair/good/excellent
TURN-TAKING	poor/fair/good/excellent
VOCALISATION	poor/fair/good/excellent
PLEASURE	poor/fair/good/excellent
INITIATIVE	poor/fair/good/excellent
RANGE OF CONTENT	poor/fair/good/excellent
RESPONSIVENESS	poor/fair/good/excellent
ANTICIPATION	poor/fair/good/excellent
IMITATION	poor/fair/good/excellent
USE OF GESTURES	poor/fair/good/excellent
FACIAL EXPRESSION	poor/fair/good/excellent
TOLERANCE OF PHYSICAL CONTACT	poor/fair/good/excellent

Length of session:

Any other comments:

Figure 4.1 Recording sheet

carry on', and a fixed distant stare may mean 'I'm not sure I like that' or 'I'm concentrating hard on the weird noises you are making'! She also showed that she was able to use a form of eye contact or gaze which did seem a more deliberate, conscious form of communication: on some occasions she would clearly look at me only when the game had stopped and it was obvious to me that this was a request for the game to be repeated.

Turn-taking: Sabrina is aware of games having a 'life of their own' with 'rules', a beginning and an end. At the moment her understanding of turn-taking is limited to showing awareness that one round of a game has finished and requesting another one. She does not yet imitate adults' actions or sounds, but hopefully this is something that will come with more practice and awareness. I often worked on feeding back to her her own vocalisations (either ones she had just produced or ones I had heard her use frequently on previous occasions). While she showed every sign of enjoying such games, she was very much the receiver and not yet the initiator or leader. She did, however, lead some games in the sense of initiating them – for example, approaching me and grabbing hold of my hands, putting them to her neck so that I would tickle her. Hopefully, once she has begun to initiate games on a more frequent basis, she may begin to develop the idea that she can be leader on some occasions and follower on others and later still that she can be both leader and follower at different times within the same game – that is, she can really begin to engage in true turn-taking.

Vocalisation: Sabrina makes very few sounds during her general play or exploration, but there was a noticeable increase in both the range and frequency of her vocalisations during one-to-one interaction sessions. Mostly she made single or repeated sounds, gee-gee, goy, mmm-mm, similar to those of an infant around 6–9 months (see Sheridan, 1977). I tried to encourage her to repeat her sounds in longer 'strings' and to give her the experience of hearing her sounds linked together in different patterns such as 'gee-goy'. Sheridan states that actual imitation of sounds takes place around 9–12 months so hopefully Sabrina may perhaps reach this stage in the foreseeable future.

Pleasure: Sabrina's pleasure in Intensive Interaction games was evident as soon as we started to use them and grew steadily as she became more aware that she had some control and influence over what happened. Her favourite games were where the adult made silly noises (preferably in her ear) which were repeated when Sabrina grabbed the adult to pull them back towards her. I tried to make the beginning, middle and end of each game clear so that Sabrina could predict what would happen and recognise when the game had come to an end. I also made the games very short so that Sabrina was not just being passively entertained but also had to do something herself if she wanted the fun to continue. It was wonderful to feel the tension of excitement growing in her as I, for example, made a noise with a rising intonation while bringing my face closer to hers, finally (after a suspenseful pause) culminating in a loud raspberry on her cheek (at which point she giggled wonderfully and grabbed me for a repeat performance).

Initiative: At first it was always the adult who started and finished the interactive games but later Sabrina began to request them. She only approached an adult in this way when they were familiar and usually when they were sitting down (I suppose because they were more 'accessible' to her in this position). This could be inconvenient if I was trying to read a story to a group of children at the time but I became adept at holding a book in one hand while tickling Sabrina with the other! One of our first indications that this approach was having an effect on Sabrina and that she realised she could influence our behaviour was when she began to grab hold of our hands and lead us wherever she wanted to go.

Range of content: The range of content in the games Sabrina enjoyed remained fairly limited, or rather revolved round two themes: bodily contact (tickling, limited rough-and-tumble, sounds made on her face, arms etc.) and sound making. The actual content of these games was probably limited by my own lack of imagination as much as by anything else. As mentioned before, she enjoyed having her hand moved with me making a sound with a rising intonation and then dropping her hand quickly (still in mine) with a rapidly falling intonation – she often then lifted her hand in mine to indicate she wished to continue. She enjoyed being tickled, especially around the neck and recognised me wiggling my hands in front of her face as a signal that this game was about to begin. She loved being sung to. Initially I used to sing lullabies to her as I stroked and rubbed her back; she seemed to find this very restful and pleasant and this was the only time I felt that she was really cuddling me rather than just being held by me. Later she preferred more lively games but still enjoyed some sung content to her games – I often made up little rhymes or ditties which she enjoyed but I had great problems in repeating the games on another occasion as I could not always remember the tunes! I also experimented with putting her own vocalisations into little tunes and this certainly seemed to fascinate her.

Responsiveness: This category may seem similar to the 'Pleasure' one, but there were some occasions (as described above) where Sabrina was content to be totally passive in these sessions (although this became less and less common) and at such times I could have described her pleasure as relatively high, but her responsiveness as quite low. In this category I looked for active responses to the stimulation received.

Anticipation: 'Anticipation' describes the degree to which Sabrina holds herself in readiness for the 'punchline' of the game – as described above the pleasurable tension experienced by Sabrina as she waits for the tickle, raspberry or whatever. Sometimes she could not bear the wait and would reach impatiently for my hands to tickle her or begin to giggle before I even touched her.

Imitation: This is an area which Sabrina found difficult, but it seemed hopeful that she might be moving towards a developmental stage where this would be within her reach. She did show some signs of being able to imitate movements if not sounds as she could repeat my actions such as lifting her hand up in mine to request the rising intonation game, or placing my hands at her neck to request a tickle.

Use of gestures: Sabrina used to request more tickling by frantically grabbing at (and pinching) the adult's arm and more noises by grabbing a handful of hair and pulling the adult's head down to her ear, but over time she had moved on to what were almost symbolic attempts at the same actions. Instead of pinching the adult's arms she would grab their hands and put them to her neck, instead of pulling the adult's hair she would reach towards (but not touch) the adult's head and incline her own head. This illustrates the importance of the adult's behaviour being consistent and responsive as Sabrina had to experience the same reaction each time to know that she was causing it. It was easy (and understandable) for adults who did not know Sabrina quite so well to react with an 'ow!' and a pulling away action, rather than a move towards her, when she pulled their hair or pinched their arms. With time this process of learning may continue with Sabrina's attempts at physical imitation becoming slowly more abstract and symbolic until she is truly using simple gestures.

Facial expression: As mentioned previously Sabrina generally showed very little facial expression, but during interactive play sessions she looked alert and interested and frequently smiled and laughed.

Tolerance of physical contact: This has never been a problem for Sabrina although it can be for some children with special needs. Sabrina seems to thrive on close physical contact – first came a tolerance and then enjoyment of cuddles and later real pleasure in more boisterous physical contact. She can still be unsure if physical play becomes too active or lively, but is gradually becoming more robust (particularly as her balance in walking improves) and looking for more interactions (so we adults need to keep fit!).

Conclusion

Sadly Sabrina's progress did not continue at the same pace and, after one term of rapid change, she became less willing to become involved in interactive play sessions. However, I feel this was partly (and possibly largely) because there was a 'spurt' in her motor development when she finally began to walk independently around the time of her fourth birthday. This meant, practically, that she was simply more difficult to contain in one place, choosing to 'escape' every time we tried to interact with her, but I feel that it was also a natural and positive reaction to the experience of new-found independence. Sabrina wanted to explore and was concentrating on extending her ability to walk over greater distances; it was very pleasing to watch her attempt over and over again to walk from one point to another in the room, dropping to the floor repeatedly but going back to the beginning and trying again. I felt hopeful that further development in interactive skills could follow once Sabrina had fully explored this phase and once we had both adjusted to how our play might be adapted to the new circumstances.

I was unable to examine this theory, however, as Sabrina then moved up to the 'main school' the next term and my contact with her became limited to one lesson a week when I, the Nursery Nurse and some of the Nursery pupils joined Sabrina's class for a PE lesson. When I now see Sabrina each week it is clear that she continues to have a very significant developmental delay which is becoming more and more apparent as she grows older. The staff working with her now confirm that she continues to progress at a very slow rate, but it is pleasing to see that she soon responds to my approaches and slips into some familiar interactive games with evident pleasure.

Appendix

Examples of recorded Intensive Interaction sessions with Sabrina follow.

Date: Tuesday 19 September 1995
Length of session: 15 minutes
Comments: Lots of burst/pause – interacting well, then switched off, then interested again. Interrupted from time to time because I had to check on another child. Sabrina wanted to lead me round by the hand (it was playtime outside) but I kept her sitting instead because I wanted to try some interaction games rather than just let her lead me around the Nursery again (this is all she wants to do at the moment). Tried a variety of games, all introduced by me – she likes it when I hold her hand and raise it up with me saying 'up' on a rising scale, then 'down', Sabrina then moves my hand up again to request 'more'.

Date: Wednesday 20 September 1995
Length of session: several brief (2 minutes +) sessions during the morning
Comments: Sabrina liked me singing long single notes close to her face – when I stopped she pulled my hair to bring my face close to her as a 'request' for more. She often just raises her eyes to look up at me when she wants me to repeat a game. Later when I tickled the back of her neck she caught hold of my hand and made me do it again (7 or 8 times).

Date: Thursday 21 September 1995
Length of session: 4 minutes
Comments: Sabrina was in a great mood – I was copying her 'goy-goy' sounds close to her face and she giggled with delight and pulled my coat to ask for more. She seemed also to enjoy me laughing at her laugh and a close cuddle/squeeze as we laughed.

Date: Monday 16 October 1995
Length of session: 5 minutes
Comments: Sabrina again enjoyed me singing long notes very close to her head. When I stopped she pulled my hair to bring my face close to her as a request for more. After a while I varied the note, going quieter and stopping as she put less pressure on my hair and singing louder as she pulled harder – she definitely began to experiment with pulling and releasing my hair. Eye contact only when I stopped – she looked away when I made a noise again.

Date: Tuesday 31 October 1995
Length of session: 10 minutes
Comments: Lots of huge smiles and real laughs. Games: making noises and saying words ('hello, hello' in a deep voice) in her ear (reached up to pull me towards her again when I stopped). Up/down game moving my hand as I said it (then she moved her hand spontaneously). Also running my nail gently over the palm of her hand so it tickled (she seemed to have mixed feelings about this game).

Date: Tuesday 7 November 1995
Length of session: 20 minutes
Comments: Took a very long time to get going – I was following Sabrina around trying to engage her and she was only responding very briefly and occasionally. Tried all sorts of games and she finally responded to a tickling game (tickling her round the neck and chin). She roared with laughter, looked right in my face with a huge smile and kept nudging my hands to ask for more. The session ended because she wet herself.

References

Sheridan, M. (1977) *The Developmental Progress of Infants and Young Children.* London: HMSO.

Waldon, J. (1983) 'Understanding understanding'. Privately published and circulated paper. One of occasional series of such papers on 'Functional Learning'.

Chapter 5

Commentary One: Practice and Progress

Dave Hewett and Melanie Nind

Introduction

One of the purposes for us in producing a follow-up book to *Access to Communication* (Nind and Hewett, 1994) was to build on the practical guidance contained there on how to do Intensive Interaction. The contributors' chapters in this volume, with their insightful reflections on their practice, are full of such guidance. Our own continued involvement with staff development on Intensive Interaction means that we are continually working to improve how we convey in words the practice of Intensive Interaction. This commentary highlights some of the contributors' guidance and brings this together with some developments in our own thinking.

Being an Interactor

We begin this section with an anecdote. One of us (*DH*) was visiting a day centre. The purpose of the visit was to meet a person who presented some severely challenging behaviours and to talk to staff about their work with him. The challenging client, Roy, was thirty-seven. He seemed to have few communication abilities, rarely using eye contact or looking at other people's faces, seeming to understand little speech, preferring his own corner, discouraging social approaches from staff. He had regular outbursts of violence and destructiveness, prompted often understandably by environmental events, sometimes arising though for no reason that anybody could identify.

I was there as the 'challenging behaviour bloke'. I don't think anybody there knew me also as the 'Intensive Interaction bloke'. During several hours of conferring with staff I tried to be as wise and helpful as I possibly could about managing the quite difficult incidents they were experiencing with Roy. They were a good bunch of people, caring and committed, and prepared to stress that they were not particularly technically knowledgeable about their work. However, at one point someone said to me 'Oh, Susan will be here this afternoon, you should see her with Roy – she gets loads out of him. He likes her, she's got a great personality.'

Susan turned out to be a tiny woman of about forty years of age who did indeed have a nice personality. She was somehow simultaneously quiet, calm, composed and sort of bubbly, full of fun, but that wasn't it; she was really good, terrific at interacting. Indeed, she was doing what appeared to be Intensive Interaction, though she had never even heard of the approach. Roy lit up when she entered the room, made eye contact with her and they had an enjoyable few minutes of him attending to her during turn-taking based on his noises and movements. Susan tuned-in well, based her responses upon his behaviours, transmitted fun and warmth, used pause effectively, had intentionality implicit in her behaviours, gently left him when she judged he had had enough.

Susan was astounded when I told her that she was skilfully using an approach derived from years of thought and research. I think she thought me a bit stupid. She told me it was obvious you had to behave like that with him if you were going to make contact. She had never thought about it any other way. She was aggravated though, that most of the other staff didn't do what she did.

In the accounts by our contributors, you can see mention of two extremes of staff ability in attempting to use an Intensive Interaction approach. At one extreme, some personalities find it very difficult to adopt the style of behaviour. Judith Samuel and Jaqui Maggs describe staff who experienced such difficulties. At the other extreme, they also describe the young man working as a volunteer with Rodney at the local gym. The staff described him as behaving in a wonderfully natural way with Rodney, which looked just like Intensive Interaction, and getting good responses. This young man presumably had no knowledge of the approach. However, he had used his personal resources to adopt the most natural and effective manner he could contrive for relating with Rodney. Val Stothard mentions her teaching assistant, who 'took to the approach like a duck to water'.

We have so often had the experience of staff at Intensive Interaction workshops declaring that we had simply put a name, a structure and some legitimacy to what they were already doing naturally with some of their service users. One accused us (rightly perhaps) of advocating 'packaged common sense'. Many staff arrive at a responsive, process-orientated way of working with people who are pre-verbal because their intuitions about communicating get them there. Like Susan they may also enjoy the advantages of having a relaxed way of looking at the world and a certain ease with their own behaviour. We suggest that there is nothing particular about some kind of 'fit' between the personality of the practitioner and the effective deployment of interactive approaches. This 'fit' or 'non-fit' is an issue for any approach to teaching:

> I have probably already made it quite clear that I have always been intuitively dissatisfied with teaching approaches for such students that are based solely on behavioural technology; working with such programmes just did not seem to 'fit' with my personality. I did not enjoy the teaching very much, finding the rigidity of the teaching programmes pedantic and irritating ... I am not amongst the most organised and fastidious of teachers, so such work brought the methodology into direct confrontation with my personality. (Hewett, 1989, p.86)

We acknowledge the point that the practitioner referenced above nonetheless has a professional responsibility to overcome personality 'fit' difficulties and use behavioural techniques to good purpose where it is judged that they are the appropriate ones to use. We would reassure also, however, that we have had the frequent experience of working with staff who find the Intensive Interaction approach quite difficult at first, but nonetheless develop good techniques gradually, in their own time at their own pace. This may happen especially if they have access to observing someone like Susan, especially if there is a supportive, communicative atmosphere amongst the staff group.

The purpose of this section is to review and discuss once again the application and techniques of the Intensive Interaction approach, related especially to the experiences of the contributors to this book. We wanted to commence with the issue described above however. It is a central one, or at least it is central for staff to whom a responsive style of behaving and reducing the reliance on session objectives and moment-by-moment task sequencing comes as a professional trauma. They may say something like, 'well yes, that's all very well, but you have to have a certain kind of personality for this teaching.' This may be true, but it is true for all teaching approaches. In this case, you do indeed need to be, or to become, a good communicator.

While personality may have some relevance for the ease with which practitioners use Intensive Interaction, there are also other personal elements which may have as much or more relevance in terms of the 'fit' between an individual and the approach. The philosophy of learning that we hold, our individual politics, these also affect how we might respond to an approach like Intensive Interaction. Special education is a relatively unpoliticised area of study and so we are perhaps not accustomed to thinking in terms of what our politics are in this field, we may even be unaware that we hold political views. It may transpire, however, that approaches based on empowering and 'listening' to learners fit well with our view of things. Alternatively it may be that we struggle with some of the concepts of shared control of learning and the right to behave in ways which step outside of the norm. These examples illustrate that individual responses to Intensive Interaction may be a mixture of personality and personal belief. Making more explicit some of our unspoken beliefs about power and control in special education can be helpful in understanding why practitioners might respond quite strongly, either in favour or in opposition to the approach.

Responsiveness

For the moment, we would actually like to play down the issue of needing to have some kind of exuberant or extrovert style of behaviour oneself in order to 'do' Intensive Interaction, to be prepared to give and receive lots of physical contact, or even romp. This boisterous extreme may well be helpful, necessary even for the development of some students/clients. There are dangers in being extrovert though, there is a temptation for extroverts to produce too much of their own behaviour and not leave enough space for the behaviour of the other person. Different staff have different personalities which lead them naturally into different kinds of interaction. The main issue is to be responsive in one's own communication style and this responsiveness operates across a very wide spectrum of possible human behaviours.

This spectrum is illustrated in the contributions to this book. Christine Smith describes a very quiet, low-key approach she used to responding to and joining in with Jamie's self-absorbed activity, with minimal use of physical contact. On the other hand, her colleague, Debbie, had a more boisterous sort of personality and seemed able effectively to promote rough and tumble activities with Jamie at an early stage of their interactive work with him. Both extremes of having his behaviours responded to and joined in with are likely to be effective for Jamie's learning. It is difficult to make judgements about which may be more significant or effective, simply that they both seem important and that the contrast between them is probably important also for Jamie. The vital, crucial aspect of the staff behaviour is that Jamie is having his behaviours responded to, and activities are then built up for Jamie by staff successively responding to further behaviours that Jamie produces.

Similarly, Lynne Knott describes little use of boisterousness or physical play with Ben, but he seemed to make good developments because the staff around him became progressively more responsive and tuned in to his behaviour. This again can be contrasted with Carol Peters' account illustrating the exuberant nature of the use of noises and physical contact with Sabrina from an early stage of working interactively with her, made all the more necessary due to Sabrina's difficulties with seeing and hearing other people clearly.

We could go on giving illustrations of the two extremes of responsiveness. But the central issue is: respond. Respond particularly to any attractive-seeming behaviours produced by one of the people you are teaching or caring for. Respond frequently, 'celebrating' (Nind and Hewett, 1994) in your behaviour what the person just did. The responsiveness can operate at many levels of practitioner behaviour. Smith (1989) argues that parents maximise their children's interactions by responding to their interests, inclinations and feedback. It may be best, then, to start by giving some special time over to 'responding sessions' – activities where we deliberately give time to using the behaviour and interests of the service user as the focus. All of our contributors give good advice or examples on this. After your response to something the other person just did, look carefully for the effect of your response. If a response to your response is evident, respond to that. You have started turn-taking sequences (see Hewett, 1996).

It is through responsiveness that we can facilitate what Sameroff (1975) described in early development as 'transactional learning'. Once we establish the complex process of two-way influences then the learner cannot be, or be seen to be, a passive recipient of our stimulation. S/he becomes instead an active, influential partner in the learning relationship. Without our responsiveness the learner can become passive, can learn that s/he cannot affect the world – learned helplessness (Seligman, 1975).

As already emphasised in chapter 1, this issue is brought out eloquently and at length by Ware (1996). She is sensitive also to the difficulties staff may have in becoming responsive, pointing out that her earlier research had shown how few opportunities for interaction may be available to pupils with PMLD. Even those opportunities that were available tended to be dominated by the adult, with only a small proportion of the pupils' spontaneous behaviours being responded to. This situation is likely to be a danger for all of us in our work, particularly if we have been around for a number of years, and have been, as we were, 'brought up' on approaches involving extensive use of task analysis and other behavioural techniques. It can become second nature for us, as a member of staff, to view ourselves as the provider, driver and controller of activities. Starting to share control in certain activities, moving on from, or changing this position, can be a trauma.

Effective responding operates at many levels of behaviour. Even practitioners who are less naturally 'playful', or may be concerned about 'age appropriateness', should nonetheless be able to find room in their behaviour as staff to be very responsive. Good responding can also be a low-key affair, simply a very friendly sensitivity to the service users' behaviours.

Sharing control

Beth Taylor gives us a vivid account of the process of changing what she and Steve were doing with Gary. They began by relinquishing much of the control that they were attempting to exert over Gary and his learning –

literally to the extent of freeing him from being on the chair, trapped behind the table where tasks were carried out. Gary was then free to indulge his lifestyle and behaviours and the onus fell to Beth and Steve to find opportunities to be with Gary by joining in with what Gary was doing. Inevitably, for this to be effective in Gary giving attention to them, accepting 'joint focus', participating in doing something with another person, then it would be with Gary's consent, under his own motivation. Beth describes their early attempts and the growth in small moments of joint focus from Gary.

Relinquishing control in this way can be one of the more difficult steps that a member of staff in our work might take. Again, you can meet staff everywhere whose personalities seem naturally and effectively attuned to sharing control in activities. The rest of us might need to think about it more (I had to. *DH*) and take decisions, have perhaps awkward discussions with colleagues.

In a sense it may have been so much easier for Steve and Beth to change their outlook in their own home, with their own child, but they do not describe it as an easy thinking process. Perhaps it was easier for them however, once decided, to recognise their own early reactions, that it felt so 'totally right to be with Gary in this way, so absolutely natural'.

Judith Samuel and Jaqui Maggs report the discussions they had with the other staff on this issue. Sharing or handing over control felt strange, the silences and pauses felt uncomfortable and they needed to resist a desire to prompt. For Lynne Knott, this was not so much of a difficulty. She is, we think, a personality who took to the concepts relatively easily, recognising the crucial principles in developing communication sequences with Ben. It was necessary to have a more responsive role and follow Ben's lead, be 'sensitive to Ben's world' and accept the responsibility to join him there, first and foremost in his world.

None of this implies accepting chaos in your workplace, no longer having a working structure, routine or timetable. We are supposed to be the controllers of our workplaces in many senses. However, the accounts of the contributors surely point to maintenance of working structures going hand-in-hand with a rethink on staff behaviour in communication teaching, but together with progressively more flexibility in the way that the day unfolded and activities were promoted. Routine is important, structure is vital, controlling elements of the lives of people with the more severe learning difficulties is essential – for many reasons, safety first and foremost.

The sensation of the control of the activity being shared between the learner and the more experienced person is essential to the learner learning about communication. To communicate is an exercise in personal power (Harris, 1994). Recognising the potential for something you do to have an effect on something someone else does, seems to be one of, if not the earliest piece of social learning that an infant conducts. We often portray this as an early realisation we are attempting to promote with Intensive Interaction: 'I do something, and it causes her to do something – that's very interesting'. This concept of social cause and effect can only come about with the more experienced person sharing power and control, doing things on the other person's terms, looking for opportunities to respond to things the person does. As with Gary, it can take time to get started on these realisations and move on to more developed sequences of turn-taking.

Sharing control means also that you are doing your best to get the learner to be an active participant in the activity. Responding to something that person does and looking to build a mutual activity from there guarantees it. It is so much more likely that an active participant will enjoy the activity and wish to repeat it gladly. It is more likely, too, that the more experienced person will also enjoy it. The activities should then become self-motivating for the learner. Taking part in the activities, having your behaviour responded to, is in itself rewarding. In an earlier publication (Nind and Hewett, 1990), we resolved these aspects of Intensive Interaction into these three principles:

- The learner is active
  The learner is a fully active participant in the activities, intellectually and emotionally engaged with the content and the teacher, taking decisions, exploring and experimenting, exercising personal power.
- The learning activity is intrinsically rewarding and motivating
  The reward for participating in the activity is the pleasure of participating. The learner will be motivated to return to these activities by the knowledge that they are so pleasurable.
- The learner shares control of the activity with the teacher
  In interaction sequences the learner is able to exercise or share control over the intensity, content and duration of the activity. This sharing of control is essential for the activities truly to be 'interactive'. Learning to exercise and to share control and power is also one of the important pieces of learning.

We suggest that these principles seem evident in Intensive Interaction. The principles can be identified both theoretically and practically – when watching people interacting together. We also suggest that these are good principles for promoting activities of all sorts. We discuss their application further in the section on 'Making Progress'.

From accessing to turn-taking sequences

In *Access to Communication* (Nind and Hewett, 1994) we used the term 'accessing' to describe the stage of work where you achieve the 'sensation of getting through to a student/client, establishing mutuality with a person who was formerly remote from social contact' (p. 89–90). There seem to be two particularly difficult stages that staff experience in using Intensive Interaction techniques. One is often this initial stage, simply getting through to a person who is remote from social contact. The other difficult stage comes with thoughts about what to do next maybe one to three years later, when the person has become more active, social and communicative. We will return to this second issue in the section 'Making Progress'.

All of our contributors, in various ways, describe aspects of the process of accessing. For some of them, notably Judith Samuel and Jaqui Maggs, they achieved access as a result of a very deliberate and almost methodical application of interaction techniques. They seemed well-prepared for what to do at this stage, patient and knowledgeable about the potential difficulties, sensitive to recognise the results of what they were attempting.

Beth Taylor and Christine Smith both describe similar revelatory moments during the very early stages where contact is made right at the end of energetic unsuccessful attempts to achieve it. For both, part of the revelation was that they had been doing too much with their own behaviour, and that once they were tired and relaxed, their behaviour actually became more secure-looking and therefore accessible to the other person.

As described in the previous section, making access can be difficult not just because of the social remoteness of the person you are trying to help, but also because of the difficulties associated with the member of staff learning to share control. The elements of this in accessing are various and well illustrated by the contributors. Be relaxed and informal; enjoy yourself and make sure that the activity is clearly intended to be enjoyable for you and the other person; don't do too much, put in too much of your own behaviour; use pauses and allow inactivity, thus allowing time and space for the other person to do things to which you can respond; don't try hard in one session for a long period of time; rather, have frequent attempts; be imaginative; be patient about lack of success.

> It was not easy to start. We had to learn to be sensitive and responsive to Ben's behaviours or interpret potential signals. We had to learn new skills as teachers for this kind of activity. The sessions could not be planned in the sense we were accustomed to . . . We had to learn to have the confidence to observe and watch Ben for those moments when we could follow his behaviours. (Lynne Knott p. 191)

Having made access, you then come to what is in a sense a central issue of doing Intensive Interaction – getting turn-taking going. It is then possible to promote gradually more complex sequences of turn-taking where the learner has potential situations to learn many things: to take turns with another person; to give attention and concentrate; non-verbal and verbal signalling; learn the fundamental routines of communication (this learning is described extensively in Nind and Hewett, 1994).

We mentioned earlier that we are attempting to bring about for the learner a realisation of 'I do something and it causes someone else to do something – that's very interesting.' The next step is for the learner to have the further thought 'that is so interesting that . . . I think I'll experiment with it.' Our experience is that the learner then gradually builds, in partnership, a repertoire of communicative behaviours and activities by experimenting with and rehearsing things which work to get responses from other people. Christine Smith describes her colleague Debbie getting turn-taking going with Jamie by echoing back his sounds.

> Jamie was surprised about this at first and would stop and look before repeating his sounds – this would be repeated until Jamie changed the pattern of his sounds and then Debbie would change also. This could go on for some time and develop into a sound conversation. (Christine Smith, p. 53)

Turn-taking helps to structure the interaction sequence, we could perhaps say that it is the backbone of it. Many other things are happening in and around the turn-taking, but one of the aims is to get turn-taking sequences established. Measuring the length, the number of turns, the variety of turn-taking sequences with a learner is one of the things we can do which gives an indicator of the person making progress with the activities we are promoting.

The central importance for the practitioner of using watching and waiting, picking up on and celebrating learner behaviours can give the misleading impression that the member of staff must always wait for the learner to have the first turn. This is not actually so. Again the contributors' chapters give numerous accounts of staff trying something out to see if it gets a response from their student/client. Good examples are given by Lynne Knott and by Samuel and Maggs. Staff prompting, doing something judged and crafted in order to 'light the other person up' need not be at odds with the overall issue of responsiveness. It can be seen as part of it. Put simply, it is all right to do something, offer something you judge the other person will respond to. If she/he responds to what you did, then a behaviour has been produced to which you can then respond. Our diagram (figure 5.1) helps illustrate this process by describing two possible scenarios for starting up interactive turn-taking sequences.

If care is taken not to bombard the learner with our own initiations, and if, as we say, 'prompts' are carefully crafted to be things to which the other person will probably respond, it is good technique sometimes to try to get a sequence going by taking the first turn. The skill is to marry the initiation with good tuning-in for any potential response which can, in turn, be celebrated with your behaviour, and not to try even harder if the attempt at initiation does not have the desired effect. This should become all the easier over time as the person with learning disabilities builds up knowledge and confidence and as you progressively build a secure relationship. The repertoire of possible activities which are enjoyable and which work for both partners should give many possibilities for the practitioner to select something to offer as initiation.

Making progress

In figure 5.2 we have listed some of the comments made by the contributors to this text about things happening for their student/client which they view as indicators the person is making progress as a result of Intensive Interaction. The list has no particular rank ordering, it is simply

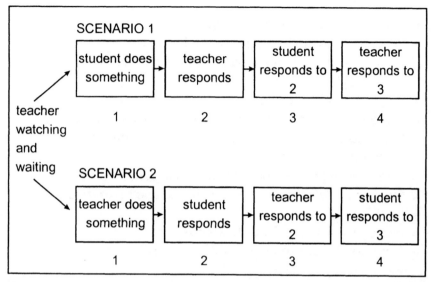

Figure 5.1 *Two scenarios for teacher responsiveness in Intensive Interaction.* These scenarios help to explain that teacher initiations (taking turn 1) do not violate the overall principle of responding to student behaviours, since the teacher initiation can be seen as an attempt to provoke a behaviour from the student (turn 2), to which the teacher can then respond (turn 3). The technique known as burst-pause may frequently be seen to be used as a way of taking turn 1 in Scenario 2.

illustrative of the staff observations as reported. It is not an exhaustive list of such items from the contributors, we merely selected a fairly random sample to enter into the chart for the purposes of this discussion.

Some of the items can be seen to be things which have happened or developed during interaction sessions, other items are things which happened generally during the person's day but are judged to be related to the interaction work. We suggest that these are the important sorts of achievements to be looked out for and recorded. These are the things which are typical of the developments which one would expect to occur if you are trying to help someone become more social and to take part in communication with other people.

Use of communication assessment tools such as the *Pre-Verbal Communication Schedule* (PVCS) (Kiernan and Reid, 1987; see also Kiernan, 1988) may help with the identification of some of the student/client's achievements. Such assessments, though, will never be fine enough or specific enough, on their own, to enable identification of

- Gives eye contact more consistently
- Regularly seeks to interact with adults
- Communicates when she wants to interact and when she has had enough
- Requests physical contact
- Has begun to 'lead' adult in the direction she wants to walk
- Eye contact – many incidents often quite prolonged
- Many meaningful smiles
- Frantic eating of non-food substances lessened slightly
- Much more 'with me' – alert, interested and responsive
- Increased affection
- Increase in his confidence to approach staff
- From no obvious response in the first session, by the fifth Levi was initiating contact
- Chose to stay close to us
- Increased smiles and laughter
- Stood up un-prompted and turned in her chair to face the rest of the group
- She did choose to watch, stayed in close proximity to the action
- Laughed and smiled and interacted with the two support workers for much longer than usual
- Participates more
- Is both more responsive and communicative
- Spends far less time alone in her bedroom
- Members of the staff team who have not been directly involved in the Intensive Interaction trial have mentioned that Alice is choosing to be with them more and is initiating more interactions
- More tolerant of using her hands and participating in activities (for example, cooking)
- More interested in what is going on around the house
- He is content to have her near him and he finds pleasure in another human being
- Being relaxed around people means he begins to take notice more in what she is doing

Figure 5.2 Comments made by contributors about progress

all the progress. It is also worth staff noticing and recording all of those often inconsequential-seeming occurrences which might nonetheless point to growing success in what you are trying to achieve with the person. The fact that the student/client makes eye contact for five seconds instead of two is important information. Significant other occurrences may be things like their personal space seeming to be smaller; becoming more comfortable somehow with people being nearby; a little more use of facial expressions; less of the day spent rocking; interaction sessions now lasting about a minute by comparison to about thirty-five seconds two months ago; the person making a greater range of noises.

This underlines the issue discussed by Ware and Healey (1994) (see chapter 1) in their debate as to just what constitutes quality of life for people with PMLD and how we go about assessing it and recording desired progress. Formalised assessments can help us to be sensitised to positive changes in the person. We have previously asserted (Nind and Hewett, 1994) that it is very important too that staff use their subjective knowledge and sensitively observe the person they are working with to allow them to be subjectively perceptive to all of the perhaps minute changes which nonetheless are potential indicators of progress. Carol Peters (p. 72) makes the point that the early items of progress were not miraculous, but were significant changes for the better for the person.

It is thus very important that ongoing changes in the person, however minute, are discussed by staff, preferably recorded in a fashion that the staff team finds effective and manageable within working routines, and used as positive feedback to themselves that they are getting somewhere. It is important that Val Stothard's attitude is emulated. Students/clients being a little more able to look at other people and a little more secure with sitting near others may not be earth-shaking developments in the grand scheme of things, but for that person perhaps achieving this for the first time in her/his life these are truly 'significant changes', fundamentally enhancing quality of life. A less positive view might be that, by comparison to what we would really like the person to do – some housework, go to the shop without screaming, table-top activities, put on their own shoes, stack four bricks successfully – little has been achieved. This view would miss out on the pleasure of recognising the considerable achievements actually made and that for the people we teach or care for who have such fundamental learning difficulties 'we need to attempt to see progress from their perspective' (Ware and Healey, 1994, p. 13).

95

In Lynne Knott's account it would seem to us that the quality of life for Ben has radically altered with his developing ability to make contact with other people and have a less isolated daily experience (see figure 5.3). He has made substantial progress with communication, even to the point of starting to attempt to use the spoken word. It may be the case that he had some 'hidden capabilities' (Detheridge, 1997) with regard to language understandings that had never formerly shown in his behaviour, though we would not wish to disavow the possibility that the dedicated work of his staff had totally brought about this development too. They certainly made possible the circumstances in which he would attempt to speak by teaching him some fundamental routines of communication, developing his motivation to attend to other people and experiencing greater confidence and security.

The speed of progress in individuals varies enormously, and the progress for an individual can occur at different rates at different times. The factors influencing progress are many, we probably cannot even estimate what they all may be. We assume some of the major factors to be: the knowledge and ability the individual already has with communication at the start of work with her/him; the cognitive potential the person possesses for continued learning; the manner in which the person already possesses some understandings which have not formerly been evident in her/his behaviour; the person's emotional state, whether she/he is happy, emotionally secure, experiencing reasonable self-esteem, having in some general sense an agreeable lifestyle; the person's physical state and general health; the ability of the staff in carrying out interaction activities; consistency of staff; the ongoing recording and reflection on practice by the staff; the working atmosphere – staff teamwork and relationships.

In one sense, we suggest the important sense, Ben has made beautiful progress quite quickly and Lynne Knott is full of optimism for further developments. In another sense, he is still a person who needs full support, who finds it difficult indeed to make contact with people who do not 'cross the bridge' to him, whose behaviours seem strange and may draw attention when he is out and about in public. It is not the intention to 'cure' him of those things by using Intensive Interaction. The central aim is fundamentally to affect his quality of life by helping him to be less isolated, to learn more and more about the pleasure and fulfilment of being with and relating effectively through communication with other people, probably limited mainly to the people who teach him and care for him, and

Our first few progress tracks show that Ben was:

- giving eye contact without flickering his eyes
- starting to allow staff to play alongside him and giving a turn

After six months Ben was:

- giving sustained eye contact
- acknowledging the presence of others by laughing and grinning
- starting to give people attention, sometimes sustained attention
- allowing others to play alongside him and share his activity
- having fun with others
- allowing others to take turns when he was imitated
- starting to initiate communication by making requests, even verbal ones
- realising that the sounds he made were important, respected and listened to
- becoming more aware of his environment and letting people into his world

Over the next two and one half years Ben was:

- less anxious in new places and situations – more confident out and about
- attending to staff instructions and responding
- making more effort with signing
- more confident to move out of his corner and take part in other activities
- trying to say words
- making the first steps in relationships with peers
- less self-absorbed generally – fiddling and far away

Figure 5.3 Summary of progress with Ben over three years

his peers. In so doing, many other aims are fulfilled. He may well gradually exhibit fewer and fewer behaviours which draw attention to him because he is so much less self-involved. He may well become more 'independent' in terms of self-care, due to the increasing ability of staff to engage him in a wealth of activities. He will hopefully progressively generalise his knowledge about communicating and relating, so that even people he meets who are not expert interactors may nonetheless make contact with him.

The discussion above is related to something that happens sometimes in workshops on Intensive Interaction. We show videos of a person who developed from a lifestyle of more or less total self-involvement and stereotyped behaviour to one where this isolation is less evident, and the person is seen to be attending to and interacting with another person for five minutes non-stop. A member of staff asks a difficult question: 'Yes but what happens next, where is this leading to?' One immediate answer is, well it almost doesn't matter as an issue, look what has happened already in the benefits to his quality of life by working with him in this way. If this is all that is possible to be achieved with his communication development, it is plenty. Of course, further than that, it actually does matter as an issue, but not all the answers to it are clear.

One answer is that, in developmental terms, the approach we are using is borrowed from a natural model of human learning and development. We operate with some kind of assumption that we are working along the developmental pathway that leads to, for instance, language acquisition. Of course, for the young man being discussed, and for many people with the more severe learning difficulties, particularly the older they get, the possibility that they will make the whole journey is not a realistic expectation. Nonetheless, we like working with the thought that this is one of the ultimate aims, to move along the pathway towards full sociability and communication ability. If nothing else, this thought helps maintain high expectations about further achievements. We may not, probably will not, get to the end of the developmental journey towards language with almost all of the people we work with, but there are good and important places all the way along the journey. Arrival at all of those places will almost certainly enhance the quality of life of the person and, for that matter, everyone else around them.

Perhaps we should look no further than Beth and Steve Taylor's story about Gary for reassurance on some of this. Gary is personally known to one of us (DH) and the progress he has made has been wonderful, and, as they report, his lifestyle and well-being and that of his family have been substantially changed by it. We have to be careful that in our modern climate of often fervent desire for people with learning difficulties to have community presence, an 'ordinary life', to learn skills and behaviours which are more socially acceptable, we may remain grindingly dissatisfied with what Gary has achieved. We may need to be careful that our aspirations for what Gary should be doing are so high in these terms that we overlook issues of quality of life from his point of view.

Another answer to the 'well, what next' question relates to our concepts of 'interactivity' and 'spill-over' (Nind and Hewett, 1994). Briefly, once work on communication and relating reaches a certain stage, the learner is more competent at attending to others and engagements are longer and more motivating, this work spills over into other activities. It becomes easier to engage the person with something on a table-top, attract her/him into self-care activities, include the person in group-work with a variety of objectives. Steve Taylor makes this point:

> Once the child accepts you as something that isn't a threat, even something that gives pleasure in itself, you can then start to introduce new objects, actions and tasks. You have then reached the stage that the 'directive' teacher starts from, in that you can dictate more of the actions of the child, but the difference is that you have a child who gains the stability they need from your actions and is therefore much more accepting of the learning situation they are now in. (p. 224)

Figure 5. 4 shows what we mean about the types of progress we can expect from using Intensive Interaction. In the first place Intensive Interaction work is focusing on attainments in communication and relating, shown in the upper section. However, it is inevitable that developments will gradually take place in other ways. A usual effect is that the learner may be starting to be more secure and confident in various situations. This gives potential for judgements to be made about deliberately employing the power of what has been established with that person in order to work at attainments in other areas, as shown in the lower section. Simply, having learnt how to engage the learner and sustain attention, it is then possible to engage them in a variety of activities.

'Interactivity' describes a corresponding process for the teacher. We found in our early work, that the interactive style we were developing quickly became a central principle in all our teaching because 'as a natural process, this style of being with the students started to be influential in everything that we did' (Nind and Hewett, 1994, p. 143). We found we were being more relaxed and light-hearted in leading all activities, but also generally using elements of interaction such as tuning in, responding to learner behaviours wherever possible, staying sensitive to tempo, allowing pauses, and knowing when to celebrate and extend. The contributors' stories show this effect too:

> Sam and Marie said that once they had learnt about the principles of Intensive Interaction it was impossible not to use the techniques when interacting with Alice, or the other residents, within their everyday work. (Samuel and Maggs, p. 136)

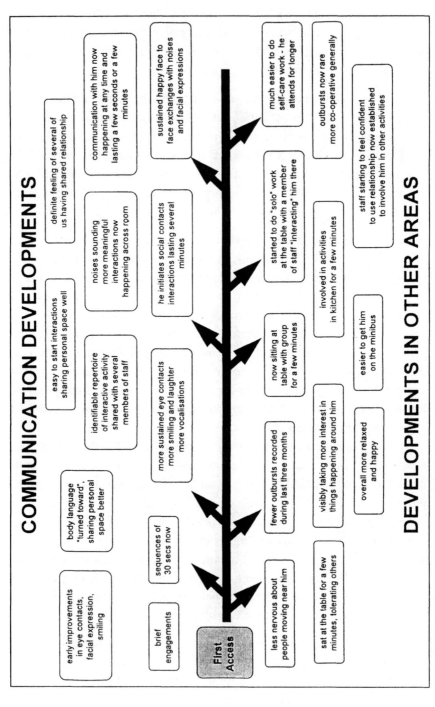

COMMUNICATION DEVELOPMENTS

early improvements in eye contacts, facial expression, smiling

body language "turned toward", sharing personal space better

identifiable repertoire of interactive activity shared with several members of staff

easy to start interactions sharing personal space well

definite feeling of several of us having shared relationship

communication with him now happening at any time and lasting a few seconds or a few minutes

noises sounding more meaningful interactions now happening across room

sustained happy face to face exchanges with noises and facial expressions

brief engagements

sequences of 30 secs now

more sustained eye contacts more smiling and laughter more vocalisations

he initiates social contacts interactions lasting several minutes

First Access

less nervous about people moving near him

fewer outbursts recorded during last three months

now sitting at table with group for a few minutes

started to do "solo" work at the table with a member of staff "interacting" him there

much easier to do self-care work - he attends for longer

sat at the table for a few minutes, tolerating others

visibly taking more interest in things happening around him

involved in activities in kitchen for a few minutes

outbursts now rare more co-operative generally

overall more relaxed and happy

easier to get him on the minibus

staff starting to feel confident to use relationship now established to involve him in other activities

DEVELOPMENTS IN OTHER AREAS

Figure 5.4 Types of progress with Intensive Interaction

This may also be the point where the practitioner starts sober consideration of the three principles of communication learning mentioned earlier – the learner is active; the learner shares control of the activity; the learning activity is intrinsically rewarding and motivating. Can we technically reflect on the way that we go about designing and carrying out activities? Is it possible to prepare all activities with these three principles in mind and do everything possible to make them present? It may well take careful thought and reflection on practice over some period of time to become well versed in working this way. It will of necessity involve being an interactor, being prepared to share control, making sure that the learner is accessed. It will mean having thoughts about communication in the forefront of everything that is happening, a continuing recognition that communication is also the basic tool with which we carry out everything we do with people on a moment-by-moment basis.

An analogy to a popular game seems appropriate. Communication is our 'cue ball' and we must keep our eyes on it. In snooker, the white, or cue, ball is the central focus of the game. It is the only ball the player strikes, its impact with other balls and its movement around the table is the key to reaching all the objectives of the game – potting the other balls. The best snooker practitioners invest large amounts of time in refining their artistry with manipulating the cue ball. There are, of course, so many other balls on the table.

It seems appropriate to end this section with one more consideration of the 'well – what next?' issue. We would be the first to admit that we are all still in the early stages of developing our artistry and technique with the use of interactive/process approaches to helping people learn things. We welcome and look out for all of the work that practitioners everywhere carry out on developing and evaluating Intensive Interaction. We suspect that there will be many more exciting developments yet and that some of them will yield increasingly authoritative statements on what is achievable for individuals.

References

Detheridge, T. (1997) 'Bridging the communication gap (for pupils with profound and multiple learning difficulties)', *British Journal of Special Education*, **24** (1), 21–26.

Harris, J. (1994) 'Language, Communication & Personal Power: A Developmental Perspective'. In: Coupe O'Kane, J. and Smith, B. (eds) (1994) *Taking Control: Enabling People with Learning Difficulties*. London: David Fulton.

Hewett, D. (1989) 'The most severe learning difficulties: does your curriculum "go back far enough"?'. In: Ainscow, M. (ed.) *Special Education in Change*. London: David Fulton.

Hewett, D. (1996) 'How to Start Doing Intensive Interaction'. In: Collis, M. and Lacey, P. (1996) *Interactive Approaches to Teaching: A Framework for INSET*. London: David Fulton.

Kiernan, C. and Reid, B. (1987) *Pre-Verbal Communication Schedule*. Windsor: NFER-Nelson.

Kiernan, C. (1988) 'Assessment for teaching communication skills'. In: Coupe, J. and Goldbart, J. (1988) *Communication Before Speech*. Beckenham: Croom Helm.

Nind, M. and Hewett, D. (1990) 'Teaching pupils with very severe learning difficulties by means of Intensive Interaction'. In: Maunder, S. (ed.) *Portage – Into the Nineties*. Proceedings of the 1989 National Portage Association Conference. The National Portage Association.

Nind, M. and Hewett, D. (1994) *Access to Communication: Developing the Basics of Communication with People with Severe Learning Difficulties Through Intensive Interaction*. London: David Fulton.

Sameroff, A. (1975) 'Transactional models in early social interactions', *Human Development*, **18**, 65–79.

Seligman, M.E.P. (1975) *Helplessness: On Depression, Development and Death*. San Francisco: W.H. Freeman.

Smith, B. (1989) 'Which approach? the education of pupils with SLD', *Mental Handicap*, **17**, 111–15.

Ware, J. and Healey, I. (1994) 'Conceptualizing Progress in Children with Profound and Multiple Learning Difficulties'. In: Ware, J. (ed.) (1994) *Educating Children with Profound and Multiple Learning Difficulties*. London: David Fulton.

Ware, J. (1996) *Creating a Responsive Environment: For People with Profound and Multiple Learning Difficulties*. London: David Fulton.

Chapter 6

Addressing the Needs of Adults with Profound and Multiple Learning Disabilities in Social Services Provision

Cath Irvine

Introduction

This chapter is about a day service project involving fourteen service users with profound and multiple learning difficulties. While much of the content will be around the implementation of Intensive Interaction, other issues will, from necessity, be discussed owing to the fact that the whole service to people with PMLD had to face a radical change before this new way of working could be introduced. Those of us involved in the project realise that the many exciting changes in the people with whom we are working are not totally attributable to the therapeutic approach, but also partly due to the major changes in service delivery that was necessary before Intensive Interaction could be used.

For a number of years the focus of the Speech and Language Therapy department has been on implementing a 'total communication' approach around the county of Somerset. Co-ordinators from each resource centre and residential establishment were trained in the use of signing and using symbols and this is now widely used around the county. However, some staff were beginning to realise that not all of our service users were benefiting from this approach and so they began to demand that something more was done for the service users who were not yet ready for a formal communication system.

Staff working in the places where the service users had predominantly PMLD were getting frustrated at the lack of knowledge and support they were receiving. In some houses bedrooms were being redecorated twice a year in order for the staff to feel that they were earning their salaries in care work! They were desperate to be working effectively, but didn't know where to start.

In 1993, a multi-disciplinary working party was set up to examine the needs of the staff working with this group of people. The initial result of this working party was the setting up of a six-day modular course where staff learned about language development, the development of physical and sensory skills and the development of cognition. They learned about empathic handling and, as far as is possible, they were encouraged to see the world from the perspective of a person with PMLD. Many staff reported that the course had a profound effect on their working practices. Some staff returned to their work places to face the reality of being unable to implement what they had learned.

The setting

Six Acres is a large resource centre in Taunton, providing a variety of services for more than 200 people with vastly varying degrees of learning difficulties. There had been a commitment to inclusion for people with PMLD which many staff felt to be politically correct. However, staff returning from the training began to express their frustration and anxieties about the conveyer-belt style of assisting with eating and personal care that was necessary to ensure access for people with PMLD into the centre's time-tabled sessions.

Some staff were voicing their doubts about the appropriateness of the actual sessions themselves. Each session had a group of people with a wide variety of degrees of learning difficulties. Many of the service users were very vocal and a noticeable percentage also displayed behaviours that required immediate and prolonged staff attention. This often meant that the people with PMLD were sitting on the edge of an activity with little involvement in their environment or other people around them.

Many of the staff were vocal in their beliefs about the ethics of inclusion and yet, when a confidential survey was carried out asking them to comment on the appropriateness of the sessions that were being offered, only 10 per cent were deemed, by the staff themselves, to be adequate. Not surprisingly, music sessions figured largely in the effective 10 per cent.

Whilst we were all aware of the possible positive aspects to inclusion, we had to face the reality that within present budgeting and staff shortages the policy of inclusion was intensifying some people's tendencies to withdraw and self-stimulate. Inclusion wasn't working. Service users were miserable and under stimulated. Staff felt guilty and ineffectual.

A radical rethink of services was necessary. Months of discussion and negotiation resulted in the PMLD project being presented to the staff team. It was initially presented as an experimental six-month long project, the continuation of which would depend on evaluation of progress and emotional security in the relevant service users.

Staffing and staff preparation

During preliminary discussions, the staff expressed their reservations about working in an environment which could be seen as the traditional 'special care', with all the bad associations that this had for many of them. Their experience had been that special care was seen as a place where new, inexperienced staff could be placed, from which staff could be withdrawn when there were shortages in the rest of the centre. Often, staff who had no interest in people with PMLD were placed in special care whether they liked it or not! It was perceived as a place where very little work satisfaction was gained owing to the focus being on personal needs. Very little progress was apparent so staff got discouraged and nobody really seemed to know how to work effectively with this group of people. Plans for the project, therefore, had to take into account some of the worries of the team.

Firstly, staff who wished to work on the project and become part of the 'core team' needed to volunteer rather than being volunteered! Secondly, we proposed to encourage a specialist approach to the core team through training and support. Thirdly, we had a commitment from the management that staff would not be withdrawn from the project to cover other sessions in the main centre. (Once appointed, all of the core team did request one day a week in the main centre to continue their involvement in sessions that they were loath to give up – for reasons of effectiveness or enjoyment.) The issues around work satisfaction were largely resolved by the proposal to use Intensive Interaction, with detailed record keeping (discussed later).

Four staff volunteered to work on the project. We also had a commitment from the residential network managers that they would provide a member of staff each day – giving us an ideal link between day services and residential.

All of the core team had been on, or were quickly put on, the PMLD training course. In additional to this, the whole of the Six Acres staff team were given a three-hour introduction to Intensive Interaction and the necessary record keeping.

It was hoped that further training could be given to the core team prior to the start of the project, but this became difficult owing to time constraints. We did some video footage of the core team interacting with a baby with the intention of using it as a training and self-evaluation tool. It seemed like a good idea at the time, but in reality we never used it as the staff found their own styles of interacting with each individual on the project. This lack of training was initially seen as a problem but, with hindsight, the staff have mostly become very comfortable with the use of Intensive Interaction and have used it intuitively and naturally rather than in a trained fashion – one of the beauties of using this approach. What we have found all around the county is that one of the most powerful teaching tools for staff wishing to use this approach is to see others using it. Certainly this was our experience on the project. It was new to us all and we learned a lot from watching one another. Core staff, physiotherapist, psychologist and speech therapist could all be regularly seen engaging in sessions of one-to-one interactions.

A system of room management was implemented in which one member of staff would organise the practical aspects of the environment and protect sessions of one-to-one interactions being carried out in the room. The room manager role was organised on a rota among all the core staff. This method of organisation also gave the staff the option of juggling the rota to enable staff to opt out of one-to-one sessions if they were feeling stressed and therefore not in a playful, relaxed mood.

One aspect of good and mutually supportive team work is having individuals within the team who are strong enough to admit to their own needs. Staff were encouraged to take ten minutes out if necessary. In this way an attempt was being made to have a routine in which staff could maintain their equilibrium in order to create an atmosphere of acceptance and calm.

Service users in the project

Recommendations were invited from the staff at Six Acres and the multi-disciplinary team for service users who would benefit from intensive work. The criterion for inclusion was predominantly around issues of communication. The aim was to choose people who were at a 'preintentional' stage (a term we radically questioned once we got to know the people as individuals). Fourteen service users were accepted onto the project, four of whom had wheelchairs, the remaining ten being mobile with a wide range of physical exploratory behaviours!

The environment of the project

After much discussion, negotiation and sacrifice on the part of a staff team already working in an overcrowded resource centre, an Eliot hut, previously housing two key groups and the music sessions of the centre, was offered as the most suitable environment. The Eliot building was decorated in a nondescript boring beige colour and furnished with uncomfortable chairs and tables. The room could be physically divided into two using a folding door. There was a large store cupboard (now a kitchen area), two toilets and a personal care area.

The first job of the core team was to overhaul this environment. We discarded most of the uncomfortable chairs and replaced them with easy chairs. The tables were put into the kitchen area and only used during lunch time. We painted one half of the room in bright, stimulating primary colours. The other side of the room was decorated in restful pastel colours in the hope of providing an area conducive to chilling-out! We gathered toys and interactive stimulating materials from wherever we could. Since the project began this environment has continued to be adapted to the needs of those using it and working there. The core team have added colourful and stimulating touches to the room as the needs of the service users were recognised.

On the first day of the project the service users walked into the room, sat down and waited to be 'done to'. It took them around a week to realise that they were free to wander, choose their own activities and sit or lie wherever they wished.

Observation period

The project began by having a six-week observation period. The core team were initially resistant to this idea as they had worked with some of these people for a number of years and felt that they knew them rather well. Nonetheless, during the observation period many new communicative behaviours were identified, staff tuned into the personalities of the service users to a degree that had not been previously possible. In the reviews following the observation period, the core staff requested that observations be extended on three of the service users as they felt they hadn't quite 'tuned' into these three in the way that they had with the others.

The observation period preceded the main project for a number of reasons. Firstly, for baselines of service users' behaviours to be identified and hopefully committed to video footage. Secondly, so the staff could stand back and look at behaviours without attempting to make individual interpretations. The project was implemented in a new, homely type of environment and there were some adjustments to be made on this account for both core staff and service users.

During this period, also, core staff began to experiment with the use of Intensive Interaction. The reviews following the observation period were attended by as many people who were involved with a specific service user as we could get to attend. We wanted as much communication and consistency as we could get. For some of the service users this meant residential staff attending the reviews, and for others parents would be represented. We gained incredibly valuable insight from people who observed service users in their own home. They saw the kind of behaviours we were hoping to see in the coming months.

Behaviours of service users were discussed and for many types of behaviours clear communicative intent could be seen, where previously these actions would have been irrelevant, obsessional, irritating or inconvenient! One man walked to the toilet door when he needed the bathroom. He hadn't had the opportunity to do this within day services before and staff were unaware that he was able to do so. Another man handed core staff his coat if he wanted to go out; again, another communication that could not have been reinforced in his previous environment.

Some regularly occurring behaviours were difficult to attribute meanings to but, in the way that parents respond to their young children using rich interpretation and intentionality, we decided to interpret some of these behaviours as though they had meaning. In this way service users could learn that their actions had communicative value and a response would be forthcoming.

An example of this was one of the service users who regularly pulled his T-shirt up. During the observation period one of the most successful interaction sequences with this man had been 'tummy-tickling', so we began to interpret his manipulation of his T-shirt as an initiation of contact rather than an irritating habit that had to be responded to by tucking him back up in case he got cold.

Record keeping

The questions we are most frequently asked about the project are around the areas of record keeping. Good record keeping is essential when working with people with PMLD and when using Intensive Interaction as a communication tool. Changes in behaviours can be minute and difficult to detect or remember over time. Staff needed written and video records to peruse at times when they feel that few changes have occurred over a period of time. Intensive Interaction is an approach that can result in an action-expecting manager accusing staff of 'sitting around doing nothing' so staff need their activities recorded on paper to prove the effectiveness of the approach being used.

Record keeping was one of the biggest headaches of the project! Social services staff had not been expected to maintain such thorough records in the past, time was precious, and taking the option of spending five minutes longer involved in an interaction rather than using the five minutes to record what happened was a great temptation. We streamlined the record keeping as far as we possibly could without feeling that we would be losing valuable information. Basic interaction forms were used, along with a day sheet recording who had maintained this routine, coming over to the 'hut' at around ten o'clock. A number of the service users did not arrive at the resource base until around ten so missed their morning keygroup time.

As it was obvious that a great deal of quality observations and communication work would occur during meal times, the service users stayed in the hut for lunch, the core team being supported by a few extra members of Six Acres staff to aid with lunches and personal care.

From the beginning we wanted to implement a system of choices, not because we really expected service users to be making valid choices, but because we wanted to introduce good working practices right from the beginning. We wanted to avoid the attitudes behind statements like 'He always drinks tea with two sugars'.

Choices of drinks were introduced using different colour and shape cups for each drink, and dinner choices were offered by showing the service user the options and watching their responses. We were amazed that many people did actually make definite choices by either taking the preferred option, eye-pointing or pushing a rejected option aside. Some people had never had a consistent opportunity to choose for themselves in this way before – especially in day services.

Personal care was provided as and when needed rather than the conveyor belt style that had previously been implemented in order to have the service users accessing the structured sessions. A couple of the service users began to request the toilet by going and standing next to the toilet door – again something that had been impossible in their previous day service provision. Personal autonomy was most definitely on the increase – for better or worse!

Intensive Interaction

I have no intention of explaining what Intensive Interaction is. This has been recorded most thoroughly and inspiringly in *Access to Communication* (Nind and Hewett, 1994). However, I have found that what most turns people on to the philosophy of the approach is personal accounts of how it works, so some examples of this I will relate.

We tried to avoid having only one member of staff working with each service user, so the examples given of interactional sequences and progression of sequences could become most confusing if I bombard with names of at least four different members of staff. I also have an aversion to using 'staff member' all the way through the descriptions of situations which were exciting and most positively emotionally charged. (I thought of using an acronym of the core team names but this would be Bach and would possibly look a little pretentious to anyone flicking through this chapter and missing the explanation!) I settled on Julia.

Simon

Simon is a man in his mid-thirties who has a diagnosis of autism. In our old thinking, he had no communication and spent his day in total self-absorption. During the observation period he occupied his time by shuffling a set of duplo bricks around the floor, using either his hands or his legs to manipulate them into position. He gathered all of the bricks into a group directly in front of his body and was most protective about them.

The first thing we did with Simon was to gradually change those duplo bricks for colourful wooden blocks – a change that he accepted unquestioningly. This was done for a number of reasons. Simon was unable to build these bricks so their value as an extendable interaction tool was limited. Also when we viewed some of the video data, we could hear nothing except the noise of duplo bricks being shuffled around!

Intensive Interaction with Simon began by just sitting next to him. After a few sessions of doing this, Julia would simply touch the bricks very briefly and continue to sit by him, repeating the action every few minutes. As Simon learnt to accept Julia's presence and her occasional forays into his territory, she began to 'interfere' in more innovative ways. She would build a tower, only managing three bricks before Simon would gather them in again. This would be greeted by Julia with a celebration of Simon knocking over the tower as if he had done so intentionally. She would briefly withdraw the red bricks or the yellow bricks. She would 'steal' one of his bricks and hold it against her temple, leaning on it in a relaxed fashion and giving him a big smile and verbal encouragement when he scanned her eyes whilst looking to retrieve his brick.

It didn't take Simon long to learn some of these routines and begin to anticipate some of the reactions he gained from allowing a member of staff to join him. Within a couple of weeks Julia was able to build a tower of nine bricks before Simon would very intentionally knock them over, then look up to enjoy the reaction. She could withdraw all the red bricks and all the yellow bricks before Simon would gather them in, seeming to look more carefully at what he was gathering in. As soon as Julia lifted a brick towards her face, Simon would make eye contact and smile – reducing the time he had to wait to get his brick back but also very obviously enjoying the positive responses he gained from looking at another person.

Within two months it was obvious that Simon's time alone had changed and his play activities were extended. He no longer just shuffled bricks. He now pushed his bricks towards a member of staff as an initiation, using eye contact to invite someone to join him. He picked up bricks of the same colours and examined them, on a number of occasions placing them next to an object in the room that was the same colour. His shuffling changed to piling bricks on top of one another (not in organised tower building – that comes next year!). The main change was that Simon was extremely happy to have others join in his activities. On one occasion, during an interaction, Simon picked up a brick, placed it against his temple, leant against it and giggled when Julia retrieved it.

Ella

Ella is a woman of thirty-two who spent the whole of the observation period either lying on the floor or sitting on a chair as far away from other people as she could find. Ella rocked constantly, groaning to herself and holding her stomach.

The first thing we needed to do with Ella was to make sure that where she chose to lie was going to be a place where she wouldn't be trampled or block access. We wanted to encourage her to lie on the mats rather than on the harder (and colder!) floor surface. When she threw herself on the floor, we moved a mat over to her and gently eased her onto it. We tried to identify her favourite places to 'flop' and pre-empted this by placing mats in these spots, then gradually moving towards safer locations. Within a few weeks Ella was using the mats rather than the floor. Ella tolerated physical contact for personal care, but most definitely rejected even close physical proximity at any other time.

Intensive Interaction with Ella was very much slower than with Simon. An approach over to the mats where she lay rocking would invariably result in Ella getting up and moving elsewhere. Julia began by lying four feet away from Ella and just being there in a non-threatening way. There were quite a few occasions when she thought that Ella was beginning to accept her presence but on moving close, Ella made her usual protest of moving right away.

At the end of the observation period, Ella was one of the service users we struggled to identify any intentional communications from. She was obviously happier, calmer and more in control of her new environment,

112

but we were all struggling to see how we could get through to her. At her review meeting, residential staff reported that Ella was much more tolerant of physical contact – something that hadn't been evident in the project. Her parents reported that Ella initiated contact when she was at home if she wanted food or drink. These were insights that the core team found encouraging. Owing to lack of reciprocation from Ella, it had been fairly discouraging to work with her. We had to refocus seriously on the priority of continuing to make Ella feel secure with other people.

Over the next month, the interactions with Ella continued to be not too interactive! The breakthrough came one day when Julia had once again moved too close too soon. Rather than getting up and finding somewhere else to lie, Ella turned her back on Julia and grunted. Julia responded to the grunt with a similar vocalisation – and Ella smiled.

Vocal turn-taking became the only way we could reach Ella. Interactions are still two feet apart. The use of the video footage has been invaluable in learning more about Ella. There have been times when she has been approached and shown no interest. Even more, she has appeared to be rejecting contact by turning her back on us. Close video scrutiny has shown Ella doing what we've interpreted as rejecting us, then turning and following us with her eyes while we walk away. We no longer take the rejections so easily. We lie down near her and wait, sometimes for up to ten minutes, for her to give a signal that we can respond to.

Amazingly, considering that the pace of interactions has hardly changed, there are some obvious developments in Ella. She will now come and sit at the table with staff and service users when the drinks are served. A number of times she has handed a member of staff her empty cup rather than leaving it on the table or floor. She will tolerate someone sitting next to her in one of the two-seater sofas. She is obviously a much happier and more relaxed person.

Sue

Sadly, one of the service users in the project died during the sixth month so was not included in the final evaluation. However, it would be wrong not to mention the progress that she made during her six months.

Sue was a very solitary person at the beginning of the project. She would find a chair well away from anyone else and occupy her time rocking, grinding her teeth, twiddling wool or pieces of material (she could be very resourceful in obtaining pieces of material if there were none immediately available), and manipulating her own saliva.

Any approaches towards Sue would result in being firmly pushed away. We puzzled over this for a while as she was indicating a definite preference to be left alone. This was an intentional communication and surely we ought to respect it as such. However, it was difficult to see how else we could get alongside of her. After much discussion and seeking of advice, we agreed to turn this pushing away into a game. Julia would approach Sue and sit in front of her on her haunches. When Sue pushed her away, she 'fell over' backwards, sprung up and cheered. Sue immediately responded with smiles. It became part of the routine of getting closer and building a relationship with Sue.

Other routines were established, shared wool twiddling, pushing a large ball over to her and diving to where she returned it. All very simple stuff and again, as with Ella, we didn't really feel that this was enough. We weren't getting any closer physically and she rarely initiated an interaction. However, Sue noticeably changed. She was far more relaxed, she smiled more and she looked around at what was happening in the room, rather than keeping her head down and showing no interest in anything. The change in Sue was also obvious to the staff in the residential unit in which she lived. Her key worker from home wrote the following after her death:

> Sue made a lot more eye contact and laughed much more. She became a lot more assertive, leading us to things, pushing us towards what she wanted. Generally her moods were happier, despite any pain she may have suffered.
>
> We feel that the time spent in the PMLD sessions contributed to making Sue's last six months among the happiest of her life.

The evaluation

Initially, it was hoped that we could analyse the difference in service users' communicative behaviours through the use of Intensive Interaction. It soon became apparent that it would not be possible to prove that Intensive Interaction caused all the changes for service users. Thus the evaluation focused on the effect that the whole of the PMLD project had on the service users' communicative behaviour.

Firstly, the environment the service users had been accustomed to had been drastically changed from inclusion with groups of more able service users to an environment which was very much focused on their particular needs. Therefore any changes in behaviours could be partly due to the changes in day service provision generally.

Secondly, evaluation of Intensive Interaction would require an adequate amount of video footage which had proved difficult to obtain. Some of these difficulties have now been resolved. The project now has a video camera within the hut so staff no longer have to go and search for the one belonging to the main centre. We are all much clearer about why we need video evidence of our work.

One of the major advantages of the structure of the project was that the core staff have had the opportunity to become more knowledgeable about the service users and their communication skills. Some of these skills which began to develop within the new day service setting may have already been evident in residential settings. This does not distract from the fact that progress was made within the project – the progress being that the staff now have a consistent picture of the service users' communicative abilities on which to encourage further development. Further progress can also be claimed in that most of the service users are now feeling secure enough in their new environment to display and experiment with communication behaviours not previously observed by day service staff. For some individuals, we have been pleasantly surprised that some progress has been obvious to residential staff – an aspect we did not anticipate in such a short period.

At the end of the six months we plainly had inadequate video data for thorough analysis of progress. This was not such a disaster as it could have been as everyone involved in the service provision could already clearly see the benefits of the project and the effect it had had on the service users. We didn't need high powered evidence to ensure the continuation of the project – the evidence was daily obvious to all who knew the individuals.

However, we had promised an evaluation and perhaps the people who needed the evidence in black and white most were the core team. The temptation for them throughout the project had been to focus on the things that could still be improved. They overlooked the success of their work and often disbelieved anyone who praised them or commented positively on their achievements.

115

Information from staff was gathered on project feedback forms covering staff views on service users' progress. This information was compared to analysis of the data on a sheet recording New Developments. There was a reassuring consensus between all of the information gathered from these forms. Individuals' review notes also supported this information so for the sake of ease I will summarise the information from the Core Staff Feedback forms.

- 12 of the service users were considered to be happier
- 12 of the service users were considered to be more relaxed
- 12 of the service users were considered to feel more secure.

(One service user did not appear to gain much from the new environment and the new approach. This is reflected in his emotional response to the project.)

- 7 of the service users had gained more independence
- 11 of the service users were thought to be more alert
- eye contact had noticeably increased in 9 of the individuals
- 8 people were allowing more physical contact
- 9 individuals were initiating interactions
- 12 people had clearly identifiable intentional communications
- 9 people were making choices of drinks and food.

There were many other benefits to the individuals that have not necessarily been measured.

There were opportunities for those in wheelchairs to have some time sitting or lying elsewhere. This is something that had only been possible during physiotherapy sessions previously. One gentleman became quite proficient at swinging himself around on his bottom in order to change his scenery.

Although no direct work was done on reducing behaviours previously seen as problematic, six of the service users drastically reduced such behaviours as faecal smearing, constant screaming, sleeping for long periods of the day and eating and drinking difficulties.

Including the heading 'Using more diverse solitary activities' on the Core Staff Feedback form was a little unfair. It was a difficult question for staff to answer as changes in solitary behaviour are likely to be minute and very gradual. These would usually be identified by close analysis of video tapes. However, there had been obvious changes in the way that Simon occupied his time and we were interested to see if staff had noticed this in any of the other service users. They identified four people who had clearly developed in the way they chose to spend time alone. Subsequent viewing of recent video data compared with the base line data revealed many other changes in this area.

The lessons learnt

There can be little doubt that the project has improved the day service provision for people with PMLD at Six Acres, and that a great deal of individual progress has been made. However, there have been, and undoubtedly will continue to be, many areas in which improvements and further progress can be made.

While our main focus has been to establish links of communication between us and the service users, we have struggled to find time to ensure that other essential communications are taking place. This was particularly a problem between day staff and residential staff. Not all residential staff had been trained in the philosophy of Intensive Interaction and there were some misconceptions. Hopefully, this has now been resolved by a blitz of training.

Obtaining video material was also a problem, despite reducing the amount of video required and introducing check lists to attempt to ensure that everyone was videoed once a fortnight. The major lesson learnt here was that staff need to know that the videos are going to be reviewed regularly. We set up regular meetings in which to do so, but often these meetings were overtaken by the need to resolve practical problems. A compromise was reached in that every fortnight we would view videos and the alternate weeks could be used for practical matters.

The project also has a video camera of its own now, which means that not so much staff time is involved in obtaining that required data.

The future

The project will continue and continue to develop. A number of individuals would now benefit from an environment which could consistently encourage more formal use of communication. These people, who so thoroughly rejected the company of others, have now learnt to enjoy it so much that the staff are having difficulties in consistently responding to their initiations. Once again, they are finding that those who still require sensitive, accepting one-to-one time are not getting all that they need.

At present, two solutions to this problem are being examined. One is a 'next step up' project, for whom there are a further twenty-two candidates still within the main centre as well as the people coming from the PMLD project.

Another possible solution is to investigate more varied ways in which people can be encouraged to occupy the periods of time when staff cannot be with them. Discussions with residential staff revealed many of these people's preferences. Swings, roundabouts and rocking equipment featured heavily in these discussions. In a service where yearly financial cuts are the norm, we are investigating ways in which the PMLD environment can be extended to include an outdoor leisure area.

Somerset Social Services have responded quickly to a philosophy that has so many obvious benefits for this group of service users who have been so poorly served in the past. Issues of age appropriateness, inclusion for people with PMLD and physical contact are in the process of a sympathetic review.

The Six Acres project has been greeted with a great deal of interest and many people throughout the county are now seeking to implement the use of Intensive Interaction in their own work places.

Intensive Interaction is a wonderful tool. As many staff point out, it's nothing new. Some of them have been doing it for years, particularly in residential settings. It is our belief that Intensive Interaction is such an instinctive tool that many people distrust its simplicity. It feels as though there should be much more to it. Many people feel that they can't possibly be doing it right because it comes so easily to them. (This is where the temptation is to 'do' too much, rather than just 'be'.)

References

Nind, M. and Hewett, D. (1994) *Access to Communication: Developing the Basics of Communication with People with Severe Learning Difficulties Through Intensive Interaction.* London: David Fulton.

Chapter 7

Introducing Intensive Interaction for People with Profound Learning Disabilities Living in Small Staffed Houses in the Community

Judith Samuel and Jaqui Maggs

In this chapter we describe our initial attempts to introduce Intensive Interaction to people with profound learning disabilities living in small community houses staffed by learning disability nurses and support staff employed by a learning disability NHS Trust. We write from the perspective of our disciplines as a clinical psychologist and an occupational therapist, and from the perspective of being involved as members of the Trust's Multiple Disability Resource Team (MDRT); a specialist multi-disciplinary team for people with profound learning and multiple disability.

The move to community care

Influenced by the North American version of the principle of normalisation (Wolfensberger, 1972), community services for people with learning disabilities have been encouraged to accomplish: image enhancement (both in the view of society and in terms of individual self-esteem), the affording of respect, the enabling of community presence, community participation and choice making and the building of individual competence (O'Brien, 1986). It has been found that the move from institutional care to small houses in the community for people with learning disability, where sufficiently resourced with adequate attention paid to staff training and working methods, has been a tremendous improvement in the quality of life for clients. This is on all measures such as interaction with and assistance from staff and time spent in purposeful activity. As a consequence, clients have experienced greater developmental progress and enjoyed greater community and social participation than in institutional settings (Bratt and Johnston, 1988; Perry and Felce, 1994; Mansell, 1995; Emerson and Hatton, 1994).

The move to community care for people with profound learning disabilities

The British 'ordinary life' philosophy (Kings Fund, 1980) promoted the development of a comprehensive locally-based residential service as the ideal for all people with learning disabilities without much reference to the degree of their learning disability (Towell, 1988). The most researched example of this (e.g. Felce and Toogood, 1988) resulted in a 'how to do it' guide: Mansell *et al.* (1987). Nevertheless, several studies of the transition to community from institutional care (Bratt and Johnston, 1988; Felce and Repp, 1992; Perry and Felce, 1994) and from segregation to integration in day services (Pettipher and Mansell, 1993; Rose, Davis and Gotch, 1993) have shown that quality of life on various indicators is related to the ability of clients. As was indicated in 1980 by Raynes: 'The less you've got the less you get'. Bratt and Johnston (1988) found that there was little evidence of integration being achieved in the local community for a group of young people with profound learning disability who had moved to small houses. Mansell and Beasley (1993) evaluated longitudinally the effectiveness of community-based residential services for people with severe or profound learning disabilities and challenging behaviour. They compared outcomes with life in the ordinary institutional wards or special units for challenging behaviour from whence the clients came. These authors found that small staffed homes were able to produce improved client experience in leisure, self-help and practical tasks or domestic chores. However, to do this required particular attention to the quality of staff performance as well as to basic materials and social resources. Perry and Felce (1994) examined outcome data on fourteen recently provided staffed houses in Wales for people of all levels of learning disability. They found that quality levels on many indicators (i.e. quality of housing provision, social and community integration, social relationships within the houses, resident engagement in activity, developmental progress over time, and opportunities for autonomy and choice) were related to residents' ability.

Hatton *et al.* (1995) note that, concerning the quality of services for people with severe learning disabilities and sensory impairments,

> purchasing an expensive service is no guarantee of quality, nevertheless all the specialised services [they] evaluated were more costly than general service provision for people with learning disability. (p. 59)

These authors stress that to be good enough, services must have adequate financial and human resources in terms of appropriately skilled and motivated staff, in particular for people with sensory impairments: 'a total signing communicative environment', clearly defined management structure, staff training, supervision, support and feedback, a mission to provide individualised and structured programmes, mechanisms for review of quality, etc.

In the 1980s, Mansell *et al.* (1987), Felce and Toogood (1988) and others questioned the idea of promoting the use of toys and recreational materials by adults with learning disabilities and suggested that involvement in domestic and household tasks is a more meaningful and valued way of spending time. Their project for people re-settled from severely deprived institutional settings used behavioural techniques to enhance skills and image and reduce challenging behaviour and made tremendous strides in terms of addressing physical and medical health care needs. They also built positive relationships with parents. Nevertheless, they do not seem to describe life in terms of much fun and the one client for whom they admit the least success in terms of gaining compliance, even via extensive physical assistance, was a woman with profound learning disabilities and severe stereotypical behaviour (Felce and Toogood, 1988).

The quality of life of people with profound learning disabilities depends on the support they get from carers: 'It is staff who enable client access to opportunities provided by the setting, its location, its goals and policies and human resources available' (Mansell, 1995). Community services for people with the most profound learning disabilities have struggled to decide what their goals should be for clients. In the 1980s, the rationale was that the most valued social role open to such clients was that of home maker (Felce and Toogood, 1988; Mansell *et al.*, 1987), enabling people to participate in everyday domestic and community activities. However, more recently there has been a cultural shift. In the 1990s, British society appears to place more value on relationships, leisure and work than doing one's own cooking, washing up or cleaning. So why not the same for people with profound learning disabilities? Why should people with learning disabilities be physically prompted to comply with domestic activities, just because it *looks* good? In fact, they do not often anyway, it is the support staff who do the chores and the houses are often not usually resourced sufficiently to engage clients in the activities all the time even if they wanted to. Still, someone has to get the meals on time, do the cleaning, obtain goods and services, manage financial matters and maintain health and safety.

Age appropriateness

The political correctness of age appropriateness has become a tyranny, especially for those with the most profound learning disabilities: 'What began as a way of saying "Let's make sure we don't insult a group of people who have been insulted enough" has become a practice that says "Don't do what you want or be who you are. It embarrasses us".' (Lovett, 1996, p. 12). There is a perhaps a difference between those people with learning disabilities who for their entire life may have been denied age-appropriate opportunities and expectations, so they may continue to prefer age-inappropriate activity in the absence of alternatives, and those for whom it has been not so much a matter of denial but rather that the opportunities offered (age-appropriate or not) have not been accessible to them because of the profound level of their learning disabilities, perhaps complicated by sensory and physical disabilities. Nind and Hewett (1996) propose instead that: 'in order to treat people with learning difficulties with respect, our behaviour in relation to them must surely have to take into account their level of language development, their understanding of the social world and their emotional maturity' (p. 51).

Staff support

As has been indicated above, at best, small staffed houses have been found to use the greater resources they have more efficiently than larger settings and thus achieve greater effectiveness in terms of client participation in meaningful activity without overall increases in problem behaviour

(Mansell, 1995). However, at worst, they are under-resourced with staff doing double shifts, woken when they are supposed to be sleeping in, isolated and demoralised. Staff who themselves may be frightened to go outside the front door because of the nature of the neighbourhood. Felce, Lowe and Beswick, (1993) found that staff turnover is extremely variable in small staffed houses but that most have a core of long-serving staff providing continuity over time.

Residential support staff have to fulfil many roles (Mansell *et al.*, 1987): teacher, housekeeper, nurse, administrator, accountant etc. without it always being clear how to prioritise them. Increasing legislation and residential home registration requirements, and the consequent wrath of management via disciplinary procedures, exist for badly kept drug records, the mal-administration of money or poor food hygiene etc. rather than for when a client has not been interacted with in a way they understood between breakfast and lunch; or for when a client has not received regular health screening such as eye tests at the recommended frequency so that staff are aware of the extent of the client's actual disabilities; or for when a dietician's advice, physiotherapy, speech and language therapy, occupational therapy or psychology programme is not carried out as recommended.

Denial of history

Given the influence of the philosophy of normalisation and the passage of time, institutions had begun to be construed as all bad, thus indicating no need to look back. It had been forgotten, for example, that developmental models may have been used effectively to influence the provision of play or music therapy, or that relationships between hospital residents described 'high grades' and 'low grades' could be loving and caring. Developmental assessment past or present had begun to be viewed as irrelevant: OTs have not been taught development in their training and 'take that with a pinch of salt!' was the recent response by a team leader when a speech and language therapy assessment suggested a client's functioning was at about six months.

Social relationships

Research has shown that the move to community care in small houses with an increase in staff:client ratios has resulted in increased client functioning in domestic activity and interaction with staff and a markedly higher provision of opportunity to engage in activities (Felce, de Kock and Repp, 1986). However, there seems to have been more concern for facilitating social integration with people without disabilities (Mansell *et al.*, 1987) than with examining the nature of relationships with the staff who support them day by day. Adherence to a policy of age appropriateness has been interpreted in some services as a reluctance to do things that staff may have done in the past, for example, give and receive hugs with their clients (Nind and Hewett, 1996). It is likely that concern about the potential for abuse has fuelled a desire to keep at a respectful distance from clients except when having to facilitate intimate personal care. However, the clients in question *de facto* do not understand why they have stopped getting or being able to give a hug, stopped being touched, stopped being talked to in a familiar tone. The likely consequence of such a change in policy is learned helplessness: depression, withdrawal and the development of stereotypical and self-stimulatory behaviours (O'Brien, Glenn and Cunningham, 1994). Nind (1997) goes so far as to suggest that such lack of physical contact except for intimate care is itself abusive. It gives the individual the message that they are 'untouchable'.

Our local experience

Oxfordshire had two large mental handicap hospitals. These were closed by 1984. Clients moved to a range of provision in centres of population throughout the county. This included a number of ordinary houses as group homes and seven Community Units (four of which were purpose built) comprising three or four adjoining six-bedded bungalows or flats with offices attached (*Development Team of the Mentally Handicapped. First Report: 1976–1977*). Initially, a number of clients with the most severe challenging behaviours and/or physical disabilities were accommodated in the wards of a small redundant hospital site in Oxford. This site also contained the new HQ of the service. Subsequently, these wards closed and the clients living therein moved on to more local provision. The site now contains the resource base of the MDRT, a specialist assessment and treatment service for people with challenging behaviour and/or mental health problems (STATT), and a five-bedded medium secure unit (MSU) which has enabled Oxfordshire people accommodated in special hospitals to return to the county. In 1993, the Service became a separate NHS Trust. The Trust has a Clients' Charter (based on O'Brien's [1986] five accomplishments) which recognises all clients' rights to:

> ... individuality, status and respect, choice, continuity, relationships, community presence, competence, health and comfort, representation (advocacy) and access to a professional service.

The Trust is committed to moving its residents into smaller more dispersed housing which is as ordinary as possible. A Housing Association was established to enable residents to gain access to ordinary benefits. The residents of some of the Community Units have already moved on. The challenge has been to find within budget accommodation which fulfils the requirements of all the clients involved, for example, friendship patterns, physical space, adequate staffing levels etc.

The Trust residential accommodation was initially managed by nurses organised into a nursing hierarchy. This has changed. The homes are now managed by appropriately experienced staff. Residential support staff are encouraged to engage residents in ordinary domestic, community and leisure activities. A 'centre-less day service' has been created. Before this, clients received six or so hours per week with an 'activity support worker' and some clients attended local Social Services day centres on a part time basis. Unfortunately, recently such places have been cut owing to Council budget capping by Central government. There is specialist health professional input from seven locally based multi-disciplinary community teams (CTPLDs) containing representatives of the following: community nurses, dieticians, physiotherapists, psychiatrists, clinical psychologists, occupational therapists, speech and language therapists and social workers.

The CTPLDs are supported by the Trust Specialist Services and include staff with time linked with the MDRT and with STATT. The residential placements are monitored by Care Managers employed by the Joint Commissioner for Health and Social Care (NHS and Community Care Act, 1990).

Introducing Intensive Interaction to the local service

We have had several sources of inspiration for our introduction of Intensive Interaction to the local service:

- Reading RNIB (1993a) Focus Fact sheet *Stereotypical behaviour in people with visual and learning disabilities; Access to Communication* (Nind and Hewett, 1994); Nind and Hewett's (1996) chapter entitled 'When age appropriateness isn't appropriate'; Nind's (1996) journal article summarising her Ph.D evaluation of Intensive Interaction.
- Workshops: by Dave Hewett (1993), Playtrac (1996) and Melanie Nind (Nind, 1997).
- Personal experience: becoming a parent oneself (JS; JM just about to!).

Initial attempts to access some clients

Rodney

Rodney is a man of 58 with Down's Syndrome and profound learning disabilities. He is blind in one eye and has partial sight in the other but no clear hearing or major mobility disabilities. He has no speech or signing. Rodney was institutionalised at the age of six. Since the age of about 49 he has lived in one of the bungalows of a Community Unit with five other residents with severe or profound learning disabilities. Rodney was referred because of stereotypical behaviour (i.e. flicking a sock in front of his face) which support staff thought was putting his image at risk. His sock flicking was something he was thought always to have done.

> I (JS) had observed Rodney before; however, when I first met him on this occasion, he was at home, sitting in his preferred position on the floor, flicking and mouthing a sock, rocking and vocalising. Inspired by reading about 'augmentative mothering' in RNIB, (1993a.) I sat on the floor near him and imitated his movements and sounds with an enquiring posture and gaze. Momentarily, Rodney stopped flicking his sock and looked at me. On another occasion my assistant met him and tried a similar approach standing. Rodney immediately made eye

contact, approached and gave her a hug and kiss. Their interactive sequence continued for about five minutes then he wandered off. At an individual planning meeting shortly afterwards, I described the process of 'augmented mothering' and wondered if the staff team might consider using this as a rationale for some work with Rodney. A member of staff exclaimed that what I was describing seemed to be exactly what a volunteer was doing with Rodney when he attended a session at the local gym. She said that Rodney and the volunteer appeared to have a wonderful relationship. The volunteer was able to encourage Rodney to participate in ways that his residential key worker, who had known Rodney for many years, had not. On arrival at the gym Rodney clearly sought out his friend again in a way he did not do with staff at home. However, my colleague was concerned because the intuitive techniques the volunteer used included conversing with Rodney using the vocalisations Rodney made. She had wondered what to do about this as it was obviously not age-appropriate . . . The independent confirmation from the literature that what Rodney needed was this style of interaction inspired the team leader of that house staff team to try out the techniques with Rodney at home. At that point, unfortunately, I left to cover another patch of the county. However, the team leader attended a workshop on Intensive Interaction that we organised facilitated by Playtrac, and was supported by another psychologist whom I supervised. Although the staff varied in their willingness to try, she encouraged her staff team at a set time each evening to try mirroring Rodney's vocalisations and movements 'to have a conversation' without words and to note his response. The outcome was, in her view, increased affection from Rodney and increase in his confidence in approaching people for a hug or to pat or kiss their head. There followed eight months of considerable disruption in the staff team for various reasons, during which time many agency or bank staff were employed. The team leader did not think she could expect these temporary staff to do such work with Rodney. At the time of writing this situation is now resolved and the team leader intends to try again.

It would appear that for Rodney those who became responsive to his style of communicating showed him that there was someone to communicate with after all. Was this new learning for him or for us, in being able to truly listen, the 'interactivity' described by Nind and Hewett (1994) or the responsiveness described by Ware (1996)? Rodney's situation shows how fragile the system is. It is so reliant on the stability of the staff group and other workers involved. In terms of agency or bank staff who are employed frequently in services for people with learning disability, it is interesting to speculate what is expected of them. Ideally it must be to communicate with clients in the way *they* understand rather than simply to ensure their physical well-being.

Levi

Levi is a man of 54 years with late detected phenylketonuria, profound learning disabilities, congenital hip dislocation and possible cerebral palsy. He has cataracts, nystagmus, a squint and severe hearing loss (hears low tones only), he also has swallowing difficulties. He has been described as having tactile defensiveness. He uses a wheelchair but can shuffle on his bottom. He has a variety of self-stimulatory behaviours including hums, rocking, teeth grinding and head turning and severe self-injurious behaviour (hitting his head and hip very hard with his fist). In terms of developmental level, Levi had no language or manipulation skills beyond five to six months and well practised care skills to about 13 months. Levi was institutionalised from the age of four years. At the age of about 44 he moved to his present home in one of the bungalows of a community unit with five other residents with learning disabilities. Levi was referred for an assessment of his quality of life as part of an internal evaluation of the Home Support Service in the local area.

I (JS) visited Levi in his home and spent some seventeen hours with him over six sessions (including an evening and weekend visit) within nine days. For a jobbing clinical psychologist that was a considerable length of time and was highly enjoyable albeit personally difficult to negotiate! Levi's preferred position was suspended in a hoist, rocking or turning himself by tapping the floor with his foot. I sat on the floor near to Levi, using touch, tapping his hand and arm and vocalising using low sounds in a singsong voice repeating his name and pausing. From no obvious response to my presence in the first session, by the fifth Levi was initiating contact. He put his arm round my neck and

128

gave me a hug as we listened to music together with the bass turned up very loud. Levi was happy to sit in his wheelchair hugging me thus for nearly an hour, until offered a drink by a member of care staff – I had begun to wonder what would happen if another preferred activity had not been offered but was very pleased that Levi had wanted to engage with me. Again I introduced the principles of Intensive Interaction to the team leader. Six months on the service, having gone through re-structuring, we are planning some staff training to introduce Intensive Interaction in Levi's house.

Nind (1997) notes the importance of Intensive Interaction being tried by people who want to do it. It is not necessarily every person's preferred style of interaction. As Levi liked to sit on the floor I asked a member of care staff if the staff team ever sat on the floor with him. Their response was 'I know what has been on it . . .'. Rodney liked to touch your hair. Some people were uncomfortable with this especially as his hands were often covered in saliva from the sock or cloth he held and mouthed.

Stefan

Stefan is a man of 34. He has rubella damage, and profound learning disabilities. He is totally blind and can only hear sounds above 90 decibels. He has epilepsy and osteoporosis. He uses a wheelchair but can shuffle on his bottom. He has no signing or speech. At the age of 29, Stefan moved from his family home to one of the bungalows in a community unit with five other people with severe or profound learning disabilities. He was referred for general advice about how to engage with him.

> I used tactile techniques, copying and reflecting back actions, then very slowly introduced objects as an extension of myself, which seemed to work. I used principles of Intensive Interaction as part of my approach (I now find it impossible not to!). I did not advertise the fact that I was using it, but it gave me a way in that I desperately needed with Stefan.

Our experiences with Rodney, Levi and Stefan confirmed our view of the importance of the principles of Intensive Interaction in accessing clients with profound learning and multiple disabilities. Caldwell (1996) talks about the importance of looking for and finding the 'correct key' to make contact and attract the person's attention. In the case of Rodney, Levi and Stefan, a stranger was able to quickly interact with each of them in a way that day-to-day staff did not appear to do, either through ignorance of methods to use or through fear that such contact might be received with disfavour from management for not being in line with the assumed philosophy of the service. This is where the debate between Nind and Hewett (1996) and Porter, Grove and Park (1996) with a commentary by Smith (1996) as well as the comments of Lovett (1996) about age-appropriateness have been timely!

Starting more formal Intensive Interaction

What follows is a more in depth example of our attempts to introduce Intensive Interaction to a client living in a small staffed house.

Alice

Alice is a woman aged 31 with profound learning disabilities, tuberous sclerosis (with hypersensitive finger nails and gums) and epilepsy. She is ambulant and has no sensory impairments, but has been described as autistic with tactile defensiveness. She has chronic constipation and PMT. Alice was institutionalised at the age of twelve. Since the age of 22 she has lived in a small staffed house in the community with two other people with learning disabilities with whom she has no attachment. Alice communicated by leading staff to places or objects (e.g. kettle for a drink). She vocalised a repertoire of sounds but staff were unsure of their meaning. She chose to spend a great deal of her time alone in her bedroom. I (JS), with my trainee, assessed Alice's developmental level using Vineland Adaptive Behaviour Scale (Sparrow, Balla and Cicchetti, 1984) and Griffiths Mental Development Scale (Griffiths, 1970) as interview checklists with staff. This was the first experience for this staff team of considering a client in a developmental way. Although some gross motor skills were above the two year developmental level, her remaining skills were a long way below it. In particular, she was described as rarely exploring or manipulating objects. The assessment helped the staff team to see that Alice did not 'understand everything we say to her' but was responding to key words and situational cues. Recommendations were made to build on the use of her hands to explore and manipulate objects and her ability to communicate her needs through the use of objects-of-reference (Ockelford, 1994; Park, 1995).

JM took on a practitioner role with Alice in her work as profound learning and multiple disability outreach worker from the local CTPLD. This work was carried out under supervision from the first author.

Why we decided to use Intensive Interaction

During the first two or three sessions, it became quickly apparent that Alice would not engage in sensory activity with me. She would only tolerate functional objects in her hands and rejected me if I put the slightest pressure on her or even maintained my encouragement. Desperately, while trying to find stimulating objects/materials/sounds/ contingency experiences, anything that would interest her, I decided to try using some principles of Intensive Interaction. This meant removal of emphasis of task/object; instead I placed the importance on the interaction applied intentionally, I emphasised my body language/facial expressions, tried to join Alice in her world, let her lead, used imitation/reflecting back her breathing, movements and vocalisations. I introduced some objects (e.g. a vibrating cushion) towards the end of the session, using no pressure and a playful approach with which she successfully engaged, all be it very slightly. The consequence was the first real positive interaction between Alice and myself. We had a great time together that afternoon and I couldn't help feeling a little guilty, though, as I had disregarded my initial objectives and genuinely had a great time at work! Alice's two key support workers, Sam and Marie, were interested in the approach and how I had been successful in introducing the use of objects. We discussed Intensive Interaction, despite my lack of experience and patchy knowledge. Many things had been tried with Alice and failed in the past, so why not have a go! We did a couple more times. Alice responded positively, for example: increased eye contact; chose to stay close to us; increased smiles and laughter; initiated social interaction

Having discussed these findings in supervision and with the team leader, it was agreed that Sam, Marie and I would try Intensive Interaction with Alice for a three-month trial to see if it continued to increase her responsiveness and to allow time for us to build our skills and confidence in using the approach. The rest of the staff team were not involved at this stage but they were given the principals of Intensive Interaction.

How we developed our skills

We had lots of discussion about the theory and techniques, modelling the approach with Sam and Marie observing me working with Alice and vice versa. I provided them with reading material, we had many reflective discussions after sessions talking about our performance and Alice's responsiveness. I attended Melanie Nind's workshop organised by MDRT (Nind, 1997) and used supervision with Judith to discuss progress.

The form of the Intensive Interaction trial

Objectives

We started by setting objectives for each session: for Alice:

- to initiate interaction on three occasions
- to give eye contact on three occasions
- to show interest in an object (glancing at, reaching to touch)
- to enjoy the session (smiles and vocalisations).

These objectives were recorded on paper as achieved or not for each session with brief comments. The sessions were either formal (i.e. planned) or informal.

Formal sessions (weekly where possible) were usually initiated by or involving me, either directly interacting with Alice or observing Sam or Marie in their individual interactions with Alice. These sessions were planned in advance and were to be recorded on video both to monitor progress (Watson, 1994) and to inform the rest of the staff team at a later time.

Informal sessions would take place when Sam and Marie used 'interactivity' while working with Alice throughout the day, during her daily activities and to capitalise on times when she is feeling sociable.

Reflective discussion would take place generally after the formal sessions, to be written up by me rather than by the support workers.

The techniques used within the formal sessions

We attempted to apply all the principles of Intensive Interaction (Nind and Hewett, 1994; Nind, 1997) and whilst we did introduce some objects (toys, musical instruments, vibrating cushion) and some activities (such as foot massage) this was without pressure to perform. We gradually learned the strategies which were effective with Alice (see Outcomes below).

Monitoring progress

The reality of video recording was that it was often difficult to get hold of the video (we used one of the support workers' own, but it was a problem for her to obtain/remember because of shift patterns etc.). We were self-conscious (at first) so this must have affected the quality of the interaction. Alice also appeared distracted by the video (initially). The video did not pick up subtleties of communication owing to the position of the camera (for example, eye contact, what we were saying quietly, facial expressions etc.). We did not take enough footage and finding time to view the video was difficult. In retrospect we do not think the objective setting and monitoring was very useful as it made social interaction seem so artificial and uniform. We became even more sceptical of its usefulness after discussions with Melanie Nind, who recommended a more subjective form of recording (Nind and Hewett, 1994: Nind, 1996; Nind 1997) which I began using. The support staff fed back their impressions at our reflective discussions.

Regular reflective discussions

We spent a great deal of time reflecting on the work: how the formal sessions had felt to us, how we felt Alice had responded to different strategies and what we might have done differently, and the 'interactivity' which had occurred between the formal sessions. I kept notes of our discussions.

Outcomes

Music session – local day centre Alice had been attending a music session for several years but had always sat away from the rest of the group with her chair facing outwards. Recently, she stood up un-prompted and turned her chair in to join the rest of the group.

Birthday Alice has never seemed interested in the experience of opening presents at Christmas or birthdays. On her birthday recently, Sam and Marie were on duty. They used playfulness to create a participative mood and were able to involve her in opening her cards and presents. Although she did not get stuck in with her hands, she did choose to watch, stayed in close proximity to the action, laughed, smiled and interacted with the two support workers for much longer than usual.

Participation in daily activities Sam and Marie have found that using principles of Intensive Interaction while involving Alice in daily activities has enhanced her enjoyment. She tolerates more contact, participates more and is both more responsive and communicative. The support workers also find their time spent with Alice is more enjoyable too.

Less time alone Sam and Marie have noticed that when they are on duty Alice spends far less time alone in her bedroom. She chooses to remain in the parts of the house where they are, in close proximity throughout their shift. Importantly, some of the other members of the staff team who have not been directly involved in the Intensive Interaction trial have mentioned that Alice is choosing to be with them more, and is initiating more interactions.

Responsiveness Other members of the staff team have mentioned that Alice appears to have become more tolerant of using her hands and participating in activities (for example, cooking). She has become happier to remain in situations for longer periods and more interested in what is going on around the house.

Playfulness Sam has turned the following around the house into a game, using anticipation, tension and expectancy, for example, chasing after Alice, 'peek a boo' and hiding games. The consequence has been mutual hilarity with Alice choosing to maintain contact. However, when Alice has approached other staff (for example, grabbing and laughing) they have not known how to respond, and perhaps have even been more concerned to get on with the job rather than feeling able to play with her.

Changes during formal sessions Alice uses a repertoire of sounds, touches her body, rocks, places her hand over her mouth and alters and exaggerates her breathing patterns. When we reflected back these actions she appeared to find it both intriguing and at times hilarious! This was often a good way of gaining her attention. This imitation with pauses and used contingently led to long interactive sequences with lots of turn taking, which sometimes felt like huge conversations! When Alice realised that her actions were controlling ours this led to wonderful eye contact. Alice clearly enjoyed the control and definitely led the interactions. She would experiment with this by leading me around, in or out of her bedroom, and experimented with sounds to see if we would copy her. She enjoyed the playful approaches that were used, especially the games that increased/built up to a climax. Alice used to initiate cuddles as one of the only methods she had learned to get people's attention. She initiated even more physical contact during these sessions. The lack of task confused Alice at times as she did not seem to know what was expected of her. Previously she was only really approached for functional reasons, not simply for someone to be with her. Physically we respected her personal space, reacted to her body language and did not crowd her. This seemed to have a positive effect also, everything was on her terms.

Formal sessions versus informal interaction We had planned to use a mixture of both forms of session but it became quickly apparent that the interactivity that occurred naturally throughout the day was far more effective. It was extremely difficult for me to arrive at the house at an arranged time and perform! That is, turn on my 'sociability' and playfully interact with Alice for a set period of time. The support workers were reluctant to do formal sessions when I was not there. Also the formality did not take into account the fact that either Alice or her key workers may not be in the mood for being bubbly and interactive! The pre-planned sessions felt very artificial and, for me especially since I did not know Alice very well, not altogether genuine. It was also demoralising at times to have planned sessions or set up the video for only a few seconds/minutes of interaction; this wasn't very fulfilling. Alice appeared far more responsive to Sam and Marie than to me, presumably because of their already established relationships. They also both have children so have more 'strategies' to call on. They could be far more playful than I felt I could be. The formal Intensive Interaction sessions appeared more successful when carried out by them. The support workers felt far more comfortable using Intensive Interaction principles in more natural situations and this seemed to all of us more appropriate and genuine and seemed to be the method that was gaining the best results.

Reflections

Reflections of the practitioner Sam and Marie have become very tuned into Alice whilst other members of the staff team remained less responsive. This is because the latter had other priorities and have not been sufficiently involved in Intensive Interaction yet. Perhaps it would have been better to involve the whole team from the start. However, if we had waited for that we may never have begun! My expectations of success were unrealistic at first. I think that this was because I didn't know Alice as well as her support workers, who seemed much more impressed with progress. I was also impatient with ourselves for missing opportunities during interaction and needed to allow for our learning of techniques without the benefit of an experienced practitioner with whom to be apprenticed (Nind, 1997). We sometimes strung out the formal sessions too long in the initial stages rather than responding sufficiently to Alice's signals to end. This was possibly because visiting the house on limited occasions led to an expectation to achieve a lot in one visit. Success of sessions depended a great deal on Alice's mood, and on ours. This is okay as we all feel more sociable when we are happier than we do when in a sad or bad mood. Tasklessness felt strange at first. I felt our objectives were not specific enough. We worried about how sessions looked to others who were not involved or did not know about Intensive Interaction. We had not developed guidelines about safeguards but probably should have done (Nind, 1997).

Reflections of the key support workers Sam and Marie said that once they had learnt about the principles of Intensive Interaction it was impossible not to use the techniques when interacting with Alice, or the other residents, within their everyday work. They feel it has provided them with a more effective communication method and enhanced their enjoyment of their work. They feel very strongly that attempting Intensive Interaction has given them permission to just spend time with clients, socialising and enjoying one another's company. They said they still feel guilty at times as it feels a bit like it is not really work; on the other hand, it was hard work to be up-beat and engaging! They have also appreciated the importance of noting progress and reflecting on their practice via the feedback sessions. They found it difficult, at first, to sit back and let Alice lead. Silences and pauses were uncomfortable. They said they wanted to prompt, but gradually became accustomed to handing over control. They both admitted to feeling a little embarrassed and self-conscious at first, and extremely worried about breaking the 'age-appropriate' rule! Sam said she felt this strongly, not only because it has been drummed into them about how age appropriateness is so important, but also because Alice is older than her. I encouraged Sam and Marie to try to use tension expectancy games. On one occasion, as part of foot massage, Sam starting playing 'this little piggy . . .' and turned to me (and the video camera) and asked 'is that going too far?' This became less of an issue as they saw how Alice responded so positively to a playful approach.

Other influences on outcomes Our impression is that the above changes were influenced by both the formal Intensive Interaction sessions and the increased interactivity of the two support workers. However, it is possible that other factors also influenced the likelihood of success and the speed of progress. At the same time as this intervention trial, an Objects-of-reference trial was introduced for Alice, with agreement by the whole staff team to encourage their use for key activities: cup (a cup of coffee), sponge (bath), Jacuzzi pipe (Jacuzzi), door chain (going out) and Jaffa cake box (biscuit). Use depended on staff initiating the process and this varied. Interestingly, Alice learned to initiate use of the cup. It also became clear that she was using this to initiate social contact and did not always want a cup of coffee, so staff were beginning to ask which she wanted and to offer interaction instead. At the same time, the service was going through a re-structuring which was putting immense strain on all concerned. The second author had to re-apply for her own job and Alice's house was shortly to lose its present team leader.

The next step Our next step is to work with the new team leader and the whole staff team to present them with the results of the trial, offer useful strategies, and encourage general 'interactivity' within agreed safeguard guidelines. We shall negotiate allocated time to continue supervised formal Intensive Interaction sessions (even just half an hour) by Sam and Marie in order to develop their skills and to further Alice's development. We shall develop a system for support staff to record their reflections and will continue the feed back session. We intend to repeat the initial baseline developmental assessments but wonder if we should have used other ones as employed by Nind (1996), i.e. Kiernan and Reed's (1983) *Preverbal Communication Schedule* and Nind's adaptation of Brazelton's cuddliness scale (Brazelton, 1984).

Issues of using Intensive Interaction in small staffed houses in the community

Philosophy

Nind (1996) mentions that the institutionalisation of the subjects in her study could not be separately evaluated as a factor in their communication ability. Our experience of community services with an emphasis on normalisation or 'ordinary life' philosophy would lead us to suppose that the difference in *setting* from institutional to community care has not been sufficient. What is required is a significant change in interactive style from the distance, as a consequence of low staff ratios in the large institutions, to the greater potential for proximity, but the apparent formality of age appropriateness in small community houses, where an individual's subjective experience may not have been sufficiently addressed.

The external professional's role

One must never underestimate the time it takes to set up intervention. We all have competing demands on our time. Unlike a day service setting – where the same staff are around on the same days each week more or less – in a residential setting a great deal of time is required to meet all the potential support staff involved; you have to contend with part-time work, shift work rotas, sickness, leave and very limited/no face-to-face time with clients (for meetings, reading programmes, writing notes or watching videos etc.). Nine staff work in Alice's house, including sleeping-in staff, plus a team leader, to support three clients. In the Community Unit bungalows, to keep two support staff on duty for six clients there could be ten whole-time equivalents on the team, and more with part-time and bank and agency workers. It takes a long time to inform all the staff team of an intervention, ensure their understanding and pass on relevant skills. Watching videos, monitoring, evaluating and maintaining enthusiasm are equally time-consuming. Unless you invest sufficient time the intervention will not be successful.

The role of support workers

Individual support workers clearly have different perceptions of what their role is and place emphasis on different aspects of their work. This can cause considerable conflict within the team about who is or is not doing what. There are immense pressures on the support workers for upkeep and running of the house, fulfilling health and safety regulations and supporting all the clients with their complex needs. There may be staff shortages, with those remaining covering rotas by doing double shifts; for example, staff may have been on a sleep-in night before but woken in the night, and the professional arrives expecting them to be full of enthusiasm and interest and to have prioritised her work!

In our experience, as professionals working within a staffed small house, intervention with a client is more likely to be successful when support workers who show genuine interest are involved. We would usually prefer to work with the whole staff team through linking with a committed team leader who can positively monitor fulfilment of agreed action. However, in our opinion, it can be effective to collaborate with the team leader and two enthusiastic support workers who can be relied on to encourage the staff team when the professional (or the team leader) is not there.

Environment

It can be frustrating to work in an individual's own home. The environment may not be ideal, the space cramped and shared with other

139

clients who want to be included too. However, it is perhaps more helpful for clients to develop sociability and communication skills within a familiar setting where transference of learning is easier and there is more chance of 'interactivity' to occur naturally throughout the day.

Team work

Nind and Hewett (1994) advocate the importance of Intensive Interaction as team work. Ware (1996) notes that the development of a responsive environment for people with profound learning disabilities makes life more enjoyable for staff and shows them that people with profound learning and multiple disabilities are valued and respected as individuals. She also notes that individual interactions are not interchangeable and the different ways we do things are important to our personality. This is different from the behaviourist view of consistency at all cost. Ware (1996) suggests that in the school setting limiting the number of familiar staff and volunteers can help ensure that the person's behaviour is understood and responded to. In a residential setting, large numbers of staff (including bank and agency) can be working with individual clients, frequently alone.

Are we always able to respond?

How does a service respond when a formerly passive client now demands interaction, and what if the client does not want to stop? (I was worried that Levi would not want to stop hugging me, staff in Alice's house have been worried that Alice would not stop wanting to interact.) Carr *et al.* (1994) note that being approached to make requests (i.e. being *nagged*) is the hoped for but temporary consequence of rapport building. For functional communication to be developed (e.g. object-referencing or signing) *all* attempts must be responded to consistently every time the client initiates their use (RNIB, 1993a). Nind and Hewett (1994) give helpful advice about ending formal Intensive Interaction sessions and indeed natural human interaction has bursts, pauses and endings so there is no reason to suppose a client will want to carry on forever! It is incumbent on services to work out ways of being more responsive.

140

However, carers cannot always respond immediately and the activity requested cannot always happen. We all have to learn to tolerate delay. Nevertheless, for people with profound learning and multiple disabilities waiting for something to happen is the rule rather than exception (Pettipher and Mansell, 1993; Rose *et al.*, 1993). In a sufficiently resourced context, if the way such clients are enabled to wait is via interactivity it will probably be more successful. With an aim of maintaining interaction rather than keeping clients 'on task', various room management techniques (Porterfield and Blunden, 1978; Ware, 1994) could perhaps be adapted to enable staff to interact with several clients sequentially or indeed with one client occasionally whilst carrying out domestic chores.

Planning

An 'active support' model in community services for people with learning disabilities includes the use of clearly defined organisational procedures for determining what will happen, when, where and with whom, how it will happen and how it will be evaluated (McGill and Toogood, 1994). Planning specific time for Intensive Interaction is important and although each 'formal' Intensive Interaction session may not have objectives in the way we initially tried with Alice, the programme should have aims and be recorded in some way (Nind and Hewett, 1994). These general aims for each client should be stated both for formal sessions and for general 'interactivity' strategies. For Alice, recording the spontaneous 'interactivity' was difficult. It was impossible to capture on video (without CCTV) and difficult to record on paper, as interactive sequences happened frequently throughout a long shift. Nevertheless, it is important to be reflective about this work and in order to do this some form of written record is necessary both to monitor development (Nind and Hewett, 1994; Watson, 1994) and to maintain accountability (Nind, 1997).

Safe practice guidelines

Nind and Hewett (1994) recommend using Intensive Interaction 'within the group environment to emphasise that it is every day teaching, to share

141

good practice and as a precaution in the light of possible allegations of abuse' (p. 151). Herein lies a dilemma in small staffed houses where there may be only one member of staff on duty in the house at a time. We have encouraged video recording and openness to observers sitting-in where possible. We acknowledge that we have not gone far enough in addressing this issue sufficiently in our service. However, in all the cases above, the team manager and supervisor were aware of the aims and strategies.

Having a go

Although there must be support from management and, ideally, encouragement from colleagues, from our experience, we would recommend having a go as a small group of interested staff. Try out Intensive Interaction with time to reflect on practice even when the staff team is not of one mind about it. In effect, piloting the intervention at a local level may be crucial in gathering the specific evidence of success with a particular client which convinces the rest of the staff team of its importance by making an impact in a way that no amount of hypothetical discussion about theory would do. For the client's sake, however, it is important not to try out Intensive Interaction completely alone or the client, whilst forming a positive relationship with you temporarily, will be bereft if you move on. It is hoped that the work fulfilment gained by doing Intensive Interaction may enable support staff to be more likely to remain in their jobs.

Conclusions

Using a developmental approach for people with profound learning disabilities is not new (Dunst, 1980; Coupe and Levy, 1985; Hogg and Sebba, 1986). However, in community services with an emphasis on normalisation/ordinary life principles it seems at best to have been forgotten and at worst to have been actively discouraged. Doing nothing has been preferred to breaking the politically correct 'rules' and offering non-chronologically age-appropriate experiences. In our local service, the Multiple Disability Resource Team is widely promoting the need to address the communication and social development of people with profound learning disabilities through a variety of methods. In order to communicate intentionally, RNIB (1993b) notes that people must have:

- someone to communicate with
- something to communicate about, and
- a means of communication.

Consequently, Intensive Interaction seems the appropriate place to begin developmentally.

However, one must also address people's idiosyncratic sensory preferences and unique learning histories. Other methods of building relationships are important for those with whom engagement with objects may have become the preferred medium through which to communicate (Caldwell, 1996) or via music, movement or dance therapy. Bunning (1996; 1997) stresses the importance of assessing preferences in a variety of sensory modalities, including vestibular and proprioceptive systems, to create an Individualised Sensory Environment for the individual to enhance object and person engagement and to reduce stereotypical behaviour. The work of Williams (1996), based on a Piagetian approach to development, is helpful in determining strategies for intervention. Microtechnology can be used effectively to teach contingency awareness and provide augmentative communication (Bozic and Murdoch, 1996), and objects-of-reference (Ockelford, 1994; Park, 1995) provide a link between non symbolical and symbolic communication. Carr et al. (1994) in their book entitled *Communication based interventions for problem behaviour: a user's guide for producing positive change* use a behavioural approach to the building of rapport through pairing one's self with preferred stimuli (such as food) and putting clients in a good mood using humour and playfulness, with no clear reference to developmental theory.

In our service we are currently pondering over which technique to use with whom. In particular, as revisiting a developmental approach represents a cultural shift in our service as it currently exists, the MDRT is introducing the ideas in a number of ways: through direct intervention with clients together with carers and support staff in a range of settings – residential, day service and further education. For some support staff introducing 'permission to be playful' has been like turning on a switch. However, to show that Intensive Interaction actually leads to the developments claimed by Nind and Hewett (1994) – sociability, fundamental communication abilities, cognitive abilities, emotional well being, constructive interaction with the immediate environment – and to promote and teach other ways of spending time than in organised self-involvement (stereotyped, ritualistic and self stimulatory behaviour), we must reflect on our practice.

Within the Trust we have started a supervision group to which we intend to invite Melanie Nind (who, fortunately for us, is working locally at Oxford Brookes University) as an external supervisor. We intend to use this group to agree user-friendly recording systems and to develop safe practice guidelines. The Trust is currently introducing Essential Lifestyle Planning (Sanderson, 1996) as the new method of individual planning. This emphasises 'spending time with and listening to the person' and those who 'know and care' about them in order to create their Essential Lifestyle Plan. We feel that, for people with profound learning and multiple disabilities, unless the principles of Intensive Interaction are used, this new planning process is unlikely to be as effective as it could be. We have also been making comments to management concerning the resources required in order to carry out Intensive Interaction effectively (i.e. sufficient staff, easy access to a video camera and a commitment that this is an important activity to which to allocate time). Where Intensive Interaction is introduced to small staffed houses step-wise via keen key members of staff, it will be interesting to carry out some research to compare the client's response to those staff implementing it and to those not, then to repeat the observation when and if more of the staff team become involved. We are interested to evaluate the progress of people such as Rodney, Levi, Stefan and Alice and to see if Ephraim's (1997) prediction of early rapid progress holds, enabling the individual to show what skills they already have in other circumstances (for example, with their family). Nind and Hewett (1994) note that progress in Intensive Interaction led staff to re-evaluate pre-conceived ideas about levels of intelligence. Alternatively, we may discover in the clients new learning of, for example, behaviours which encourage others to be with them, making facial regard and eye contact, developing alternative ways of being other than occupying oneself in ritualistic behaviour, and initiating social contact as demonstrated by Nind (1996). Moving on to what next: a plateau in development reaching the limit of their potential or continued progress?

Acknowledgements

Thanks to clients and staff of Oxfordshire Learning Disability NHS Trust who have shared their experiences with us, in particular our colleagues: Sam Bowers, Marie Goodchild, Marcia Samuels and Chris Daffue; Karen McSweeney for typing; and John Sharich, Nicholas McInerny and Nicholas Maggs for support.

References

Bozic, N. and Murdoch H. (1996) *Learning through interaction: technology and children with multiple disabilities.* London: David Fulton.

Bratt, A. and Johnston, R. (1988) 'Changes in lifestyle for young adults with profound handicaps following discharge from hospital care into a "second generation" housing project', *Mental Handicap Research*, **1**, 49–74.

Brazelton, T.B. (1984) *Neonate Behavioural Assessment Scale.* London: Heinmann Medical Books.

Bunning, K.T. (1996) 'The principles of an individualised sensory environment', *Royal College of Speech and Language Therapy Bulletin*, January 1996, 9–10.

Bunning, K. (1997) 'The role of reinforcement in developing interactions'. In: Fawcus, M. (ed.) *Children with learning difficulties: a collaborative approach.* London: Whurr.

Caldwell, P. (1996) *Getting in touch: ways of working with people with severe learning disabilities and extensive support needs.* Brighton: Pavilion Publishing, Joseph Rowntree Foundation.

Carr, E.G., Levin, L., McConnachie, G., Carlson, J.I., Kemp, D.C. and Smith, C.E. (1994) *Communication based interventions for problem behaviour: a user's guide for producing positive change.* Baltimore: Paul H. Brookes.

Coupe, J. and Levy, D. (1985) 'The object related scheme assessment procedure', *Mental Handicap*, **13**, 22-25.

Department of Health and Social Security (1977) *Development team for the mentally handicapped. First Report 1976–1977.* London: HMSO.

Dunst, C.J. (1980) *A clinical and educational manual for use with the Uzgiris and Hunt Scales of Infant Psychological Development.* Baltimore: University Park Press.

Emerson, E. and Hatton, C. (1994) *Moving out: the impact of relocation from hospital to community on the quality of life of people with learning disabilities.* London: HMSO.

Ephraim, G. (1997) Intensive Interaction Abergavenny: British Psychological Society Division of Clinical Psychology Special Interest Group (Learning Disabilities) Annual Conference.

Felce, D., de Kock, U. and Repp, A. (1986) 'An eco-behavioural comparison of small community based houses and traditional large hospitals for severely and profoundly mentally handicapped adults', *Applied Research in Mental Retardation*, **7**, 393–408.

Felce, D., Lowe, K. and Beswick, J. (1993) 'Staff turnover in ordinary housing services for people with severe or profound mental handicaps', *Journal of Intellectual Disability Research*, **37**, 143–152.

Felce, D. and Repp, A. (1992) 'The behavioural and social ecology of community houses', *Research in Developmental Disabilities*, **13**, 27–42.

Felce, D. and Toogood, S. (1988) *Close to Home*. Kidderminster: BIMH Publications.

Griffiths, R. (1970) *Griffiths Mental Development Scales*. High Wycombe: The Test Agency.

Hatton, C., Emerson, E., Robertson, J., Henderson, D. and Cooper, J. (1995) *An evaluation of the quality and costs of services for adults with severe learning disabilities and sensory impairments*. Manchester: Hester Adrian Research Centre.

Hogg, J. and Sebba, J. (1986) *Profound Retardation and Multiple Impairment, Volume 1 Development and Learning*. Beckenham: Croom Helm.

Kiernan, C. and Reid, B. (1983) *Preverbal Communication Schedule*. Windsor: NFER Nelson.

Kings Fund (1980) *An Ordinary Life*. London: Kings Fund.

Lovett, H. (1996) *Learning to listen: Positive approaches and people with difficult behaviour*. London: Jessica Kingsley.

Mansell, J. (1995) 'Staffing and staff performance in services for people with severe or profound learning disability and serious challenging behaviour', *Journal of Intellectual Disability Research*, **39**, 3–14.

Mansell, J. and Beasley, F. (1993) 'Small staffed houses for people with severe learning disability and challenging behaviour. Special Issue Community Care', *British Journal of Social Work*, **23**, 329–344.

Mansell, J., Felce, D., Jenkins J., de Kock, U. and Toogood, S. (1987) *Developing staffed houses for people with mental handicaps*. Tunbridge Wells: Costello.

McGill, P. and Toogood, S. (1994) 'Organising community placements'. In: Emerson, E., McGill, P. and Mansell, J. (eds) *Severe learning disabilities and challenging behaviour, designing high quality services*. London: Chapman Hall.

Nind, M. and Hewett, D. (1994) *Access to Communication: Developing the basics of communication in people with severe learning difficulties through Intensive Interaction*. London: David Fulton.

Nind, M. and Hewett, D. (1996) 'When age-appropriateness isn't appropriate'. In: Coupe O'Kane, J. and Goldbart, J. (eds) *Whose Choice? Contentious Issues for those working with people with learning difficulties*. London: David Fulton.

Nind, M. (1996) 'Efficacy of Intensive Interaction', *European Journal of Special Needs Education*, **11**, 48–66.

Nind, M. (1997) 'Intensive Interaction', a multidisciplinary training day for Oxfordshire Learning Disability NHS Trust.

O'Brien, J. (1986) *A comprehensive guide to the activities catalogue: an alternative curriculum for youths and adults with severe learning difficulties.* Baltimore: Paul H. Brookes.

O'Brien, Y., Glenn, S. and Cunningham, C. (1994) 'Contingency Awareness in infants and children with severe and profound learning disabilities', *Development and Education*, **4**, 231–243.

Ockelford, A. (1994) *Objects of reference.* London: RNIB.

Park, K. (1995) 'Using objects of reference: a review of the literature', *European Journal of Special Needs Education*, **10**, 40–46.

Perry, J. and Felce, D. (1994) 'Outcomes of ordinary housing services in Wales: objective indicators', *Mental Handicap Research*, **7**, 286–311.

Pettipher, C. and Mansell, J. (1993) 'Engagement in meaningful activity in day centres: an exploratory study', *Mental Handicap Research*, **6**, 263–274.

Porter, J., Grove, N. and Park, K. (1996) 'Ages and stages. What is appropriate behaviour?'. In: Coupe O'Kane, J. and Goldbart, J. (eds) (1996) *Whose Choice? Contentious Issues for those working with people with learning difficulties.* London: David Fulton.

Porterfield, J. and Blunden, R. (1978) 'Establishing an activity period and individual skill training within a day setting for profoundly mentally handicapped adults', *Research Report No. 6*, Cardiff: Mental Handicap in Wales Applied Research Unit.

Raynes, N.V. (1980) 'The less you've got the less you get: functional groupings a cause for concern', *Mental Retardation*, **28**, 217–220.

Rose, J., Davis, C. and Gotch, L. (1993) 'A comparison of the services provided to people with profound and multiple disabilities in two different day centres', *British Journal of Developmental Disabilities*, **39**, 83–94.

RNIB (1993a) *Stereotypical behaviour in people with visual and learning disabilities.* London: RNIB Focus Fact sheet.

RNIB (1993b) *Eye Openers.* Video for RNIB Certificate in multiple disabilities. London: RNIB.

Sanderson, H. (1996) 'Essential Lifestyle Planning', *RNIB Focus*, **19**, 12–22.

Smith, B. (1996) 'Discussion: Age-appropriate or developmentally appropriate activities'. In: Coupe O'Kane, J. and Goldbart, J. (eds) (1996) *Whose Choice? Contentious Issues for those working with people with learning difficulties.* London: David Fulton.

Sparrow, S.S., Balla, D.A. and Cicchetti, D.V. (1984) *Vineland Adaptive Behaviour Scales.* Minnesota: American Guidance Service.

Towell, D. (ed.) (1988) *An Ordinary Life in Practice: Developing comprehensive community based services for people with learning disabilities.* London: Kings Fund.

Uzgiris, I. and Hunt, J. (1975) *Assessment in Infancy: Ordinal Scales of Psychological Development.* Urbana: University of Illinois Press.

Ware, J. (ed.) (1994) *Educating Children with Profound and Multiple Learning Difficulties*. London: David Fulton.

Ware, J. (1996) *Creating a Responsive Environment: For People with Profound and Multiple LearningDisabilities*. London: David Fulton.

Watson, J. (1994) 'Using Intensive Interaction in the Education of Pupils with PMLDs (ii) Intensive Interaction: Two Case Studies'. In: Ware, J. (ed.) *Educating Children with Profound and Multiple Learning Difficulties*. London: David Fulton.

Williams, K.C. (1996) 'Piagetian Principles; simple and effective application', *Journal of Intellectual Disability Research*, **40**, 110–119.

Wolfensberger, W. (1972) *The principle of normalisation in human services*. Toronto: National Institute on Mental Retardation.

Chapter 8

The Gradual Development of Intensive Interaction in a School Setting

Val Stothard

St Piers, Lingfield is a large residential school for students with severe epilepsy. It caters for approximately 120 students aged five to 16 whose ability ranges from complex and severe learning difficulties to those who are able to be integrated into local primary and secondary schools.

Six years ago, when Intensive Interaction was first introduced, the school was divided into three: one junior and two senior departments. One of the latter was for students with moderate learning difficulties while the other, called Ash, in which I worked with three other teachers, was for students aged 11–16 who had the most severe learning difficulties.

The curriculum on offer at that time was teacher led and skills based. We taught Makaton signing with a feeling that, if children could not speak, the way forward was to teach them to sign. The expectation was still that the student needed to understand our forms of communication. We had not yet taken the step of realising that they were already communicating in other ways and that it was a more realistic process for us to understand their methods than to teach them to understand ours. Communication was speaking, signing or gesturing and we missed entirely so many subtle signals. The pace was often too fast or the emphasis so strongly on achieving the task in hand that we were missing what the child was trying so hard to tell us. By not listening to them we could not teach them how to express the things they wanted to say, but instead offered words that were of no interest to them. Although signing obviously was important, particularly to help with comprehension, it still enabled the students to express only the words that we chose to teach them. Also, for many students who lacked the inner language, a signed version of a word would have no more meaning to them than the spoken word. Communication was thought of as a means of asking for something instead of being a means of building relationships, expressing feelings, making sense of the world and of expressing who we really are.

Most of the staff in the department had studied the EDY package and skills were taught and behaviour managed using these methods. Thus some of the ways that pupils had found to express frustration, dislike or hurt, for example, were seen as difficult or inappropriate behaviours and would be managed accordingly, thus blocking this means of communication that was open to them. So, although much of the knowledge learnt from EDY was and still is very useful, it did not allow us to see the students as truly communicative individuals and it was still a very controlling approach.

The ethos of the school at that time was one of age appropriateness with play in any form being discouraged. The opportunities offered then were the teaching of self-help skills such as dressing, toileting and cooking, painting, and gardening. In personal care we would remove a student from the classroom, take them to the sinks by the toilets and go through a process of cleaning their teeth! Likewise if it was time to learn how to put on a coat, the student would be taken outside and shown through backward chaining how to put it on – only to have it removed in order to start again. Looking back it seems incredible that it took us so long to question what we were doing and to see how it must have confused the students. Later we introduced objects of reference and visual timetables to try to help the students become aware of their day and the relevance of situations and where they will lead: it suggests the anxiety and confusion that was probably caused by the introduction of activities that were so utterly out of context.

Cooking sessions were also rather meaningless to the students with most complex needs. The only way that they could have access to the activity was for them to be guided with hand over hand. So many processes were demonstrated by this method and I think this sometimes accounts for some students' reluctance to be 'helped'. As I have since discovered, to have your hand held under someone else's whilst turning on taps or using scissors is not a pleasant experience and the feeling of having no control over the movements of your hands is quite unnerving: however deep your trust for the person who is manipulating you. Another reason for disliking hand over hand methods is that, if this is the method of teaching, the tasks do not need to be totally appropriate or motivating because the student can be guided to perform them anyway.

Another activity was that of matching coloured clothes pegs to coloured plant pots – an occupation which was apparently viewed as appropriate to their age but which now seems so meaningless and dull! The classroom was filled with coloured soap dishes, sink tidies, bowls, and red and yellow plastic cutlery but, for all the traipsing round market stalls and kitchen reject shops, the purchases and the uses we found for them failed to motivate the students!

Michelle, a young teacher who had recently acquired a degree in Special Education, then started at the school and introduced a sensory based curriculum, and this brought in a much more sensitive and agreeable aspect to the curriculum and allowed an element of fun. The gentler aspects of this included massage and an environment of aromas and music, while the opportunity to explore syrup and cornflakes with hands and feet introduced a playful, fun (and sticky!) atmosphere. It also made us more attuned to the students' likes and dislikes and their ways of expressing these and their rights in doing so. In fact we became generally more respectful of the students and began trying to see things from their viewpoint a little more.

Looking for a new approach

This change in our relationship with the students meant that we began to realise that we desperately needed ways to interact with some of the students whom we did not really understand and who seemed so shut off from us. These students had perhaps given up trying to communicate because they had so often been misunderstood or ignored. We also seriously questioned some of the more behavioural approaches and were looking for answers to explain the reasons for the behaviours, believing they should not just be stopped by physical control or by effective management without understanding why they were happening in the first place. We had seen over time that behaviour modification methods on their own were not successful in changing these behaviours but only in managing them for the moment and only for certain members of staff. So often we have heard it said that: 'he behaves all right for me'. While this may have given some staff a feeling of success, it was of little benefit to the student.

We were therefore moving towards a more empathic approach and, through the training and experience of the staff working within the department, we tried to offer a more appropriate and relevant curriculum. However, in retrospect, we were unaware that we were teaching on the surface only and still were not reaching the child within. This was particularly so with students who were on the autistic spectrum to whom, I now believe, we may unintentionally have done a great disservice. We were not able to truly understand them, nor did we give them the opportunity to communicate in whatever way they could. We had not been shown how to actively listen. Although we were doing the best we could with the knowledge we had, it is sad to think how little we understood: how little we knew.

Working within a regime of total age appropriateness was difficult particularly because, although we were aware of what was unacceptable, nothing had been suggested in its place. We did understand the ideas behind age appropriateness and agreed with the principle of treating the students as the teenagers they were. However, the true reason behind this was to kindle a deeper respect for the young people with whom we worked and for this to happen it requires more than the removal of brightly coloured equipment and all physical contact. True respect and value come from a deep empathy with others and communication and interaction on equal terms.

The staff working within the department had been unhappy with some of the enforced policies and we had known that we were not successfully teaching all of the students using the curriculum we had on offer. We had felt that what we had been doing was not enough but we had not known how to move on. Some of us were also unhappy about the use of control approaches in the school, but we had little experience or knowledge of what ways could be offered as a viable alternative. We were therefore proactive in looking for something that would enable us to work in a way that we would find comfortable and acceptable.

It was at this time that I saw advertised the course on Intensive Interaction led by Dave Hewett and Melanie Nind which was described as an approach to teaching and relating to people who are difficult to reach. It appeared that this might be the answer for which we were searching. I attended the course and, in a very short time, I began to see how this could be the way forward for one particular student whom we felt we had failed to reach. All through the course I thought of him and could not wait to return to school to be able to try it out on him.

Starting Intensive Interaction

As soon as I had the opportunity I set up a session with the student in the adjacent area, just as Dave Hewett and Melanie Nind had recommended we did not do! Although the first few times the pupil showed little response, this was not surprising since I sat rather stiffly a few feet away and stared at him, waiting for him to make some sort of movement. I offered no explanation or introduction; I just sat and waited. What he thought of this strange behaviour I have no idea! Eventually he lifted his arms above his head, probably just to stretch, but I did the same and he clapped his hands against mine. He sat still again until, a few minutes later, he repeated the action and, as I once again joined in, looked at me in a way I had not seen before. Fleetingly we had made contact.

This raising of his arms and clapping my hands was the only action he initiated for a long time, but the looks he gave me as I responded were wonderful. His growing interest in me and what I did made the sessions very special and caused me to become more relaxed and more natural and to begin to really enjoy this time together. I felt that I was beginning to understand him a little more each time. The first time he showed a definite awareness of what I was doing by initiating an action and waiting for the response, it was a tremendous break-through and very exciting. Such a small action and yet with more meaning than anything he had achieved through task analysis. This small action was indeed the start of a change for us. A change that was to bring new meaning, understanding and empathy to everything we did and to challenge all that had gone before.

Having tried a few sessions, I explained the principles and approaches to Ellen, an assistant who took it in turns to work in isolation with this particular student. The fact that we worked in isolation at least meant that we needed to talk about the way sessions had gone, and therefore others working in the team and in the department began to hear and know what was going on. The enthusiasm of the assistant, who took to the approach like a duck to water, was also instrumental in making others curious and interested. At this time the only method we used was imitation. I think this was because we lacked confidence to try anything more intuitive and because we had to shake off gradually our roots of age-appropriate learning and taboos on physical contact. We would have been uncomfortable in the climate of the school and of attitudes in Special Education generally at that time to take any bigger step. It was also the easiest part of the Intensive Interaction approach to understand and start using. For this reason it is the approach most often seen and many people, it seems to me, believe that imitation and Intensive Interaction are synonymous.

Even with only this approach available to us we saw worth in what we were doing. The recognition and the interest in the eyes of the pupils, their involvement and concentration in the sessions and their evident enjoyment made us realise how little we had really known them and how much we had underestimated their contributions. We were getting responses where nothing else had worked and we were realising that these responses were more important than anything else we had worked towards.

Intensive Interaction offered us the chance to tune in closely to the students and to begin to recognise reasons for certain behaviours in a way that we had previously missed. The more we became aware of their needs and their means of communication, the more we were able to avoid the build up of behaviours and, by offering a more fun approach, many of the earlier problems did not arise.

Intensive Interaction was a way forward that nurtured empathy and empowered the students to have some say in the type of interactions that were meaningful to them – thus being a much more respectful education. Delivering a curriculum that is truly appropriate is the only way to show respect for our students and only then, I believe, can we work with utter conviction.

We now knew that this new approach was the right way to go, but we were unsure how it would be viewed by others not working with these students and felt that, in the beginning, we had to work 'undercover'. This had the effect of delaying it being fully acknowledged by the rest of the school. It soon became apparent that, having adopted an interactive approach, we could not easily encompass a strongly behavioural element within it. By feeling the depth of empathy and respect for the student and the relationship between staff and student that the interactive approaches engendered, one could not readily step back into the role of controller. We had to find ways to compromise, often a harder path to take but one which did not jeopardise the relationship and trust that we were trying so hard to develop.

One or two staff still felt a little wary and, although they were happy to see the worth of Intensive Interaction within a session, they did not feel happy to give up the behavioural strategies at all other times. The idea of a playful atmosphere and a more fun approach using distraction instead of over correction, and trying to avoid triggers rather than expecting students to face up to them and pushing them through the resulting outbursts, made the staff feel that the student was 'getting away with it'. This was obviously a big obstacle to the Intensive Interaction developing more fully as it would only partially work unless everyone was convinced of its value. For us it was necessary, therefore, to reach a compromise in order to make the scheme a workable one. It was an enormous step to take from well-used approaches to a completely new way of life, not just a new way of working but a complete turn around in our thinking.

Continuing with Intensive Interaction

Although we had been very keen to find a new way to work, the interactive approach was so different from anything else we had done that it required a great deal of rethinking – we had concerns and questions and quite a few difficulties in putting it into practice.

I worked most closely with three classroom assistants at that time. One of these had been at St Piers for several years longer than I had, one had arrived at the same time and the other was relatively inexperienced. Between ourselves we questioned, challenged, assessed and modified our approaches. Talking it all over, voicing our concerns and having to justify what we were doing, helped us to strengthen our resolve and conviction. Of course it meant that we had to question much of what we had done in the past, which was not an easy or comfortable thing to do and took a certain amount of courage.

The biggest bone of contention was that of relinquishing control. This was so opposed to our former thinking that some people could not at first see that this could possibly be right. If students were not physically prompted to do things, and if they were allowed to have more say in what happened to them, then it could be construed that they were 'getting away' with too much. It was a difficult dilemma and we needed to move slowly rather than rush this issue or we would not have been able to move forward in agreement. Even after working in this way for two or three years we continued to challenge ourselves. If we questioned why it was considered so necessary that a student must conform to certain requests and we could not be convinced that there was a very good reason, we had to be prepared to adapt and change. Today we still continue to question each other and ourselves and to check out our reasons in order to ensure that we have thought out thoroughly any strategies we use and any decisions we make. I think that the relationship we had as a staff team, and our ability to challenge one another and to be able to be honest about our doubts and fears, made the change a positive and lasting one. Eventually we made the step with conviction and have never since doubted its worth.

It was very strange to start a session with no resources and no definite plan to guide us and no tick sheet to record each step. It was particularly awkward for us as we have frequent visitors coming to look round St Piers. To be interrupted and observed when sitting facing a student, just the two of us and no equipment, was hard to explain. Especially considering that, as soon as a visitor walked in, any interaction immediately stopped, owing to embarrassment on my part and distraction for the student. We realised how hard this was for the child, who would not know why a halt had been called, and as Intensive Interaction was becoming more and more evident on the timetable, we had to learn to continue and to overcome our self-consciousness. Gradually, as our confidence in what we were doing increased, and, more importantly, as we became more intensely involved in the interactions, so the interruptions affected us less.

We also had to allow ourselves to 'lighten up'. We were concerned that if we had too much fun, we may 'lose' the students and be unable to calm them down and regain control of the situation. There was also the problem that we felt that what we were doing was not really work.

As we became more and more involved with the use of Intensive Interaction, so we found that it became an integral part of everything we did. Thus, when we put on school plays, we naturally included an interactive dance. In the past, we had included all of the children no matter what their ability and to enable them to take part, we would physically move them around the stage. However, allowing them to move freely to music but with us mirroring them meant that the dance became their own. For the first time they were able to contribute something on truly equal terms and could demonstrate their own creativity.

This was the way that our senior managers first came into contact with Intensive Interaction and their interest helped to promote it within the establishment. Our medical director in particular found the dance very moving and spoke highly in praise of it. He was most influential in promoting Intensive Interaction at St Piers and in voicing its worth to parents. As parents heard more about the introduction of the interactive methods – through consultation days, including watching videos – so they joined in our support of it. One parent said to me: 'This is what I have been wanting to hear.' So there was no difficulty in persuading the parents! It actually gave them confidence to find that what they felt they wanted to do naturally was now officially formalised and recognised. When a new headteacher came to St Piers, she supported our work and allowed Intensive Interaction to be included in the curriculum.

New developments with Intensive Interaction

In the classroom we now took every opportunity to respond to the students' sounds or actions, making the most of every chance to communicate. We were aware that the more verbal children were claiming more of our attention as they were able to ask questions that demanded a response and had better skills at attracting attention. We had to offer an equal chance to the students who lacked these abilities and so I began a circle time that incorporated aspects of Intensive Interaction and we called it Group Interaction. Each student took a turn in the middle of a circle and we reflected back every action or sound. These sessions had a very different feel from the intimate intensity of the one-to-one sessions; the mood and tone of each session was dependent on the student who was leading. The sessions often tended to be noisier, livelier, less intense and more boisterous and incorporated the use of the whole body. The mood that one student brought to the group often appeared to affect the subsequent interactions. For example, if the student was noisy, often the atmosphere would remain noisy, while if the first one was quiet and subdued, this mood often carried over to the next student. This showed us how much the other students were participating in the group: by feeling, sensing and experiencing the different moods offered by the student who was leading. We were all able to share in the laughter and benefited from the sessions being great fun. It was noticeable that some students responded more in this situation than in a quieter one-to-one session although, conversely, some were more comfortable with just one other person.

There were a number of advantages that the group sessions can offer for both staff and students. Being in a circle meant that we could support one another. Some of the concerns we had felt in one-to-one sessions came from working in an atmosphere where physical contact was discouraged. It took some time to feel easy with some of the interactions and to know how to divert actions with which we were not completely comfortable. In group sessions we were able to learn from one another and to feel easier about accepting the students' approaches. By its very nature the interaction was public and we no longer needed to feel self-conscious, as we were all as involved as the others – we were all in the same boat. Because it became so open, it felt more and more comfortable to interact in this way. It was also an excellent way of introducing the approach to new members of staff, who very quickly fitted in. The sessions are often quite lively and can be great fun, although it is obviously dependent on the leader in the middle for the mood and style of each interaction. It is a means of encouraging teamwork and similarity of approach, and shared fun is always good for strengthening a group and providing a positive ethos within it. The public nature of Group Interaction enabled more people to become aware of new methods and, because the sessions were such fun and so productive, people saw more readily the value of the work. Also, on a more practical level, it was easier to offer quality interaction to all of the class in this way as it is not as staff intensive.

For the students, the circle offers security. They are given the freedom to choose the person with whom they wish to interact and, although they usually choose an adult, they also have the opportunity to approach their peers. As we would want from all group activities Group Interaction teaches turn-taking and awareness of others and helps to bring the group together through shared experiences. For the student to be able to influence several people at once gives a very strong response and is a very powerful experience for them.

A student who might be very active, and finds difficulty in sitting or staying in one place in order to recognise the responses in a one-to-one Intensive Interaction session, is given natural boundaries by being within a circle and can look for a response from anywhere within the circle. Another very powerful element that has come out of Group Interaction is that of changing some unacceptable behaviours. We had to decide whether or not to respond to every action and generally felt that we should not if it was not acceptable to us. This is actually very effective because the student so enjoys the strength of the response that, if s/he does an action such as spitting, and we do not repeat it, the absence of a response will often eliminate the behaviour. During a turn, the student is the most powerful person in the group and is often very reluctant to relinquish the position!

Although the students developed their social and communication abilities in interactions with staff, most of them did not make relationships with their peers and took little or no notice of one another. I decided, therefore, to start up Joint Interaction sessions in which two students are encouraged to respond to each other, to notice each other's behaviour and to be aware of each other. This is a less dramatic method and its successes are much smaller but it has still brought about progress where no other method has had any effect.

We all had such belief in what we were now doing that we looked for ways of developing it into other areas wherever we could. At that time one of the assistants, Margaret Corke, who had become steeped in Intensive Interaction and who has some musical skills, began to see how music, itself a powerful medium, could be used to enhance the interactive processes. She composed songs for anticipation games and used music and instruments to elicit communication and so evolved an exciting project.

Interactive music

Margaret had practised Intensive Interaction for some time and asked to be given the opportunity to use her musical skills within some of the sessions. With the knowledge and experiences gained from Intensive Interaction, she introduced a unique approach. Interactive Music enhanced many of the aspects of Intensive Interaction: using songs and instruments such as hooters for anticipation games, articles such as feather dusters and tambourines in burst/pause activities and sung running commentary. Alongside these, to motivate and gain attention, she also introduced all manner of interesting objects – bought or made – to fascinate the children and enrich the interactions. New items were introduced at frequent intervals, in order to stimulate the curiosity of both students and staff! The group sessions often included songs, instruments and objects to create an atmosphere that reflected the season or topic of the term.

At first, she was able to offer all this only to the class in which she worked as an assistant. However, as we saw the work that she was doing and the benefits it had for the students, so we felt that staff should be reorganised to free her to work throughout the department. This was given support by the head teacher and we were therefore able to go ahead. Margaret set up a pilot scheme which was to last a year and clearly showed the benefit of using an interactive music approach to elicit communicative responses from the students.

Throughout the year, she worked with individual students, in small groups to encourage interaction between two or three students and in class groups. She evolved different skills that would best capitalise on each situation. At every stage, students participated at their own level. Activities were offered to motivate but, importantly, we responded to students' initiations, suggestions and ideas throughout.

Concentrating wholly on developing the approach enabled Margaret to gain experience with students of different abilities and interests and thus the Interactive Music Project grew alongside our increasing use and knowledge of Intensive Interaction. The professional relationship between Margaret and myself was very important with this development. At that time, I was passionately trying to encourage the growth of Intensive Interaction in the school and she to show how valuable her musical approach was. Because of our friendship and our ability to challenge each other at every step, we were able to move forward together; we were able to support each other and borrow ideas and find ways to evolve them. We drew strength from each other.

The nature of the Interactive Music sessions meant that other people could not help hearing them and could see the value of what was being done, thus helping to spread the knowledge and worth of Interactive Music, and therefore Intensive Interaction, throughout the school.

Interactive Music has gone from strength to strength within St Piers and beyond, with visitors coming to observe the way that Margaret works. What she offers is a wonderful way of encouraging interactions. The approach extends respect, empathy and positive regard towards students and staff alike and an atmosphere of utter enjoyment is often created. Her undying enthusiasm, her willingness to try anything and be prepared to see it fail and to start again, and her great need to reach the true spirit of the students, all contributed to the project being successful. The establishment supported and valued the project and Interactive Music is now part of the

St Piers English curriculum, recognising its invaluable contribution to communication.

Difficulties encountered using Intensive Interaction

Even with our dedication and commitment to Intensive Interaction, there have still been some students who did not respond to any of the methods that we used. One student in particular appeared to take no notice of us or what we did – we felt we were unable to get through to her.

She spent a lot of time over-breathing and rubbing her fingers together and this distracted her from anything that we were doing. It succeeded in blocking us out completely. Anticipation games brought no change of expression from her. We searched for a way forward and I fear that if she had been the first person we had worked with we may have given up and not taken the project any further. We may never have been aware of what we were missing. However, we felt sure that there must be a solution but that we were not yet skilled enough to find it. It was extremely important to us that we should discover the 'way in' as we were convinced that, if we could, it may well change her life. So we did not give up and, eventually, we found a way to reach her. She is a quiet, gentle girl, and because of this we had used a quiet approach with her. This had not been effective. It took boisterous 'rough and tumble' games and dramatic anticipation games to finally elicit a response and, from then onwards, she never looked back. Indeed she has become one of the most rewarding students to work with. She now responds delightfully to quiet whispering interactions and she smiles and laughs at even the quietest anticipation games. She initiates physical contact that she once would reject.

Other problems were those of battling against 'controllers': some staff who, although in theory were following the interactive process, in practice were unable to allow the student to take the lead. The learning experience for these members of staff must be a very gradual one and maybe some staff will never be able fully to take it on board; perhaps never feel the depth of conviction that others do.

Some of the staff continued to question and challenge, often in order to make sense of their own changes of thinking. This was a helpful part of the process of change as these people made us think, made our convictions stronger as we needed and were able to find answers. By challenging, they brought about growth of the new approach.

Altogether, I suppose the hardest times were at the beginning when our confidence was low and we were operating behind closed doors away from other people. Intensive Interaction was not at that time part of our formal curriculum and we therefore offered it somewhat tremulously until it eventually became recognised and acknowledged.

Intensive Interaction gradually became a very important part of our timetable and of the students' school day and, although both parents and we ourselves could see how valuable it was and how it was changing their lives, we found it extremely difficult to find ways of recording these changes.

It was necessary in Individual Education Plans to set objectives and so we attempted this. However, this caused problems for a variety of reasons:

- We became so focused on that objective that we failed to capitalise on other learning or even to notice other things that were happening.
- The whole tone of the session changed because something had to be achieved – it became more stilted.
- It put pressure on the students and the teacher to have to achieve a particular objective.
- Subtly, sessions became teacher-led, as there was a hidden agenda within the session.

Within Intensive Interaction, slightly more teacher-led activities could include objectives for the student, such as in established anticipation games, where we knew we were seeking to promote the student's ability to anticipate or to respond. In more student-led activities, such prediction has not been possible. The way forward for us was to be prepared for any learning that happened and recognise and record any changes, progress, new initiatives and responses, but not to try to make them happen.

If the session was to be student-led, we cannot possibly know in advance of it which direction the learning within the session would take. So, a very thorough baseline was needed, preferably as a detailed written report and as a videoed session. Subsequent sessions were then recorded with any new events noted and a summary written to update the baseline. Videos are essential as evidence of progress. This is the procedure that we now use but it has been arrived at through trial and error and we do not feel it is necessarily the best way.

Wider implications of Intensive Interaction

The most poignant effect Intensive Interaction has had on us since its introduction has been the regret we feel that previous students never had the opportunity to have access to something so meaningful and beneficial. How often have I thought 'If only I'd known then what I know now.' That is why it is so important that all students who have severe learning difficulties should be given the chance to enjoy Intensive Interaction now that it is known about.

The effect of Intensive Interaction on the department and on all who worked within it was dramatic and altered all aspects of our work to a greater or lesser extent. We began to change the way we delivered the curriculum, adapting all that was unsuitable or inappropriate. We removed areas that put the students in a position to fail and avoided any task that required using hand over hand in order to allow the student access to it.

This process of change is still on-going and it is necessary to continue to question all areas of the curriculum and our methods of delivering it and to see how we can add to it in order to enrich what is on offer. We now have elements of Intensive Interaction in our storytelling, music sessions and social group times and within Creative Arts. This has enabled the students to have genuine access to the subjects.

The benefits of all the changes have been many. There is more fun in the classroom, more openness amongst the staff, and there is an improved and more equal relationship between staff and students. The assistants take on a different role and need to offer their creativity and intuition rather than merely following a set programme a certain way. This has given a new dimension for the students and a far greater involvement from the staff and thus more commitment. Having a number of interactors each with their own style enriches the whole process.

Having had some Intensive Interaction practice at St Piers for about five years now, the name is well known across the establishment. There are classes and houses where it is practised with dedication, and management is certainly in support of its continuing development. However, the momentum of the project is sustained by individual teachers working within the classrooms and there is no formal structure at present to train new staff or to support one another in the work.

The whole structure of St Piers has changed since Intensive Interaction was introduced. The departments are now arranged according to key stages and therefore have a very wide range of ability and need within them. Some classes now comprise mixed abilities and the staff teams will move around regularly in order to spend time working with all abilities. It will be interesting to see if the new structure and strategies of regular moves and changes of staff help to spread the expertise or if the skills begin to die out through insufficient time to establish them before the next moves.

I feel certain that, having come so far, the worth and the recognition Intensive Interaction has received from management, teachers, care staff and parents will ensure its continuation and development at St Piers.

Chapter 9

Commentary Two: Getting Intensive Interaction Established in Different Settings – Institutional Issues

Melanie Nind and Dave Hewett

Introduction

In the commentary on practice and progress we looked at the issues of introducing and continuing the use of Intensive Interaction from a 'micro' perspective, concerning ourselves primarily with the interactive dyad. In this commentary we are concerned with the 'macro', that is with the issues for an institution or service in using Intensive Interaction as a primary approach. We know of many teachers, residential care workers, day centre staff and various other practitioners who use Intensive Interaction, some of whom contribute to this book. Use of the approach can occur with or without the full support of the school, centre or service. Sometimes managers have other agendas. Sometimes managers are supportive but some individuals within the staff group have spoken or unspoken reservations about using Intensive Interaction. Staff development on Intensive Interaction gives rise to as many questions about convincing others about the approach, and getting it established within a setting, as questions about the day-to-day interactive practicalities. Even the most natural and intuitive interactors who can use the approach most effectively with little support will face difficulties if their interactive work clashes with the central ethos of their workplace.

Once again the contributors to this volume provide valuable guidance on these matters. Chris Addis's account of using Intensive Interaction in a unit for pupils with multi-sensory impairment most usefully describes a setting in a state of readiness for such an approach. Val Stothard's account of a special school describes a more typical situation in which the approach has grown within a school, working outwards from a committed core of staff, in a semi-ad hoc way. Christine Smith touches on some of the

165

tensions of using Intensive Interaction in the context of a Further Education College, and Cath Irvine and Judith Samuel and Jaqui Maggs describe the process of incorporating Intensive Interaction into adult services for people with profound and multiple learning disabilities. We see here some of the differences and indeed some of the similarities between the issues for social services, health trusts and education providers.

In this commentary we will address the question of how Intensive Interaction gets going in an institution or service, how the momentum is maintained, and how some of the key practical problems and philosophical controversies might be resolved. Readers who are particularly interested in this theme might like to look at the section in *Access to Communication* (Nind and Hewett, 1994, p.145) on organisational issues, where we offered some basic advice on issues such as team work and time management. The chapter in that book on wider and related issues is also relevant to issues such as age appropriateness, which we address again here.

How does Intensive Interaction get going?

There are many different ways in which Intensive Interaction might be initiated into an institution or service, but they can probably all be classified as falling into either one of the main patterns in figure 9.1 below.

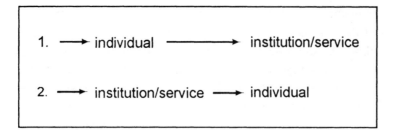

Figure 9.1 Who starts the process?

In our experience the first scenario is more common. It is often the case that one or, if they are lucky, two or three staff within a workplace or service initiate the use of Intensive Interaction. This might be because they are already attracted to doing this kind of work or because they intuitively use interaction as their central tool. It is often a response to the realisation that what is on offer to an individual (such as Alice, p. 130) or group of student/clients (such as the PMLD group in Somerset, p. 103) is failing to benefit them. This may be a private realisation or, as Cath Irvine describes, the outcome of a more public exercise. It may be that, as with us at Harperbury, these factors combine to be influential.

Reading about or participating in training on Intensive Interaction may affirm the position of these individual staff and allow them to develop what they are doing. This pattern is seen in the chapter by Val Stothard, and in the one by Judith Samuel and Jaqui Maggs who note comments by support staff that 'attempting Intensive Interaction has given them permission to just spend time with clients, socialising and enjoying one another's company' (p. 137). Formalising interactive work as Intensive Interaction also provides a language to enable these individuals to talk about previously nebulous-seeming ways of working with colleagues. These individuals can also find a strong psychological base and rationale for their methods in Intensive Interaction. This often provides the stimulus needed for the interactive approach to be shared with other members of a team, or across classes or groups.

In the second scenario, the starting point is the institution or service. In some ways it is a nonsense to separate this from an individual, because there is always a person behind the scenes, feeding in the ideas or fuelling the change process. There is a different feel, however, when Intensive Interaction is adopted as a service policy or as a whole school approach from very early on. The issues for the staff involved will also be different. Chris Addis describes all of the staff being involved in an audit of the learners' communication behaviours and Cath Irvine describes the discussions of the core staff following their observation phase. This is quite a different endeavour to one or two staff, with little discussion, imputing intentionality and doing communication work in isolation.

It may be more useful to think of the two main scenarios in terms of how it happens rather than who is responsible (see figure 9.2).

We are not advocating either one of these scenarios as inferior or superior to the other. Neither are we suggesting that the two scenarios have to be entirely separate. At Harperbury Hospital School our beginnings were very exploratory and informal, but we increasingly formalised our work as a written school curriculum with some formal

167

1. informal, exploratory, intuitive, unplanned, evolving

2. formally planned, implemented and evaluated

Figure 9.2 How introduction of Intensive Interaction happens

evaluation of it. Similarly, with the Oxfordshire NHS Trust MDRT (see Samuel and Maggs), individuals played around with the ideas and the practice and then instigated a three-month trial. At Six Acres the beginnings were quite thoroughly pre-planned, but the training in Intensive Interaction was such that ample room was left for intuitive and exploratory work with the method itself. In many ways St Piers is the most typical example of how the introduction of Intensive Interaction happens. It is also a perfect example of the first scenario:

> There are classes and houses where it [Intensive Interaction] is practised with dedication, and management is certainly in support of its continuing development. The momentum of the project is sustained by individual teachers working within the classrooms and there is no formal structure at present to train new staff or to support one another in the work. (Stothard, p. 163)

Val Stothard's account is particularly valuable in illustrating the stages and processes along the evolutionary route to this position five years on. We see the curriculum change in stages through behavioural, sensory and more empathic curricula. We see the early explorations with the method, and the gradual growth in the confidence of the key staff involved. We also see some important turning points with whole school staff development sessions, management coming on board, and parents giving their support.

There are factors, illustrated by the contributors here, which make the process of adopting Intensive Interaction as a primary approach easier (such as having allies and management support) and there are factors which will make it more effective (such as having some consistency). There are also many factors which we would argue are important to both ease and effectiveness. In this last category we would emphasise good communication and team work and good critical reflection. Samuel and Maggs offer a particularly valuable discussion of these components and their work provides a good model for team reflection with a commitment to supervision in order to further develop their skills and the necessary support frameworks.

A major issue affecting how Intensive Interaction gets going in a workplace is, as Chris Addis highlights, readiness for such an approach. This readiness may lie in the diverse terms he describes such as a suitable physical environment, appropriate staffing levels, flexible timetable, and good team work and established communication systems. The actual physical environment for doing Intensive Interaction is not an issue we have emphasised with Intensive Interaction. This is in contrast to the somewhat similar Option Method (Kaufman and Kaufman, 1976; Kaufman, 1994) where staff follow and join in with individuals with autism, but where great importance is placed on this occurring in a distraction free therapy room. At Harperbury we informalised the physical environment, but otherwise spent little energy on it. Chris Addis recognises the benefits of the physical environment the unit enjoys. Cath Irvine's team were starting anew with their environment and so gave careful consideration to what physical space would be appropriate. Judith Samuel and Jaqui Maggs reflect on the lack of space or special environment to do Intensive Interaction in the person's own home, but do recognise that in many ways this is the most natural and suitable place to be learning about communicating and relating.

More importantly than getting the physical environment right, readiness, we suggest, is about staff attitudes and the existing ethos of the institution or service. At St Piers we see that initially there was very little readiness, but that the whole school moved towards this in stages, gradually easing up on the rigidity about control, age appropriateness and physical contact. In the NHS trust getting ready to formalise Intensive Interaction within the service required something of a cultural shift (Samuel and Maggs p. 121).

In the MSI unit difficult issues over touching and physical contact had already been resolved. This would have had two benefits. Firstly, the staff would feel freed up by this policy outcome, they would be likely to be less inhibited in their interactions and less threatened by the 'judgements' of others. Secondly, they would have been through an important *process* of

169

thinking about and talking about their priorities, their duties and accountabilities and as a result of the process they would know one another and themselves better. The MSI unit were fortunate in being able to adopt Intensive Interaction as a method with this, though certainly not all, preparatory work done.

When reading the various accounts of getting Intensive Interaction established, practitioners will be able to identify with elements from their own working environments. I (MN) can think in terms of the school at Harperbury having an attitudinal (if not physical) readiness although, as with St Piers and probably every school, we had the occasional staff member who was more strongly adhered to behavioural style structure and control. I can also remember the cultural shock of then working in a community SLD school in which the prevailing culture was one of dominating the pupils, of breaking down their challenging behaviours (and spirit?), of getting them to conform and be normalised. Staff relationships were uncomfortable and the working atmosphere was tense. In this setting I continued to use Intensive Interaction as part of my individual style and to share the approach with staff 'allies', but I recognised the need for fundamental institutional change before a state of readiness for the school to adopt the approach would be achieved.

Sometimes Intensive Interaction can be the trigger to bring about much needed broader changes in a workplace. Sometimes, however, if the changes are vast, an approach like Intensive Interaction can be seen by reluctant staff as the problem or 'enemy'. This ultimately may confuse issues of what the approach is about and ultimately make its adoption less probable. When individual practitioners seek advice on this we often only have the answer that it all depends on the particular circumstance and the particular people involved. How one initiates the approach will be influenced by how much power the initiator has. A classroom assistant may be in a less influential position than a head of department, for example, to make change happen. (We do know of situations, however, where the reverse was true!) It will also be influenced by how much support the initiator has, both inside and outside of work. We are sure that Val Stothard's supportive assistant made an enormous difference in the early period. Personality also plays a role and enthusiasm can be catching. There are also advantages to having a thick skin! Commitment to Intensive Interaction is vital if you are going to 'sell' it to others, but it is also necessary to be able to see it from the perspectives of others. In the

SLD school situation described above I felt vulnerable because it wasn't just 'an' approach I would have been introducing, it was 'my' approach or at least one with which I was emotionally involved. A bit of distance can help and perhaps there is a careful balancing act to be achieved between feeling and showing our commitment to Intensive Interaction and not becoming too evangelical about it.

Whether Intensive Interaction is introduced in a planned way or whether it evolves, it is worth thinking about the readiness factors which emerge from the examples in this book. It may be that preparatory work is undertaken or it may be that these factors become markers for developments you are working towards in the institution/service, alongside developments you are working towards in the students/clients. We would, however, endorse Cath Irvine's working principle that wherever possible it is important to establish good working practices at the start of a new project.

Staff support for Intensive Interaction

It is a rare for a staff team to be wholly in favour of any new initiative. It is to be expected that some staff will need to be won over. When we reflect on effective accessing of learners in Intensive Interaction, we recognise helpful features such as not trying too hard, giving the person time and space, not expecting too much too soon. These features can equally well be applied to the broader issues of getting Intensive Interaction established by staff. Introducing Intensive Interaction may well mean that practitioners are forced to question their own practice and long-held ideas. We have all done this at some time and we should remember that we need to be able to do it with dignity; we need to feel that we are in charge of the process and the pace of change. This is feasible when Intensive Interaction evolves in an institution or service.

> Between ourselves we questioned, challenged, assessed and modified our approaches. Talking it over, voicing our concerns and having to justify what we were doing helped us to strengthen our resolve and conviction. Of course it meant that we had to question much of what we had done in the past, which is not an easy or comfortable thing to do and took a certain amount of courage. (Stothard, p. 155)

171

Other staff can observe from a quiet distance and come round to what they see in their own time. It is easier for them to do this, of course, if they have not publicly placed themselves in opposition to the approach; no one likes back-tracking. The St Piers story illustrates beautifully how effective this unforced approach can be.

There is a lot to be said then for doing what you think is right for your students/clients and sharing your very clear rationale for why you are doing it that way, but not insisting that others join you in this. We need to remember that in Intensive Interaction the 'teacher-interactor' has to be having her/his own genuine fun. We cannot force interactions on staff just as we cannot force them on learners; the whole point is to take part because you want to. This was recognised in Cath Irvine's project with its strategy of recruiting a small team of committed staff volunteering to be the core team. Judith Samuel and Jaqui Maggs's account of increasingly using Intensive Interaction in their service illustrates how natural momentum can be judiciously combined with planned initiatives to bring colleagues on board.

The questionnaire responses from the special schools/units from four counties (Nind, Oxford Brookes University project, see p. 5) indicated that Intensive Interaction was used 'occasionally', or as 'part of' the curriculum, but never as 'central to' the curriculum. Partial use of Intensive Interaction usually happens when it is used with one or two especially remote pupils, or by one or two especially innovative staff members in their particular sessions or groups. This can be quite pragmatic, for as Samuel and Maggs reflect 'perhaps it would have been better to involve the whole team from the start. However, if we had waited for that we may never have begun!' (p. 136). It may be helpful, as they do, to regard small groups of interested staff 'having a go' as 'piloting the intervention at a local level' and gathering valuable information needed for working effectively and for convincing others. These authors have a clear idea of the ideal whole team approach they strive for, but they are also aware that the less than ideal can still be effective. We would accept the need to compromise, but would argue that it is never desirable to work, as Val Stothard and close colleagues did at one time, 'undercover'.

Use of the approach by part of an organisation becomes complex when some staff within a single class/group are using Intensive Interaction and some are not, although a lot depends of course on how different the work of the others actually is. It also becomes more complex when some classes/groups within an organisation use Intensive Interaction and some do not, especially as inevitably the classes/groups impact on one another in various ways. Individual students/clients with learning disabilities may experience different approaches as they move from one class/group to another or when the staff change. In the former situation, where there is variation in approach within a single group, the option of giving staff time to come round can still work. Each individual staff member can contribute most by working to their strengths, while at the same time the apprenticeship model of working alongside a skilled interactor can be a powerful experience. As Val Stothard illustrates, patience and open dialogue are likely to be the watchwords in this situation.

The latter situation where only some classes/groups use the approach can be more frustrating. Judith Samuel and Jaqui Maggs (p. 128) are painfully aware of how fragile the system is for Rodney. He is reliant on the stability of the staff group and yet circumstances necessitate that agency staff are frequently used. Equally, if your own working unit has established the practice of Intensive Interaction and the student is about to move on to a class or group where the ethos and practice is very different we can be quite fearful of the effects on the person with learning difficulties moving through. In this situation it can be helpful to think through which of the potential threats are to the person her/himself, and which are threats to us, our practice and our pride in our work. That it not to say that we should not be aiming towards having a consistent approach across an institution/service, but that we sometimes cannot expect this to happen all at once.

Good transition practice is as relevant here as for any other transition situation. Providing opportunities for the learner to get used to the new situation and providing opportunities for the staff groups to spend time in one another's environments is obvious good practice. We need to remember that we all have different interactive styles and that our students/clients can benefit from this range of experience. We would also reassure readers that, although we know of occasional tragic circumstances (such as Jamie's change in living arrangements in Christine Smith's account) in which individuals have regressed in their new environment, or become more challenging as a result of a new lack of responsiveness or sensitivity, such incidents are rare. We have been impressed so often by the hardiness of people with learning disabilities to cope with these situations. We have also been continually pleasantly

173

surprised at how lasting their communication developments have been. Although (as with Jamie and to some extent Sabrina) new developments may go on hold for a while, and although challenging or ritualistic behaviours may disguise someone's abilities, often the change to seeing oneself as being someone who can have an effect on the world and who others enjoy being with, is not *un*learned. Sometimes, in the relatively short period of time we have to work with people, we can enable them to reach the stage where they are easier to be with. Being better company increases the likelihood of eliciting good responses in those around us. This scenario can help to make transition less traumatic as new staff are able to see the social and communicative nature of the new student/client.

We include this discussion because sometimes we cannot wait for the whole school or service to be right before we begin to make changes in part of it. We may, though, have ethical dilemmas about starting something which may not be seen through. There are difficult decisions to be made, individual situation by individual situation, but for which the discussions here may provide some help. Cath Irvine, for example, shares a number of important insights into getting Intensive Interaction going in a social services environment which can be applied to other settings. Here we are given strong pointers to what we need to get right. We need:

1. colleagues and managers to understand that we are not just 'sitting around doing nothing'
2. freedom from needing to set objectives for all activities, and alternative, appropriate and negotiated forms of accountability
3. time to communicate thoroughly about what is happening
4. practical recording systems which will support points 1–3 above
5. an atmosphere of mutual support where we do not feel under pressure to perform interaction, but do feel an obligation to enable interaction to happen
6. to experiment with the approach so we have our own personal accounts of how it works – which will help to turn others on to the approach.

Conflicts with other approaches

In most cases when Intensive Interaction is introduced the staff involved face decisions about whether it is used alongside existing approaches or practices or whether there is a conflict to be resolved. Val Stothard and Chris Addis discuss this issue in relation to behavioural methods previously in use in their schools. Cath Irvine and Judith Samuel and Jaqui Maggs discuss the conflict with the normalising drives in adult services.

Behavioural approaches

In our review of pertinent recent literature (chapter 1) we noted the trend away from behavioural methods and ideologies, but also the desire not to lose the benefits that these have brought with them. Many writers (such as Farrell, 1994; Garner, Hinchcliffe and Sandow, 1995; Collis and Lacey, 1996) advocate some mature marrying of the best parts of behavioural and interactive approaches.

In the practitioners' accounts in this book, we see some of the ways in which this is achieved, but also the difficulties with this in practice. Chris Addis is very clear about which aspects of behaviourism his unit can maintain, arguing that positive reinforcement and task analysis have their place sitting comfortably alongside their child-centred, interactive approaches. He is also clear about 'which aspects are diametrically opposed to the philosophy and practice of Intensive Interaction' (p. 35). For him these are the view of the learner as passive, and the role of the teacher as shaper and prescriber. Equally, Val Stothard has views about how Intensive Interaction can act as a reinforcer for good, communicative behaviours and as a depressor of more problematic behaviours. She recognises that Intensive Interaction operates within a different frame of thinking, however, and identifies the control element of behavioural thinking and practice as the key area of conflict with interactive approaches:

> It soon became apparent that, having adopted an interactive approach, we could not easily encompass a strongly behavioural element within it. By feeling the depth of empathy and respect for the student and the relationship between staff and student that the interactive approaches

engendered, one could not readily step back into the role of controller. (Val Stothard, p. 154)

We would argue that there are practical reasons for using behavioural approaches. They are effective for some skills learning. We would also argue that there are practical reasons for using alternatives to behavioural approaches. These centre around their inadequacy for teaching complex areas like sociability and communication and the comparative power of interactive approaches to facilitate these important and complex developments. Intensive Interaction was developed for this very practical purpose. We are also aware, however, that Intensive Interaction fits with a certain way of seeing the world, that to operate within its principles and to use its methods requires us to think in certain ways. It is because of this respect for the individuals with learning disabilities for what they are, this willingness to work with them rather than do things to them, that makes a conflict with behavioural approaches somewhat inevitable.

The conflict with behavioural approaches, however, is already becoming less of an issue for practitioners wanting to use Intensive Interaction than it was eight years ago when we first started writing about Intensive Interaction; it is less of an issue even than it was three years ago when we wrote *Access to Communication*. This is because the criticisms of behaviourism are now well-documented (see, for example, Wood and Shears, 1986). Many of its proponents have now moved their efforts to quite different areas (compare, for example, the current work of Mel Ainscow to a decade ago), and many of those working within the behavioural paradigm have shifted in aspects of their thinking.

Kroese *et al.*'s (1997) recent book on *Cognitive Behaviour Therapy for People with Learning Disabilities* illustrates the trend towards a different kind of behavioural approach. Here the disempowering aspects of behaviourism (at its worst) are challenged and the rights of those on the receiving end of the treatments are considered a priority. It is reassuring to see such a trend in behavioural psychology in which people with learning disabilities are coming to be seen as active participants in their own learning and life planning. This text even uses the language of 'working with' rather than 'treating' people with learning disabilities. Kroese's opening chapter openly discusses the tensions about whether the intentions of cognitive behaviour therapy are about social control (appropriate behaviour and productivity) or about enhancing

176

psychological well-being. We have often been aware of problems arising from staff using Intensive Interaction wanting to develop the whole person and their individuality, and colleagues using behavioural methods wanting to shape a person who ostensibly will be functioning well and who will be acceptable to others. If there is a coming together of intentions, and a greater honesty about what we are working towards, this is encouraging.

There is also a trend marked by this text in the way social learning is regarded. Reed (in the Kroese *et al.* book) shows how independent living skills are often prioritised over emotional well-being and she exposes some of the weaknesses of social skills training for nurturing good mental health. Loumidis and Hill (in the same volume) tackle many of these weaknesses with the description of an intervention concerning the social *process* and which addresses the need for emotional well-being and realistic self-advocacy. The inclusion of a chapter (by Kushlik *et al.*) on applying cognitive behaviour therapy to professional carers working with clients with challenging behaviour also marks a welcome shift in thinking. Here, the effect of the staff's beliefs and feelings about (the reasons for) their clients' behaviour is explored. The potential of, for example, re-assessing one's ideas about someone's 'attention-seeking' for making the working relationship more positive, is excitingly evident. It is possible to see from these examples the gap between behavioural and interactive approaches becoming easier to cross. We certainly applaud Clements's (same volume) concluding remark about a desire to see the strong value base of cognitive psychology emphasised in terms of needing effective interventions which do not oppress those on the receiving end. All this may seem a million miles away from EDY and other forms of behaviourial work more frequently seen in schools and adult services. This new kind of behavioural work, however, may offer a useful stepping stone for those who find the transition from behavioural to interactive approaches a little too revolutionary.

Normalisation

In adult services for people with learning disabilities, the doctrine of normalisation in general, and age appropriateness in particular, might be regarded by some as the major ideological obstacle to using Intensive Interaction. There is of course a major difference in that here there are no proven practical advantages for the age-appropriate approach, indeed there is not really a method to be evaluated or researched in terms of outcomes, just a set of guidelines (sometimes rigid rules!) on how to behave. This is often interpreted partly as a need to talk in an adult way to adults with PMLD. The success of this for engaging these adults is limited, however, for as Clegg, Standen and Cromby (1991) show, even the best talk sessions, in the most ideal environments, facilitate little client responsiveness and little turn-taking.

Judith Samuel and Jaqui Maggs provide some useful background context to the trend towards policies for normalisation and an 'ordinary life'. They go on to show the particular limitations of practice based on these policies for people with more profound learning disabilities. Cath Irvine illustrates this with her example of ordinary living being taken to mean integrated provision in which in reality people with PMLD were clearly missing out. Samuel and Maggs also identify an important shift which is in its early stages, away from an emphasis on domestic life and basic independence, as an indicator of quality of life. The growth in dialogue about what constitutes a good quality of life (see chapter 1, p. 10) has been helpful in beginning to shift the status quo about what constitutes valuable normalising experiences.

Just as we have argued that the opposition to Intensive Interaction from behavioural approaches is lessening, we would also argue that the opposition from advocates of normalisation and age appropriateness is also on the decline. We increasingly find that in staff development sessions on Intensive Interaction participants no longer want to spend so much time on the age appropriateness discussion. Often this discussion has gone on before, some resolution has been reached, or advocates of strict age appropriateness no longer assume that everyone thinks the way they do and refrain from voicing their views as if they are universal truths.

This is not to say that the issue of age appropriateness has gone away altogether. It remains a feature for discussion by the contributors here and it was cited as a challenge presented to the use of Intensive Interaction by two of the respondents to the questionnaires mentioned earlier. It is more that approaches which challenge the automatic priority for age-appropriate activity are not met with the same level of emotive response as was true of a few years ago.

Val Stothard shows how the age-appropriate doctrine permeated schools as well as adult services. She shows some of the ways in which the choice of activities for the students, such as matching coloured clothes pegs to coloured plant pots (p. 151), were influenced by this thinking. She and the other practitioners contributing to this book are amongst the growing numbers who have come to recognise that respect for people with learning disabilities as the teenagers or adults they are 'requires more than the removal of brightly coloured equipment, and more then the removal of all physical contact' (Stothard, p. 152). Judith Samuel and Jaqui Maggs note how 'doing nothing has been preferred to breaking the politically correct "rules" and offering non-chronologically age-appropriate experiences' (p. 142). They illustrate how staff in adult services have come to think in terms of clients' stereotypical behaviours putting their 'image at risk' (p. 126), but also how this thinking is open for negotiation. They cite examples of staff pondering whether good interaction which breaks an age-appropriateness rule is okay. This seems to us to be a fairly healthy state of affairs. Again we do not want to 'lose the baby with the bath water'. Constant checking of ourselves for respectful practice that is in the best interests of our clients/students must be a good thing.

We set out our position on age appropriateness quite comprehensively in *Access to Communication* (Nind and Hewett, 1994). We expanded on this in a more political essay in *Whose Choice* (1996), Judith Coupe O'Kane and Juliet Goldbart's excellent collection of work on contentious issues for staff working with people with learning difficulties. We have frequent feedback that this has been helpful. Now *Interaction in Action* shows how staff from different disciplines are tackling the issue and we are hopeful that this will boost the confidence of other practitioners for whom this is an issue also. The value placed by parents on Intensive Interaction as a developmental, interactive approach should also help to dispel the myth that what people want from us is the delivery of persons who will not offend our sense of normalcy. The quality of life aspirations of the Taylors and the Bruces should support us in putting normalisation aspirations into appropriate perspective.

Touch

We have discussed some of the potential obstacles to getting Intensive Interaction established in an organisation providing education or care to people with learning difficulties in terms of conflicts with other preexisting ways of doing and thinking about things. The fact that Intensive Interaction most usually involves making physical contact with our students/clients can also be an obstacle to its acceptance. This is linked with age-appropriateness thinking in that this becomes more of an issue the older the person with learning disabilities gets. It is also linked with normalisation as in 'ordinary life' the dominant British culture largely reserves physical contact for sexual relationships and family bonds.

There has not been a recognisable cultural shift in recent years which has made this an easier issue for staff wanting to use Intensive Interaction and other approaches which incorporate touch. What is available, however, is, first, a set of physical contact safeguards which institutions might adapt or adopt (see figure 9.3); second, a small group of schools/day centres/residential settings which offer a model of good practice for use of touch; and, third, a growing body of literature asserting the importance of touch for human development (see below). Chris Addis's MSI unit is one of these establishments which has sorted out its policy on physical contact. It may be that practitioners in services for those with MSI will lead the way on this. These practitioners do not have the option to side-step the dilemma of 'to touch or not to touch' and still communicate with their students/clients. In recognising the developmental, emotional and communication need to make physical contact they have gone on to develop policies which support this need. Much of this reasoning can be applied to students/clients with other severe and complex learning disabilities. The rationale for using Intensive Interaction, and for using touch within it, is clearly laid out in *Access to Communication* (Nind and Hewett, 1994, p. 129).

Recent literature on caregiver–infant interaction provides ongoing and new support for the need for physical contact for positive interactions and healthy development. For some time now studies (such as Montagu,1971) have shown the importance of touch stimulation for motor, cognitive and social development. Familiarity with this kind of literature helped to confirm our welcome of physical contact in developing Intensive Interaction. On the whole, however, we operated on the premise that touch is part of a complex package of optimal interaction in natural settings and that therefore this could not be removed from an approach based on this model. (Indeed, touch itself forms a complex package of elements including rhythmic and kinesthetic stimulation which are inseperable from other forms of stimulation (Korner, 1990).)

- **Know why you do it**

  Be knowledgeable on the purposes of using physical contact by discussion, thought and by reading the pertinent psychological and developmental literature.

- **Have consent from the person**

  Obey the usual conventions concerning making physical contact with another person. If you rarely get consent to touch, then go back a few stages and work toward obtaining willingly given consent. At the very least, physical contact may be necessary to carry out basic care.

- **Be prepared to discuss and explain your practices**

  First and foremost by being knowledgeable, as above.

- **Document – have it acknowledged in the school curriculum document or workplace brochure**

  The culture and working practices of the school or other workplace are acknowledged in the curriculum document or workplace brochure and this will include explication of the use of physical contact and the purposes of it.

- **Document – have it acknowledged in any individual programme for the person**

  Be assertive. If you are certain that use of physical content is fulfilling the person's needs educationally or developmentally, then state this in the documentation drawn up to support work with that person.

- **Have good teamwork, both organisational and emotional**

  Teamworking practices should literally facilitate staff working together in teams so that staff or students are rarely alone. The teamworking ethos should also include good discussions among staff concerning the emotional aspects of the work, including crucially orientations toward the issue of use of physical contact.

- **Use of physical contact should be discussed openly and regularly**

  There should be no sense of furtiveness or 'hidden curriculum'. This important aspect of teaching technique should tangibly be a matter of open discussion and study.

- **Have others present**

  The most basic safeguard for staff and students is to have other staff present in the room when in situations where physical contact is likely to be used.

Figure 9.3 Use of physical contact in work with people with learning disabilities – guidelines for safeguards

Pelaez-Nogueras *et al.* (1996) acknowledge the reality of a multi-modal composite of interactive stimuli which includes touch, but argue that earlier research based on this leaves unanswered the question of whether or not infants respond more positively to a composite social stimulus which includes touch. This question is directly relevant for the issue of to what degree touch is essential to Intensive Interaction. Pelaez-Nogueras *et al.* (1996) note recent development of our understanding of the role of touch in interaction which has emerged from studies (such as Toda and Fogel, 1993; Pelaez-Nogueras *et al.*, 1995) in which parental behaviours have been manipulated. These show that when mothers adopt a stationary, expressionless pose, touch serves to reduce the infants' negative effect and to direct their attention. Removal of touch as well as facial expression led to more grimacing and less smiling from the infant, but re-introduction of touch increased positive effect and attention.

Pelaez-Nogueras *et al.* (1996) compared the effect of a compound of adult stimulus that included touch with one that did not. In both situations the adult responded by contingently cooing and smiling; in the touch stituation the adult contingently rhythmically rubbed the infant's legs and feet. They found significantly more infant smiling and vocalising and eye contact during the touch situation, and significantly more crying and protesting during the no-touch situation. This research is important because it gives empirical evidence for touch being a significant reinforcer for infants' eye-contact behaviour and for interactions involving touch being preferred. This kind of research evidence helps to support our claims to needing to use touch in Intensive Interaction. Pelaez-Nogueras *et al.* (1996) acknowledge that individual infants may differ in their preferences for modes of stimuli and emphasise that caregivers need to individually tailor their stimulation based on their interpretations of the infants' responses. This again reinforces our concept that touch, however beneficial we know it to be, should never be seen as compulsory, but rather viewed as part of a powerful option in a responsive repertoire.

Policies of no-touch or highly-prescribed touch in institutions and services for people with complex learning disabilities represent a lack of awareness of the role of touch in human development, communication and relationship. There are whole books on touch and Montagu's (1971) *Touching: The Human Significance of the Skin* and Barnard and Brazelton's (1990) *Touch: The Foundation of Experience* illustrate that continuing ignorance of the role of touch is untenable. Rose (1990) states that touch, though recognised as one of our five senses, remains relatively ill-understood. The basis for the need to understand it better is seen in her description of touch as involving a rich and complex 'flow of stimulation' (p. 300) with a role in promoting social and emotional functioning, regulating physical and physiological development, and guiding perception and exploration of the external world. Intensive Interactions learns from how infants learn, and Brazelton's (1990) concluding chapter to the Barnard and Brazelton (1990) collection of essays on touch in infancy highlights just some of the significance of touch:

- functioning to make survival possible
- functioning to make life meaningful
- acting as a comforter
- acting as an alerter
- enhancing physiological functioning
- regulating arousal
- regulating the mother's response as well as the baby's
- providing an important source of information
- keeping the infant in contact with the human world
- providing a form of social communication which transcends almost all culture.

Seen in these terms, touch must be given a greater priority and different treatment by practitioners and policy makers across a range of services and institutions working with people of all ages whose development is delayed or problematic.

There are a few examples of interventions for people with learning disabilities which recognise the value of touch in work with this client group. Hegarty and Gale (1996), for instance, illustrate how massage was found to reduce the tension and anxiety in a young woman with learning disabilities and challenging behaviour, and they propose that we should address the question of how therapeutic touch can be incorporated into professional practice. The knowledge base we have on this, however, is sparse, possibly because writing about using touch with people with learning difficulties is still a taboo.

The case studies of using Intensive Interaction with varied learners by the various contributors here illustrate how physical contact often forms an important part of the interactions and help to illustrate that touch has a valuable role. We get some impression of how problematic or otherwise this was for the practitioners involved and for their school/centre/service. We hope that these accounts, together with the general guidance which applies equally to this particular issue, about the importance of having a clear rationale and good team work and communications, are helpful. We should be open and honest about what we are doing and why. We should remain sensitive to the potential to abuse the use of touch. We should be respectful of the needs of our students/clients at all times.

References

Barnard, K.E. and Brazelton, T.B. (1990) (eds) *Touch: The Foundation of Experience*. Madison, Connecticut: International Universities Press.

Brazelton, T.B. (1990) 'Touch as a touchstone: Summary of the round table'. In: Barnard, K.E. and Brazelton, T.B. (eds) *Touch: The Foundation of Experience*. Madison, Connecticut: International Universities Press.

Clegg, J.A., Standen, P.J. and Cromby, J.J. (1991) 'The analysis of talk sessions between staff and adults with profound intellectual disability', *Australia and New Zealand Journal of Developmental Disabilities*, **17**, 4, 391–400.

Clements, J. (1997) 'Sustaining a cognitive psychology for people with learning disabilities'. In: Kroese, B.S., Dagnan, D. and Loumidis, K. (eds) *Cognitive Behaviour Therapy for People with Learning Disabilities*. London: Routledge.

Collis, M. and Lacey, P. (1996) *Interactive Approaches to Teaching: A Framework for INSET*. London: David Fulton.

Farrell, P. (1994) 'Behavioural methods: a re-appraisal', *BILD: The SLD Experience*, **8**, 9–12.

Garner, P., Hinchcliffe, V. and Sandow, S. (1995) *What Teachers Do: Developments in Special Education*. London: Paul Chapman.

Hegarty, J.R. and Gale, E. (1996) 'Touch as a therapeutic medium for people with challenging behaviours', *British Journal of Learning Disabilities*, **24**, 26–32.

Kaufman, B.N. and Kaufman, S. (1976) *To Love is To Be Happy With*. London: Souvenir Press.

Kaufman, B.N. (1994) *The Miracle Continues*. Tiburon, CA: H.J. Kramer.

Korner, A.F. (1990) 'The many faces of touch'. In: Barnard, K.E. and Brazelton, T.B. (eds) *Touch: The Foundation of Experience*. Madison, Connecticut: International Universities Press.

Kroese, B.S., Dagnan, D. and Loumidis, K. (eds) (1997) *Cognitive Behaviour Therapy for People with Learning Disabilities*. London: Routledge.

Kroese, B.S. (1997) 'Cognitive behaviour therapy for people with learning disabilities: conceptual and contextual issues'. In: Kroese, B.S., Dagnan, D. and Loumidis, K. (eds) *Cognitive Behaviour Therapy for People with Learning Disabilities*. London: Routledge.

Kushlik, A., Trower, P. and Dagnan, D. (1997) 'Applying cognitive behavioural approaches to the carers of people with learning disabilities who display challenging behaviour'. In: Kroese, B.S., Dagnan, D. and Loumidis, K. (eds) *Cognitive Behaviour Therapy for People with Learning Disabilities*. London: Routledge.

Loumidis, K. and Hill, A. (1997) 'Social problem-solving groups for adults with learning disabilities'. In: Kroese, B.S., Dagnan, D. and Loumidis, K. (eds) *Cognitive Behaviour Therapy for People with Learning Disabilities*. London: Routledge.

Montagu, A. (1971) *Touching: The Human Significance of the Skin*. New York: Columbia.

Nind, M. and Hewett, D. (1994) *Access to Communication: Developing the Basics of Communication with People with Severe Learning Difficulties Through Intensive Interaction*. London: David Fulton.

Nind, M. and Hewett, D. (1996) 'When age appropriateness isn't appropriate'. In: Coupe O'Kane, J. and Goldbart, J. (eds) *Whose Choice? Contentious Issues for those Working with People with Learning Difficulties*. London: David Fulton.

Pelaez-Nogueras, M. *et al.* (1996) 'Infants' preference for touch stimulation in face-to-face interactions', *Journal of Applied Developmental Psychology*, **17**, 199–213.

Reed, J. (1997) 'Understanding and assessing depression in people with learning disabilities: a cognitive behavioural approach'. In: Kroese, B.S., Dagnan, D. and Loumidis, K. (eds) *Cognitive Behaviour Therapy for People with Learning Disabilities*. London: Routledge.

Rose, S.A. (1990) 'Perception and cognition in preterm infants: The sense of touch'. In: Barnard, K.E. and Brazelton, T.B. (1990) (eds) *Touch: The Foundation of Experience*. Madison, Connecticut: International Universitites Press.

Wood, S. and Shears, B. (1986) *Teaching Children with Severe Learning Difficulties. A Radical Reappraisal*. London: Croom Helm.

Chapter 10

Ben's Story: Developing the Communication Abilities of a Pupil with Autism

Lynne Knott (with contributions from Angela Curtis and Ruth Kennedy)

I first met Ben when he started at our residential school for pupils with severe learning difficulties, as a ten-year old. He came to us a young person who was remote and absorbed in himself with a diagnosis of autism. He did not initiate social interaction with his peers and he became very distressed if they approached him, visibly shrinking away from them. Sometimes he would approach adults and touch them briefly with eyes flickering. He would squeal in distress for long periods of time and this would alternate with hysterical laughing. When he appeared upset he would 'over-breathe', though there was no indication of what was worrying him. He then might run to an adult, grasp their hands and jump and down in front of them squealing and over-breathing.

Ben had no language and could not relate to symbols. His only means of communication seemed to be his crying and distressed behaviour, eyes flicking giving little eye contact. We had no way of knowing whether Ben had a problem or pain. He seemed at his happiest wandering around the classroom, picking up objects to shuffle together. He allowed the adults around him to determine his daily life. He relied on them for a drink, something to eat, or going to the toilet. Ben seemed to be full of anxieties, constantly wringing his hands, running frenetically around spaces. He appeared fearful of the world, distressed by it with no apparent reason.

I had started my teaching in an inner-city mainstream school, in 1968. I had a class of forty pupils aged five. A large majority of the class had some emotional problems because of their deprived backgrounds. This manifested in difficult behaviours and in some cases in withdrawal from the world, even self-mutilation. I suppose I started learning then that before the children would make any progress educationally they had to have a relationship with their teachers, one which would help them to see the relevance of learning. For many, it was not happening in their lives outside school. School had to be a different place with some hope and a realisation that things could change. It was frustrating because of the numbers of children in the group and the rules and regulations of the school. I feel that education takes place twenty-four hours a day and school is only a small part of that, but in my first setting school was so important.

I left the school when I moved away from the area and started a family. I worked for a year in a small village junior school, again with a group of very difficult pupils. This was followed by three years in a nursery school. In both those jobs I was fortunate to be working in places which had a sense of community, and I think I realised the importance of relationship and personal attention. This suited me and the feelings I had already developed about relating effectively as a basis for teaching.

I came to my present job in this residential SLD school seventeen years ago. I have seen many styles of teaching advocated for our pupils and adopted plenty of them. To keep up to date and to move my teaching on I have been on many courses and tried to read the latest books. It has also been very helpful to visit other schools and talk to a variety of people who have worked with other pupils with autistic characteristics.

Over the years I have had to try to adapt to the different needs of pupils I have worked with. I have worked with pupils with autism who are verbal with echolalic speech but who cannot engage in social conversation, and with the non-verbal youngsters who have difficulty being understood and difficulty understanding what is going on around them. Most of these young people retreat from interactions with others. Their lack of early interaction skills and leisure or play skills I have found to be the biggest challenges in my teaching career. It is hard to sort out how to work with such a group of pupils. Ben, in particular, has made me think and rethink.

Ben was initially assessed and given aims and objectives in the core areas of English, maths and science. The other subjects in the curriculum were taught through topic work where activities were given to the whole group, though with individual targets. Ben was now a member of a group of seven children, though much of the work in core areas took place in a one-to-one setting, with the tasks broken down into small steps. He was brought to the table to work with the adult leading the session and recording the progress. Ben was always reluctant to leave his self-absorbed activity, showing resistance and lack of attention to the educational task. Once completed, he would return to his own activities, seeking little human contact.

I had been assisting with this group for some of the week, but I then took over, for a short period, as main teacher to Ben. I continued with the educational programme, working with Ben at the same tasks, in a one-to-one situation. The tasks were at an early skills level. Ben showed some progress because some of the tasks required ordering, sorting and matching, which seemed to fit well with aspects of his personality – his desire to fiddle with things, to do something repetitively. Even in his English work the tasks were geared towards matching skills using symbols. The symbols seemed to have no meaning for him, but he could be successful at the task. He had no interest in applying any of the skills learnt during the tasks though. He was simply being led by the adult through the task and when he had finished he went back to his own world of activities that he enjoyed and that had relevance for him. He seemed to make sense of his own activities.

Ben really made me think. I was beginning to be concerned at the way we were working with him. We were taking Ben away from his world and expecting him to work at tasks at the table. It seemed to be all teacher-led and Ben saw no relevance in the task he was doing. It was in an almost robotic manner that he sat through the task. He wanted it out of the way and finished in order to get back to his collection of objects. I felt our one-to-one time with Ben was being wasted and that there was no feedback from him. I did not feel that we were reaching out to him. We did not know him and how to help him to want to know us. The scheduled 'cognitive' activities presented to Ben at a table seemed to be more for the staff's benefit to do something at least and to justify our role as 'educationalists'.

These thoughts occurred to me even more when Ben was visited by an educational psychologist. She wanted to observe Ben in the classroom setting as preparation for the annual statement review. An activity was organised for when she came into the room. Ben was sitting at the table ready to complete the task, a simple sorting one to show the world what he could do. The psychologist watched Ben and then we chatted about him. I felt self-conscious about what I felt to be a sterile activity and wanted to apologise for our poor attempts to do something meaningful with Ben. I think the psychologist maybe felt that this was a forced situation too and noticeably relied more on staff's information than observing Ben.

My feeling was that nobody was listening to Ben. By this I mean that this was not the learning environment that would stimulate Ben to want to communicate. He had no reason to communicate with people, he could be led through this type of work and then go back into the only world he knew, his own. Many of the educational activities were ones that needed skills – eye-hand skills, visual skills, sorting ability and so on that Ben possessed already, or showed ability to develop; simple mechanical skills that were geared towards some of the characteristics of his autism. I was not sure that we were seeing the real Ben.

About this time, owing to some school reorganisation, I then changed classes to a different group. I felt frustrated that, even though I had worked with Ben for a short period, I had come nowhere near to getting to know him nor had even started to build a relationship. It seemed to have been an unfulfilling time for Ben and me. I had no idea of what made Ben tick and I thought it was my inadequacy. All these thoughts would not now leave me.

I still saw Ben in the playground, running around distressed or laughing, usually in isolation. He lived in a remote world with little human contact, not seeming to want or need it. I was pleased, though, when a few months later Ben moved into my class. I was pleased and I was also worried about it. I was worried that working with Ben and trying to reach him by working at table top activities did not seem the way forward, it seemed of little relevance to him and it was all a one-way process from the teacher to Ben, with little true involvement from him. I felt that this was my problem rather than Ben's. He was difficult to reach and none of the approaches used in our classroom seemed to be useful when working with him. It was my responsibility to Ben to give his learning environment some meaning. Somehow we had to start to get to know him and 'go with him', get a better quality of attention from him, help him to become more interested in the rest of us, learn to take pleasure in other people, be with them.

We had devised a programme for Ben to give him at least some means of access to communication. In co-operation with the residential staff we introduced a set of objects of reference to be used in both places. We considered the following points: could Ben reliably name and select objects and answer easily very simple questions using objects he was familiar with, and did he understand such cause and effect?

The objects of reference were objects that had some meaning attached to them. A cup to signify drink, a toilet roll for toilet, purse for shopping, keys for going out in the bus. Naturally we wanted Ben to touch the objects at the time of each particular activity. Our main aim, of course, was that eventually Ben would touch them spontaneously to indicate thirst, need to use the toilet, desire to go out on the bus.

We had overlooked that communication comes before language. Ben needed a desire to communicate before he would use this system to initiate communication. Ben was able to touch the objects at the time of the activity but not to use them to initiate. Maybe once Ben developed the desire to communicate, he would be able to use symbols as another means to express his needs and wishes. (Actually, we have persevered with the objects of reference since that time, using them as well as interaction activities. At the time of writing, Ben has moved on from objects and now has photographs/symbols in the school and residential setting, but only ones which he is strongly motivated by such as bath, video, drink, food, soft play, playground, bus.)

At this time, several of the staff, both school-based and residential, began to go on courses on working with an Intensive Interaction approach. After talking about the content of the course and our worries concerning working with Ben, the staff who worked with him in the school, including the speech and language therapists, felt even more that we were trying to give Ben a means to communicate but that he found the process of communication meaningless.

When working with our pupils it is important that all staff work as a team. The classroom assistants play a vital role in the school, supporting the teacher and working on the learning programmes with the pupils. They are also encouraged to develop their own individual strengths and skills. By building a team around our pupils we can focus upon individuals and the most appropriate and natural way to work with them. It was up to us to give Ben the desire to want to communicate and the ability to participate and initiate. We needed to assist Ben to develop pre-verbal skills such as use and understanding of eye contact, facial expressions, physical contact, body language, turn-taking – all these early abilities that are essential to the development of communication. Even though Ben could show many 'cognitive' skills, these essential basics to relating to other people were things he did not seem to know much about.

After the course and our discussions, and with some advice from Dave Hewett, we drew up a schedule of work for Ben, stating our intentions about what we would help him to do – give sustained attention to other people, learn more about enjoying giving the attention, take part in turn-taking routines with other people, learn how to have fun, be less socially remote, use and understand eye contact, use and understand facial expressions, use and understand physical contact, develop the knowledge that any noises he makes are important, and to use all these abilities in learning all kinds of things.

Ben was to be given one-to-one sessions of interactive play, with the emphasis on these as an enjoyable and positive activity that would only proceed with his participation. If possible, time would be found to record the sessions immediately. At the end of a week the records were to be looked at and an entry would be made on a progress track.

Getting started – early engagements

It was not easy to start. We had to learn to be sensitive and responsive to Ben's behaviours and to interpret potential signals. We had to learn new skills as teachers for this kind of activity. The sessions could not be planned in the sense we were accustomed to. To get a good session we had to go along with Ben and he had to have control of how long the session lasted and the way it went. We had to have a more responsive role and follow Ben's lead. We had to learn when to take a back seat and give him time to direct. We had to learn to have the confidence to observe and watch Ben for those moments when we could follow his behaviours. We felt it really important that we stayed alert for any little noises or behaviours that he might produce at any time. We had to be sensitive to Ben's world and how to interpret the meaning, and not try to make this into our session and get something we wanted. As teachers we are often too anxious to get a result and go into an activity with a pupil with a fixed idea of what we want to achieve.

At first we started being alongside Ben in his corner, attempting to 'play' by joining in with things that he was already doing. Ben had this particular part of the room which he had made his own from his start in the class. He would go around the classroom collecting objects which interested him, which would make good 'fiddles'. We found it difficult to leave anything around such as jigsaw puzzles or bricks because Ben would put them into his corner. Ultimately we went with the flow a bit and gave him a tin with a lid to put his objects into. When he was not working at the table in a teacher-led task, he would spend much of the day in his corner, and if another pupil went up to him or touched his things he became very distressed and started squealing. We found that the activities that were created with Ben in his corner were many, but here are some examples.

Ben was playing with coloured perspex panels, looking through them out of the window. These perspex panels were part of our science resources, but Ben liked them, collected them to his corner and into his tin. Gail started to play alongside him, putting the panels up to her eyes. Ben turned and grinned, giving good eye contact for about five seconds. Ben then reverted to his 'own world'. Gail felt that, although brief, the eye contact was good and direct. She felt that she had been allowed in briefly and it felt good, but that she was only allowed in on Ben's terms. She felt that Ben's interest in the perspex panels was a useful tool to use.

Ben was very involved with sorting through toys in his box. Don placed himself on his knees nearby. We often found that it was better to place ourselves fairly close, but not too close to Ben in order to get going, but moving in gently as he gave signs of tolerating us. Don simply went with everything Ben did, using a running commentary and imitating. Don was careful not to impose anything, which was a basic rule we made for ourselves. The idea was to get the activity right on Ben's terms. Whenever Ben gave Don the slightest attention, such as flicked eye contact, Don celebrated the moment by smiling or nodding or giving him big smiling eyes, or by saying something warm. Ben was very self-involved, yet Don got brief moments of attention. Don felt fine and relaxed. He discovered a useful skill – allowing himself not to succeed in fully getting Ben's attention. This was a difficult thing for us to learn at first, allowing ourselves not to succeed, but it helped us not to be too 'pushy'. Don had therefore resisted the temptation to dominate Ben to get his attention.

Ben was in the classroom taking his cars and pieces of jigsaw out of his box. He was busy matching the cars together and examining them. I went alongside Ben and started to copy him, matching up the cars. Ben paused and looked intently at me for about twenty seconds. He continued to allow me to play at his game alongside him and when I called his name he looked at me directly once again with a quizzical look on his face. Our play side-by-side went on for about five minutes until he gently pushed me away and I went. It was important that I moved away from Ben and his activity at his request. For Ben to be in control of the session and for it to be fun for him I had to respect his decision about when to end the session and try not to take the dominant role. Ben had to have confidence to enter into other communication/relating sessions because they were enjoyable and safe. I felt too that Ben seemed pleased when I played alongside him and he also seemed interested in why I was imitating him and enjoying myself.

Overall we were sensing that Ben did seem more aware of people around him than we had thought previously, but we were now getting ourselves 'more right' for him to feel okay about giving us proper attention. Our first few progress tracks were showing that Ben was giving eye contact without flickering his eyes, starting to allow staff to play alongside him and giving a turn. We found making entries on the progress track kept us focused on where we and Ben were going and the steps he was making in communication and whether he was initiating any activity.

Ben was running around the classroom giggling and I imitated his noises. He stopped and looked at me and started to giggle more. Then Ben clapped and again I clapped in imitation. Ben waited then clapped again becoming more and more giggly and playful. This felt like turn-taking, a conversation; it felt good. Ben had obviously enjoyed leading the game and stopped to give me my turns. It was a pleasure to see this happening, Ben being playful and having fun with another person.

Tony, the music therapist came into the room whilst all this was going on. Ben immediately stopped what he was doing with me and stood by Tony, indicating that he knew it was time for music therapy. It was interesting that Ben had led the session with me yet he was aware enough of his surroundings to stop when Tony walked into the room. He enjoyed music and we felt that we had to respond to his request to go to music therapy immediately, even though he was not scheduled for it. In Ben's way he had initiated a request, clearly to us, and we felt that we needed to respond.

As we were using this approach focused on Ben, we found too that we were becoming more flexible and confident in working with the group as a whole. We were observing better the behaviours of the other pupils and responding to these behaviours more sensitively. We were learning to take advantage of 'communication moments'. Slowly we had changed the way the classroom was organised. It became much more informal, one-to-one sessions were shorter and work was not necessarily taking place at the table.

The residential staff: Angela Curtis's commentary

Ben tended to stand in a corner in the living room with his back to the wall, he appeared nervous and anxious with jerky movements – squealing and clapping in a world of his own. He seemed to need his own space and did not appear to want to communicate or interact with staff. Ben made various vocal noises and sounds to indicate his feelings and moods. For example, during periods of agitation, usually apparently caused by not wanting to do something he had been asked to do, he would squeal and scream, stamp his feet and bite his hand.

Ben had various obsessional habits such as slamming doors and eating rubbish from the floor. His main interest within the house was to watch videos or, actually, the same video continuously throughout the day. On first meeting Ben it was obvious too, though, that he had huge potential. He appeared to have some understanding of spoken English and would happily complete simple tasks in the house if he was in the right mood. He had good life skills in the areas of dressing and washing, but he needed verbal prompts and encouragement.

Ben spent a lot of time on his own and chose solitary activities such as watching videos and playing with lego on his own. He became agitated and angry when another resident chose the video or when there was a change in routine. These periods of behaviour could last some time with screaming and stamping and dragging staff around and on some occasions pushing or pinching one of his peers.

On observing staff working with Ben it became apparent that we were not getting very far with him in this area. Staff appeared to get into endless power struggles with Ben that made them as agitated and angry as he was, creating tension and low team morale. Some of the staff within the house group had used Intensive Interaction previously in their work with another group and were quite eager to adopt this in the house for Ben and the other children. Initial discussions were held at the team meetings. Staff who had attended the course and used this way of working talked about the theory and their experiences with the previous group. We talked about the benefits for Ben and how we could adapt to make the changes. Some staff found the concepts and ideas difficult to understand and take on initially as they had fixed values and training which conflicted with the ideas of Intensive Interaction.

Every one agreed to give it a go, though, and we also agreed to be very open as a team, watching and observing one another and noting and giving feedback on what went wrong and what went right and the possible reasons – constructive criticism. The first area we looked at was Ben's interaction with staff and working without a set task or expecting an end result. If we didn't have any expectations for the session Ben couldn't fail and power struggles were avoided. We set up various activities and games such as water play and puzzles and toys. Staff would not ask Ben to join in but initially played alone next to Ben but making lots of noise and fun to create an interest. Ben would usually come over to see what was going on and then join in in some way. Ben then led the session as staff imitated his actions and his noises and clapping, usually working in front of him trying to gain eye contact. Any kind of positive interaction was responded to with copious praise, clapping, laughing and generally having fun with Ben. Some sessions lasted longer than others, but if he left after a few minutes this was okay. We knew that the session had come to a natural end and quality of time was more important than quantity.

We looked at Ben's periods of agitation and aggressive behaviour and agreed to adopt a policy of distracting and diverting his attention, defusing and recognising triggers and not getting into 'no win' situations. If Ben became agitated, staff used the activities he enjoyed to divert his attention, rather than reacting strongly to the inappropriate behaviour. The most difficult thing for staff was to realise that sometimes the way in which they reacted made a situation worse. This is why we had to adopt a policy of being open and honest with one another, without getting upset or taking things personally.

Ben's progress was good, he responded well to his sessions and began to instigate and seek attention and contact. He began to become more vocal, attempting to copy words. He was generally more relaxed and happy, which allowed staff to approach him and try out new things. We began to work on his self image, choosing clothing and doing mirror work. All areas of work were tackled in a fun and game-like way; for example, Ben brushed his own hair and staff's hair, looking in the mirror and laughing at different styles. If we had an objective or aim for the session it was important not to let it take over or for Ben to be aware that he was expected to do something in a certain way.

Lynne Knott's commentary continues

After three months working with Ben in this way we felt we were beginning to get to know his unique personality, his sense of fun, his creative and original personality. We felt that we were making progress with what we wanted for Ben and that it was becoming easier to get and keep his attention.

Ben was in the classroom, very involved with a ball and his box of bits and pieces. I imitated his play and noises and talked with him. He gave me good eye contact, recognising my presence, rewarding me. He clapped his hands and I imitated this, then he clapped again after me. After two minutes or so of this turn-taking, he walked over to the computer and gazed at the patterns programme that was on the screen and then looked at me. I asked him if he wanted to sit at the computer but he returned to his box of treasures. Was he telling me that he would rather I was somewhere else then – he was finished with the game? He had been very involved with his box in his corner when I started, but I felt that I got his attention and recognition of presence. I felt that Ben had showed me when he had had enough of my presence and I respected his wishes.

In a quiet classroom Helen sat with Ben with a 'wooden clapper', an instrument he frequently liked. It took a few minutes for Helen to get some reaction from Ben, but eventually he looked at her and they played an expectancy game, with Helen saying 1,2,3, hanging the 3 out, then clapping on the 4. The pauses were amusing Ben and when Helen asked him if he wanted 'again' or 'more' he handed her the instrument. She made a sign for her name and he copied her three times. Helen again had that feeling that they had established something, had communicated and that she was being let into his world. She had a lovely feeling of being emotionally rewarded by Ben. She felt that at last she had established something with him and that they were both gaining a lot from sessions together.

All of us staff working with Ben in this way found that we were creating a partnership with him and that the sessions meant as much to us as they did to Ben. We were really seeing him for the first time and enjoying his company and he seemed to be enjoying us. He was so much more relaxed in this more informal atmosphere and he seemed to realise that he could be appreciated for the person he was. He had shown us all by now that he could use eye contact, enjoyed fun, knew or had learnt how to take turns and was amused when we imitated him. His noises were recognised by others and respected. We could now be with him, doing something with him that pleased him and enabled him to give us attention for much longer periods than was possible before. To see Ben responding to us and wanting to actually be involved with us – and we felt reaching out to us – gave all the staff motivation to get to know him even more. It felt that it was a proper two-way thing between Ben and ourselves and we were having more fun in our work with him.

Ben had always been sensitive to noise around him but he was becoming more tolerant of other pupils and we found that he was able to handle noise more easily. On one occasion the classroom was very noisy with children screaming. We had learnt that this was not a good situation for Ben and that the noise and rushing around would be likely to cause him to become distressed. However, Ben went and sat in his corner with his box, then put a ball into his mouth, squeezing it to feel air rush into mouth. Barbera went up to Ben and tried to give him a toy. He ignored her for a while then looked at her and took the toy from her and put it down. He giggled to himself, crossed his legs and looked out of the window. Barbera asked Ben if he wanted to go outside into the garden and he smiled and skipped across to the door. Barbera felt that Ben was obviously disturbed by the noise in the classroom but appeared to handle it very well, another reassuring sign that Ben was making progress generally, feeling more secure in the environment we were offering.

Sometimes the adults in a classroom are so engrossed in dealing with the immediate situation that interactions and communications are missed. We need to create an environment so that resources are laid out for pupils to experiment with and be stimulated by. We then need the confidence to sometimes observe and look for moments when the time is right to interact with pupils, to join them in their world and use ourselves or the objects that they are using to play with and have fun, imitating and sharing time. By observing we can learn about favoured activities and try to share this with our pupils. We tried hard to learn the skill of combining organising things and activities, with being flexible and responsive at all times.

Following a swimming session Ben was busy dressing himself. Suddenly Maureen heard the sound 'Mau -ree' behind her. She turned round to face Ben. He had his shoe in his hand indicating he needed her to unknot the shoelaces. He had used a name to attract attention and asked for help. The exciting thing about Ben starting to attempt words was that there seemed to be a need for him to communicate. Ben took the key to Maureen and led her to the cupboard, he then said 'swee'. He was given a sweet from the cupboard. Ben was asked by Maureen whether he would carry the blanket for her. He enjoyed being pulled, rolled or swung on the blanket. He said 'yes' very clearly. It was time for swimming and Ben found his bag and said 'towel'.

Maureen was working with Ben and looking at musical instruments in a box. She had picked up a whistle from the box and blown long continuous sounds then she put the instrument back into the box. He looked at her and found the whistle from the box and blew long continuous sounds and then he started to explore with the sounds long, short, long, short. He had listened to her with the instrument and imitated her sounds, then he had explored and experimented using his own problem-solving process.

After six months, we felt that Ben and we ourselves had learnt plenty and that was no reason why we should not continue to move on with him. He had surprised us sometimes with his abilities. We found that he already had abilities which didn't show in his behaviour previously, but we also felt that by giving him the activities with an Intensive Interaction style he had learnt new skills for relating to other people and was starting to use them more generally. From his starting point, he had achieved a great deal. He was giving sustained eye contact and acknowledging the presence of others by laughing and grinning. Even though he was still mostly self-absorbed he was starting to give people attention, sometimes sustained attention. He was allowing others to play alongside him and share his activity – having fun with others. He allowed others to take turns when he was imitated; he was starting to initiate communication by making requests, even verbal ones; he was recognising the presence of others and accepting their presence; he was realising that the sounds and noises he made were important, respected and listened to; he was realising that he could have some control over situations; he was becoming more aware of his environment and letting people into his world.

Ben had made many achievements but working in this way had been a learning time for all the staff. We had found that by going to Ben and taking the lead from him, by responding to his noises, actions and joining him in his favoured activity, we were getting responses from him. We allowed him his own personal space and waited for the moment to let him start and decide the length of the session. In this way we started to have fun and take pleasure in working with Ben. It was also important that we realised that he enjoyed working this way and knew that we were having fun with him. There was a more informal and relaxed atmosphere generally in the classroom and Ben felt no pressure from staff. We were starting in Ben's world and he allowed us in.

Further progress and generalisation

We were getting new achievements with Ben during interaction sessions, but other things were also starting to happen that showed as progress. A new pupil started at the school, a young American lad, also with a diagnosis of autism. Barbera introduced Ben to him and asked Ben to say 'hello'. Ben touched his hand and leaned forward and put his cheek against his cheek. Later, in the playground, the new pupil threw the ball to Ben who promptly threw it back to him. A small incident, certainly, but it was wonderful now to see Ben with the confidence to take so much interest in a new person. Ben spent time watching the new boy and even touched him on the arm as if to say 'hello'. We had not seen him pay so much attention to one of the other pupils before. There was obviously something about this person that was attractive to Ben, but also it seemed that he had got to a stage where he could use some of what he had learnt about being with other people, in a new and different situation.

In a session in the classroom Ben came over and sat by my side. This in itself was a lovely thing to happen. He then ran over to his box and took out two coloured paddles which he put to his eyes. I went with Ben and he then put the paddles to my eyes, giggling. He then pushed my hands away and started to clap. I clapped, then he clapped saying 'd' 'd' 'd'. I imitated this and started giggling, but he then took hold of my hand and led me to the french doors to go outside. I felt like Ben had allowed me into his world and wanted to share an experience with me and then to celebrate the event. When he had had enough he used me to communicate that he wanted some space to go outside.

As can be seen in this example, around this time Ben started to vocalise more. We felt that he was making sounds to use them to communicate. Words began to have meaning for him. Any sounds or words that we heard from Ben were imitated and responded to. We often repeated the sound and extended it into a word we thought he was grasping for and waited for Ben to respond.

We felt that we did not want to formalise this into a 'language' session where we sat him down in the old way and practised sounds and words with him, but we did monitor the sounds he made and when he made them. We tried to be alert, using the sounds ourselves, feeding them back to him in our play. We went along with Ben's noises, made them important for him in our responses. One morning in the 'hello' session when we said 'hello Ben' he said 'pl'. Later that day he was sitting at the table and said 'Ben, Ben'. That week he was playing with sounds when interacting with people 't', 't', 'pa', 'pa', 'ho ho' and, when looking at a ball in his corner, 'bal', 'bal'. During circle 'hello' and 'goodbye' sessions when he heard his name we had lots of 'Ben' vocalisations. Ben's use of word-like sounds was continuing and he seemed to be using them for 'conversation' during interactions.

Barbera was sitting with Clare another pupil, looking at a book about dogs. Barbera said 'dog' for Clare. Ben was sitting close by and looked over to Barbera and Clare then at the book and said 'do', 'do' and then 'dog'. Ben was on his way out of the classroom. I asked him where he was going and he paused and looked at me, then touched the toilet picture and said 't', 't'. We were finding that our perseverance with our objects of reference and photographs of reference was now paying off, but especially now that we were working with Ben on things like giving people attention.

Ben was becoming more aware of what was happening around him in the classroom, or at least showing now that he was more aware and finding the ability to join in. We were finding that the more we worked with Ben in this way, and the more our engagements were pleasurable to him and us, the more he was coming out of his world and showing us that he had more verbal understanding than we had known. The eccentricity of his behaviours and the extreme self-absorption which was the basic Ben originally, meant that we had underestimated his ability to comprehend things – he did not have the behaviours which demonstrated his knowledge. There were, still are probably, so many understandings and abilities which simply did not show in his behaviour and could not show until he had learnt more about being with us, and sharing attention.

Ben had always been anxious in new places and would usually start making a distressed sound, when taken somewhere new. Even if the bus went a different route and he recognised that we were not going the usual way he would start a distressed squeal, over-breathing, wringing hands and flicking his eyes. This noise would get louder as the journey proceeded and no reassurance could comfort him. However, by now he was becoming less apprehensive of new places and showing more confidence.

We had a visit to a garden centre that he was not familiar with. It was explained where he was going and what he would be doing. Ben walked ahead of Barbera and into the garden centre. At one time Ben would have clung on to a familiar person unsure of the surroundings and not enjoying the experience. However, this time he led the way. They looked at plants which Ben occasionally touched. He was particularly interested in the winter cabbages and felt one for several seconds. We were to learn more later about Ben's fondness for cabbage. They then came to the fish tanks. Ben stopped to look carefully at the tanks. Barbera felt he was more interested in the bubbles than the fish. When they came to the tank of crabs Ben leaned over the tank, looked in then sucked up some of the water into his mouth. He then laughed out loud as Barbera exclaimed 'Ben!' He continued to smile as they left the fish tanks, occasionally clapping his hands. Ben had only been to this garden centre once briefly before, but Barbera had not seen him quite so confident.

At one point he walked and led the way around a corner. As Barbera called 'Ben wait', he stopped and waited round the corner with a smile on his face. Barbera felt good because Ben seemed very happy and relaxed and she had successfully stopped him with a verbal instruction. She felt that his self confidence was growing and that he appeared to be enjoying new experiences rather than being apprehensive and worried. She thought that Ben really looked about him almost as if seeing places for the first time. She asked him if he would like to come again and he clapped his hands and gave a little whoop.

I had a similar rewarding experience on a walk around a local park. Ben had run some distance away from me in amongst some trees. I called out his name and to my great pleasure he stopped his wandering, looked in my direction and then ran to me, taking both my hands and giggling. A small occurrence perhaps, but for Ben to start taking that much notice of other people, especially at a distance, when he was involved in his own activity, this was very pleasing. It was a very good feeling when Ben took my hands, a feeling of true relationship.

Ben was still having his interaction sessions in the school but this approach was now being used in many different situations, not just in Ben's corner. In the classroom Ben was moving around more, being involved more in different situations. He continued to surprise us with new utterances. One day he went up to the computer and said 'com pu'. We were able to be flexible at that moment and he was given a computer session. Our policy is to introduce signing to all our pupils at relevant times in the day, rather than having formal signing lessons. We hoped that some of our pupils would have another means to express their needs spontaneously, if the desire to communicate was there. During the computer session Ben was asked 'the man or the teddy bear?'. He was helped to sign both. It was becoming easier to teach him some signs because we were getting better at having eye contact and holding his attention. He then initiated the signing of teddy bear by pressing both arms across his chest and repeated the action, reinforcing his answer. He clearly wanted Maureen to see his answer and was determined that she should understand.

Ben was also continuing to put himself forward into social situations. He was watching intently as two classmates bounced together on our trampoline. Ben decided to join in and persevered in getting on even when one of the pupils tried to push him away. This pupil then not only gave in but linked arms with Ben, and then the three of them bounced together, holding one another and laughing hilariously. It was a joy to see this incident, to see Ben so confident and assertive with other people, taking part in a fun situation with such naturalness.

Ben was now initiating communication in virtually every activity and setting, and becoming increasingly comfortable with people being close to him, and clearly more and more enjoying physical contact. I remember an occasion where he was sitting next to me. I became aware that he was looking at me. I reached out to touch his cheek, saying his name at the same time. He reacted immediately with a joyful laugh, taking hold of my hand to urge me to stroke his cheek more, before interlocking with my fingers. I felt honoured that Ben was able to put his trust in me and that he wanted the relationship. I felt great joy that I was able to work with Ben, that I had learnt a way to work with him and how that was changing my thoughts about working with the whole group.

As we continued working with Ben, responding to his initiations, we found that he was able to respond to a system such as objects of reference. We found the more we worked with Ben in the Intensive Interaction way, the more attention he paid to such systems. He was more aware than we had realised. Soon we found that he could move on from objects to the more abstract photographs, and when the intent to communicate was there, he was able to use them. We used objects of reference then photographs with Ben in a natural and informal manner in a meaningful context with him.

Ben was still having his interaction sessions but we were finding that the sessions were becoming more and more successful and leading to interactions in all areas of his life. He was much more confident and learning how to relate to people and enjoying them. He was a pleasure to be with as we were beginning to be amazed at what he could do and how he tackled things and solved problems in his unique way.

Ben had begun to find other means to communicate than by showing distress and frustrations which could sometimes lead to anger. He had started to realise that when he communicated with people they were willing to listen and respond. They could not always resolve a situation for him but they were aware of his feelings and conveyed that to him.

On the minibus one day Ben was sitting near to the bag of vegetables we had just bought. He seems to particularly like cabbage, and we noticed that he was munching on a cabbage leaf. I told him that we were taking the vegetables back to make soup, so he handed the bag over to me. To our pleasure about five minutes later, Ben tapped me on the shoulder, made good eye contact and signed 'more'. I couldn't refuse him after he had asked me so well and I felt it important that his good communication was rewarded, though after two repeats of this I explained that there would be no more. Ben accepted this without the distress that might have occurred in similar situations months previously. I felt that we had negotiated successfully, that he understood and accepted the explanation. I felt that his ability to give attention to me helped him understand the situation, that he was not being 'fobbed-off'.

Problems

Ben had quite a distressing time for a period suffering from sinus trouble which caused him pain. Though some days he was again more remote, he did not go back into his own world and was still trying to communicate. I think because he now had more understanding of people, he realised that the people around him were aware that he was often in pain with headaches and sympathised with him. I think he felt people were listening to him.

Ben was also now approaching adolescence which would be a difficult time for him. He was having sexual feelings and he could not understand these feelings. He became confused, with pain showing on his face as he could not understand the changes in his body and what to do when he had an erection. He would run in and out of the toilet in great distress. However, throughout this difficult time he did not go back into his isolated world, though progress with him was more slow. He was still trying to relate to the world and his motivation to communicate was still there. It was more difficult to have good communication sessions with him when much time was spent rushing in and out of the toilet, taking clothes off and trying to push them down the toilet bowl. Naturally he was having extreme difficulty understanding what was happening to him.

We were distressed and frustrated by our lack of ability to help him understand, though we also felt that it could have been worse. He may have been so much more difficult and challenging at this time if we had not at least learnt to relate to him better in our work over the previous two years. Ben did attempt to communicate his distress. I remember him rushing in to the classroom from a visit to the toilet. He was very excited, taking hold of both hands of member of staff and placing them firmly on his hips. He attempted to pull down his trousers with staff member hands in place, looking directly into her face. His excitement turned to distress when member of staff removed her hands from his grasp. Ben tried to initiate several similar interactions with various members of staff. Staff felt that he was asking for help, he was asking 'do something'. We felt very inadequate as we could see no way to explain to Ben how to deal with his feelings. However, on the bright side, he had successfully summoned his communication ability to get some message across, even when highly distressed. Even at this difficult time of adolescence Ben seemed to be becoming 'hooked on communication' and we had to listen and try to respond positively to reinforce his motivation to communicate.

Advice was sought from a consultant on how to deal with sexual feelings in some of our pupils. It was helpful to talk through Ben's situation with her as we felt reassured that we were helping Ben through this difficult time of adolescence in the best way we could. We had to deal with each situation as it occurred and we were now better able to deal with them, not seen as a challenging behaviour, more a natural process which is hard enough for any adolescent, much more so for Ben. So many of our pupils do not have the necessary comprehension for a visual sex education programme or the concentration to follow through a picture sequence. We felt that we could reassure Ben, had to give him time and space and allow his routines that were developing when using the toilet.

Conclusion – where are we now?

We have worked with Ben now in this way for three years. He now knows so much more about communicating and being with other people than he did when we begun, but it is only a start. There have been many changes for us. We had to listen and respect his wishes and come up with some answers for him, learn how to be the right kind of communicators for him. Ben now initiates communication. He has the motivation and energy inside him to learn so much and we must work on this before it disappears into challenging behaviours!

We have to be prepared to go with Ben and his choices. We may have had an effect on some of Ben's behaviours which are characteristic of people with autism, but have not 'cured' him of it. Ben is no longer remote and isolated in this world. We have helped him to learn how to socialise and, more importantly, to want to, so that he is less self-absorbed generally, fiddling and far away. We think he now recognises who he is and that he is liked and respected for the real Ben. Ben is continuing to have sessions of Intensive Interaction during the week with different staff now following a move of class. We have recognised the value of using the Intensive Interaction approach to develop the early communication skills and have placed great importance on this and included this in our curricular documentation, as a way forward with our pupils.

Ben has moved into a class with staff who had already worked with him and with whom he had had Intensive Interaction sessions. They had been on courses learning about this approach and are firm advocates of it. The teacher in the group has a natural interactive approach when working with the group and as such the learning is presented in a fun relevant manner which is right for Ben. Ben continues to have his Intensive Interaction sessions. Interaction sessions also happen spontaneously at leisure times with Ben going up to staff to initiate interactions. Staff have fun together with Ben imitating and responding to him. Ben now gives attention to others, and he will initiate his needs and wishes to them, and his use of sounds, photographs and signing is a means to do this. He is aware of other pupils and observes them and wants to get to know them. When people walk into the room he does not visibly shrink away but he will go and stand near them as if to say 'hello' and to be introduced. He is much more aware of his environment than we ever realised and now he will respond and shows verbal comprehension. He enjoys being with people and wants to be part of a group though still knowing that he can have his own time and space. He feels that he is listened to and heard and that staff respect what he is trying to communicate and will if possible respond to this communication. Ben still has some of his behaviours, obsessions and unique routines, but he is not socially isolated and he seems to enjoy his life more. He is much more relaxed and seems at ease with himself and the people around him. Ben responds positively to an interactive environment and he is gaining confidence and his self-esteem is growing.

The residential staff: Ruth Kennedy's commentary

Ben moved into the house where I work just under a year ago and appears to have settled well. In contrast to his previous group, the group in No.6 are generally physically small and less physically able. This is quite a positive thing for Ben as he is quite nervous and has exhibited fretful behaviour in the past around his peers. He does not seem to find the group intimidating and thus he is able to relax more in their company.

Ben is showing ability to make relationships. Another young boy has only recently moved into the house. This eleven-year old is also physically small, so there is no immediate physical danger to Ben, in fact the only threat that this young man causes Ben is in a shared passion for videos (the former liking Postman Pat, which Ben objects to, as it is not Walt Disney).

One particularly amusing thing happened in only the last couple of weeks. Ben had gone to bed quite early and was asleep by 9pm. Staff on shift realised that they had not seen our new resident in some minutes and guessed that he had gone into Ben's room. Naturally they did not want Ben disturbed. A rather annoyed member of staff went to Ben's room to find this new resident and evict him. The sight which greeted his eyes was of this new resident knelt on the floor by Ben's bed singing the theme from Postman Pat very quietly as if it were a lullaby. Ben was lying very still watching him, but otherwise not reacting. It seems to us to be very positive

206

that Ben responded in this way rather than being intimidated or frightened.

Ben takes a great deal of notice over who is who in the house and despite having extremely limited speech himself he appears to know which names belong to which people, both staff and peers. I know that he knows that I am Ruth as staff have said, without the use of gestures, 'Give that to Ruth' and he will seek me out and give me whatever it is that the member of staff is referring to. Not only does he know his peer group by name, but he has also shown that he is able to recognise and respond to their needs. For instance, some weeks ago the group were spending some time in the Soft Play room, which is a particular favourite for Ben as he can be energetic in a safe (and therefore unrestricted) environment. A favourite activity in this room is a circular 'swing' which works by twisting round and round. Ben delights in getting up quite a speed on it, and he will spend a great deal of time playing with this one activity. After some time another member of the group indicated through gestures that she wanted to have a go. I approached Ben and asked him nicely if she could have a go, but he gently pushed her away and continued playing. I was a little annoyed at this so I approached him again, but I was careful not raise my voice, use any physical gesture, or try to remove him from the 'swing'. I simply stated to him that this other person would like to have a go and as he had been playing on it for quite some time could he possibly amuse himself with another activity. I explained this two or three times and then gave up and took her away to play in another area. After a few more turns on the 'swing' Ben then walked over to this young woman and gently took her by the hand and led her to it, as if to say 'I just wanted a couple more turns but I've finished now'.

Lynne Knott's commentary continues

Working with Ben has affected us as teachers and assistants. We have changed our organisation of the classroom so that there are more opportunities for our pupils to interact and for the staff to respond to these times. There is much less table top work and we go more to the pupils and go along with their speed of life more, giving time to do an activity and responding during it to their behaviours and noises. If any youngster initiates communication we try to respond and act upon it right there and then. This can have implications for a rigid timetable so there is a necessary balance between planning and responding. We have to be more flexible and try to look at the timetable so that we can change it to adapt to pupils' requests, whilst still getting through planned activities. There is more negotiating with our pupils about our pupils' day and we have to think on our feet more!

We are now finding that more of our pupils are being given Intensive Interaction sessions and we are realising even more how vital it is to work on those early communication skills. We are more positive about 'difficult' isolated behaviours, seeing the behaviours of our pupils as part of their personality, and we are more confident to go along with them now. This helps reduce their social isolation because we look for opportunities to join in with what they do. Some challenging behaviours we have found are usually a way to communicate. Many of our pupils communicate negatively in this way because they have not yet learnt a more positive way. We have to listen and find other means for our pupils to communicate and try to respond to any potential communications they have.

The classroom feels a much more exciting and interesting place and all the pupils seem to thrive and start to interact with the staff and other pupils, whilst still feeling that there is space and time to be away from the group. However, it feels at the same time as though the group is much more together, which is an achievement in itself given that the majority of the group have some characteristics of autism. It was a great reward when one mother of a future pupil chose our school because it felt right for him, his behaviour and his diagnosis of autism. We are much more confident when people visit now as we find that they more easily become involved with the atmosphere and the momentum of the group.

Chapter 11

Gary's Story: Parents Doing Intensive Interaction

Beth Taylor and Steve Taylor

Beth's commentary

There's a rather inane pop song that is currently being played on the radio which, although it wouldn't usually appeal to me, I just find myself singing whenever I'm with my 12-year-old-son. It's usually when we're sitting at the table and I'm feeding him his dinner, looking into his sparkly, big blue eyes, and the chorus of, 'You're gorgeous, and I'll do anything for you', spontaneously bursts forth. My son grins broadly and chuckles, puts his arms around my neck, looks deep into my eyes, and for a moment we enjoy a precious feeling of shared happiness. It may only be fleeting but it is definitely there. We are seeing more and more of Gary's feelings, and a greater variety of them too, but more important, and what is absolutely fundamental to our approach with Gary, is the sharing of emotions. This brings him in as a part of our family, and makes him one of us. It wasn't always like this.

It is a source of great pain (and it always has been and I guess it always will be) that because Gary has autism his natural tendencies are to find his amusement and stimulation in a solitary way, away from us. He also has profound learning difficulties, which hamper his opportunities even further and, on top of that, suffers (and I use the word deliberately) with very severe epilepsy. Getting to really know our son, and him getting to know us, was not easy. The early years were painful for all of us, with days building into months spent weeping for the loss of the son I thought I had. None of my grief, however, could compare with the distress and confusion that Gary had to endure, in a world that he couldn't understand, then made a thousand times worse by frequent seizures and drug changes in a vain hope of controlling the epilepsy. Those were grim times indeed.

I have a strange mixture of contrasting and conflicting memories of Gary as a baby. He was a beautiful bouncy baby in some respects, and there are the hundreds of photos that you take of your first born that prove he had the widest smile. When I look at them, tinged with sadness, I can hear his long baby chuckle and feel his strong sturdy warm body in my arms. What we didn't take pictures of, of course, were the endless screaming sessions (colic, the GP said), the many chest infections he had and, worst of all, the dreadful nights he spent crying inconsolably for hour after hour. I worried terribly for him then and, after trying everything I knew, I resorted to taking myself and my screaming, writhing baby into the bathroom as this was the only room in our terraced house that didn't have an adjoining wall to next door (and therefore would reduce the noise getting through to our neighbours). There I sat on the floor and just held him, for hours on end, trying to soothe him but feeling totally helpless and feeling utterly useless. Those horrendous sessions seemed to last and last, and we thought that they would never come to an end.

Frequent trips to the GP eventually led us to an indifferent and arrogant paediatrician who didn't even examine our son and wrote a letter for us to hand to our GP. Well, we opened that letter, and it described us as over-reacting parents who had a perfectly healthy child, saying it was our anxiety that was causing the distress in our son! Too wrapped up in struggling from day to day, and totally exhausted, we didn't have the energy then to pursue this ludicrous diagnosis (we were polite with professionals in those days!).

We moved from London to the coast, and the repeated illnesses Gary had previously had reduced considerably. Over what seemed a lifetime, but was only two years, Gary had gone from being a screaming baby to a quiet toddler. But this new quietness wasn't a relief, it was eerie and unreal, and left me with a permanent knot of worry in my stomach. All the mothers at the local toddler group delighted in exchanging amusing stories about their little darlings (I'm trying not to sound bitter about what was denied me), while I looked on with a growing sense of panic and, I'm ashamed to admit, shame and embarrassment at my strangely behaving son. Gary would find the oddest way of playing with toys, preferring to turn them upside down and examine the screws which held them together, or to line them up and then bang them up and down on a table top. He was amused by anything except how children were supposed to play with the toys, and he never came to me to show me things, or pointed at things that should have interested him to say 'Look at this with me Mummy'. He showed none of the shared curiosity that is innate in human nature.

All I knew at this time was that my little boy didn't fit in, and that I felt a resentment towards him because his behaviour prevented me from experiencing all the usual things new mothers should find themselves being a part of. Gary didn't show any interest in other children, or appear to be aware of the natural unspoken rules of socialisation. My response to him at this time was to rush over while he was seemingly aimlessly knocking Duplo bricks together, to show him how to build a tower with them. He would instantly turn away, uninterested. In the play-group at the local church hall, the other two-year-old children would be pretending to eat from the plastic plates or cook over a wooden box in the 'home corner'. All the time they were interacting with one another. Gary would wander in, find a yellow plate to spin, and wander off again, unaware of the social game being played in front of his eyes.

The cruellest thing for me was to witness my son as the permanent outsider, with children quickly drifting away from him when he was unable to participate in their game or play 'properly', as he just didn't understand what the social world was all about. Again, my reaction was to rush over to him to show him that the pretend food that wasn't really on the plastic plate, that hadn't really just been cooked on a box pretending to be a cooker, was 'emm, yummy!'. Gary's blank expression, and his eagerness to get away from the situation I was forcing on him, would yet again ring sickening alarm bells in me, as the many other instances had done from as early as when he could just sit up. My stomach would turn as 'Daddy' got home from work and called out 'Gary' but met with no response. Then Gary would see his Daddy and that lovely smile would spread across his face. I knew Gary could hear as the tinkley sound his dummy made always caused him to turn and look for it, but he didn't turn to the conversation going on around him. It may as well have been a totally alien language and culture to Gary, as he wasn't even aware it existed, let alone that he needed to be part of it to survive and thrive.

So I spent the first two years of Gary's life, before we got a diagnosis for his problems, trying to get him to play and behave 'like children should'. With my hand over his, I would make him hold a crayon and scribble over the paper. As soon as I let go of his hand, Gary would drop the crayon, wriggle desperately to get away, and any attempts of mine at getting him to look at the marks made on the paper were useless. He just wasn't interested and couldn't understand what on earth I was trying to encourage him to do. All my desperate attempts to make him play appropriately with cars, toy people and musical instruments ended in the same way – he would be frustrated and upset and so was I. It was a deeply distressing situation. Fortunately, a wonderful doctor at a London hospital then helped us to begin to make sense of everything when she diagnosed Gary as having learning difficulties and autism. Although to know that our child had a permanent disability was news which we dreaded more than anything else, it allowed us to start anew. But even then I didn't alter the way I worked with Gary, as although what I tried to teach him may have been different my approach was the same.

I made elaborate flash cards of familiar objects, but would he look? He didn't follow my point, even as the huge red siren-blaring fire engine went past. His interest couldn't be directed and the more I tried to direct the more he withdrew. All my attempts at making and shaping his play and behaviour to look more like 'normal' simply caused him to shrink away further into what was familiar and unthreatening to him. All my attempts were a threat to him, and I prevented him from being him. Everything he did, which was natural and a comfort to him, was met with my punitive reaction. The world I created for him, his whole environment, was a negative and unrewarding one. Although I never used the words 'Don't do things this way, do it like this! Everything you do is wrong!', that in effect was the message I was giving him, loud and clear.

I didn't stop to think of the distress I was causing Gary, only being aware of my own distress. I wanted a child that people didn't stare at with puzzled and disdainful expressions, and I thought that if I could mould his behaviour and play he would become that child. The more effort I put in, the harder he struggled. It felt like a battle that had to be fought and won, not my child that needed to be loved. He was an embarrassment to be hidden, not a beautiful child that we should accept and be proud of (and 'sod everyone else').

After one particularly traumatic 'play' session with 'Push the button on the toy here – Clap your hands like this' (my hands over his, his hands wriggling and sweaty to avoid the physical contact), Gary pulled away from me and ran to the french windows. He sobbed big tears, looking up at the trees in the garden, as though desperate to be there, away from all the pressure. I looked at him then and my heart, by no means for the first time, just broke. I tried to comfort him with words and cuddles but nothing could reach him. Gary just kept looking at the trees and his little body would stiffen and pull away at the merest touch. He must have felt so tormented and alone. What was I doing? It couldn't be right, not if it was causing him such distress. Not if when anyone went into the same room as him he would get up and leave. Not if whenever anyone went up to him he would avoid looking at them, leave what he was doing and disappear.

At that time, in fact, we had very little initiated eye contact from him, and no real physical contact. He never cuddled, couldn't stay on our laps for more than a second, and then it was something at best that he endured, never enjoyed. The little tasks he did learn were carried out robotically, systematically, and with a rush to complete them and be away. By 30 months we'd taught him to rattle through his 12-piece inset puzzles, match up the correct colour and size stacking eggs, match familiar objects to the flash cards, and stamp his feet and nod his head in time to a known nursery rhyme.

However, one day I accidentally altered the sequence of an action song and Gary carried out the actions without noticing I had changed the words. After a few more attempts at making sure he had heard me I realised, with sinking heart, that he had simply learned the actions by rote and hadn't understood the meaning of the words at all. The more I observed him doing all the things he'd learnt, the more I could see that they remained totally meaningless to him. It was a slow process of realisation that the traditional methods of teaching were wrong for Gary, that they were doing him and us harm, and that we needed to stop what we were doing and start somehow afresh. We looked at our son and wanted to help him, to gain an insight into his real needs, and to get close to him. I wanted him to be happy, to show contentment, and to smile with us.

There are a few important factors about Gary's development which would be useful to mention before going on. When he was two-and-a-half he started having major epileptic seizures and from the onset of these seizures it was clear that they were going to be difficult to treat and this was going to have a lasting detrimental effect on him. The first few months and then years of various treatments proved to have little if any real beneficial affect, leaving him now frequently plagued by severe seizure activity and by the after-effects of the seizures together with the side effects of the high levels of anti-convulsant drugs that he needs to take. The misery that this causes him is another story, but it is important to know that after he was left in status (constant seizure activity) for a whole weekend in our local hospital when the paediatrician refused to come in to see him, he ended up with further and severe brain damage.

He was about three years old when this happened, and it took us many years to learn to cope with this additional trauma, especially seeing him lose all the skills that he had learnt. He could no longer do his puzzles, derived no pleasure from (and even stopped watching) his old favourite videos, and familiar tunes fell on deaf ears. This was another reason why it slowly became clear to us that we needed to look again at what we were trying to teach our son and how best to do it. I say it was a slow process because initially, after his gradual recovery from being in status, we just wanted him to be able to regain all the skills that he had lost. I believed that in time this would happen. Even though I knew in my heart that it didn't feel right, I continued to persevere with the Portage mantra 'Gary will put the blue ball in the blue bucket; Gary will stack the beakers', etc.

I can't remember the exact moment it dawned on me, but somewhere along this tortuous route I realised that even when Gary had managed to learn a task, he never chose to 'play' in this way spontaneously. He never found satisfaction or enjoyment in the things he was being taught and shown.

A typical work session would go something like this. Gary would be sat on a chair in the corner of the room his back to the wall, with the table placed in front of him and me on a chair facing him across the table. This was purely to stop him from constantly getting up and disappearing around the room. I was once told by his class teacher that he wouldn't ever learn anything if he couldn't sit down at a table so there he was, trapped in his chair, with his sole aim being to find an escape route! I would then begin to try and gain his attention, show him an array of colourful toys, make his hands push buttons and press levers, trying all the time to catch that fleeting eye contact, but he was deliberately avoiding looking at me and just not interested enough to want to look at the equipment we were using. At the end of this tense session, he would break free from his captivity and, if not totally distraught (as he sometimes was), he would take solace in gently feeling the fronds of a Koosh ball or touching the eye-lashes of his dolly. Sometimes he would closely examine the toys left scattered on the floor where they fell (after he had thrown them far from the table), but he would turn them upside down and look closely at the screws holding the things together (this was far more interesting to him!).

So, I guess what I'm trying to say is that if he was able (under duress) to press the button on the pop-up toy, but never smiled at the effect, looked surprised or showed any inclination to repeat the process willingly, then what the heck was all this for? Where was all this leading? If my son was performing obedience tasks but remaining socially isolated, in a little tormented world of his own, then what we were doing needed to change radically.

We began by a process of elimination. We visited other schools, spoke to a variety of experts in the autism field, went on every available training opportunity, read much literature on autism (and in particular teaching social communication), and from all those things took away with us the pieces of information that we could usefully apply to Gary. It was the beginning of a long road to find and shape a way of working with our son that is rewarding for both him and us, finding out what really mattered when it comes to finding a quality of life for him. We really felt that we were getting there as we learnt techniques of structured music therapy and worked on encouraging his pointing and eye contact skills. This led us along a better path for quite a while, but it wasn't it. We were still playing the director's role and leading him for much too much of the time. It wasn't until we came across Intensive Interaction with its total philosophy of a non-directive approach that everything fell into place. It felt so totally right to be with Gary in this way, so absolutely natural and, from the response that Gary gave, we needed no more proof that this was how we should move on.

Intensive Interaction from an outsider's casual observation may appear to be completely anarchic! There's my son, flitting round the room, with someone trying to keep up with him. He's choosing not only what he plays with but how he plays with it and for how long. He sits on the floor and scrutinises a tambourine for a few seconds, throws it down, and the adult is just copying him! Now he decides to run into the next room and up she gets off the floor and follows him, not making him stay put! If this article was a video then I could rewind it and you would see the complete joy on Gary's face as he looks deep into the eyes of his companion. Yes, companion, friend, whatever, not a name one could so easily have applied to anyone previously working with him. While he's looking at her, he is making sometimes soft noises and at other times loud squeals of delight, and then he turns his head to one side, his ear next to her mouth, and listens intently to her repetition of those sounds. He makes more noises and again turns his head to listen to those sounds being repeated. He looks amazed. The expression on his face seems to say 'Someone speaks my language!'. When that person copies his patting the wall or jingling his bells, again his face radiates with delight saying 'And someone wants to play with me!'. When the adult narrates what he is doing back to him, 'Gary's touching his keys', she isn't just reinforcing his actions with words and giving names to those actions and objects, she is telling him loud and clear 'It's good what you are doing'. The message is unmistakably positive. He is content to have her near to him and he finds pleasure from another human being, it's not a threat to him any more.

Being more relaxed around people means he begins to take notice more what they do, and listens to different sounds too. He moves closer for a cuddle, climbs onto laps, puts his big hands either side of our face to turn it round to look at him, and comes up to give us big sloppy kisses.

Some people feel that it lets Gary off the hook, working with him in this way, "What's he being made to do?'. What those people fail to appreciate is that it is nevertheless really demanding for Gary to have another person so close to him for such an intense period of time. The fact that he enjoys that time as well shouldn't be held against him. And, of course, he is made to do things, like getting dressed, having a bath, and all the necessary things in life, but he does those things with a willingness and trust that we would not have had without the close relationship Intensive Interaction allowed us to develop. Communication is a two-way thing, for if it is to work those participating have to be aware of the other's needs.

Intensive Interaction is not about teaching adults a way of controlling our children. What Intensive Interaction helped me to develop was a way of communicating our requirements to Gary, in a way that is sensitive and respectful to him. So, when he's playing, absorbed in his activities, I don't just walk up to him, pull him up off the floor and expect him to come passively along, without him having any idea of what's happening to him (this is something I've observed too often enough in educational establishments, and then the staff wonder why the children can go berserk – wouldn't you?). What I'm aware of now is making sure that I approach Gary quietly, sit on the floor next to him, move my head to gain his attention and eye contact, then talk to him reassuringly about where we are going, show him his shoes, and only then hold out my hand for him to take and sit him on a chair to put his shoes on. Each step of the way I try to prepare him for what's going to happen next, to give him a moment to assimilate what's going on and why. There are times when he really doesn't want to be fussed or be bothered with complying, and on those occasions he can show brief flashes of frustration or just pull away from me; but he has learnt to accept that if I persist it's because I really need to, and he understands that – he understands me. Our two-way communication has worked.

The first time we abandoned the table and the chair in the corner, opened the doors, and allowed Gary to be himself, we found that he would move from room to room, oblivious of who was with him. He didn't show any sign that he was aware of the adult talking to him and he didn't take much notice of the toys and equipment strategically placed to catch his eye. There certainly wasn't any eye contact initiated by him. We had to contort ourselves into the most uncomfortable positions to get into his line of vision without blocking him from his chosen object. Occasionally we would briefly catch his eye and, in that fleeting moment, give him the biggest smile one could, accompanied by an exclamation of happiness and praise. Then there was his definite message of 'leave me alone'. He would do this by simply getting up and leaving the room, turn his back to us or, when we were being too intrusive, he would push us away very forcefully and all without directly looking at us. Neither did he voluntarily come and sit near us.

During one of those early sessions, I had been interacting with him for about ten minutes. I was exhausted and let a moment or two elapse, just sitting back on the floor watching him, when he turned around and looked at me straight in the eyes for several seconds with almost an expression of expectation which said 'Where is she? Is she coming?'. So he was aware of me then, and he did want me to stay with him. At that point I both physically and mentally relaxed, and realised that I could have been much more relaxed from the start. While it was important to follow his moves and imitate his sounds, it was just as important to allow him time to recognise that I was not intruding or interrupting, but giving him the opportunity to control my participation.

Gary was playing excitedly with a tin wastepaper bin, picking it up and throwing it down on the floor (it made a wonderful noise that reverberated around the room). When he made to leave the room, I picked up the bin and let it crash down. He looked on in total fascination when I joined in with this game, flapping his hands and grinning, waiting for me to pick it up again. Another crash and this time I waited to see if he would take this as the game was over and leave the room, or would his interest be

217

rekindled and he start to play again? He came back and patted the tin (another good sound!) then went to the edge of the room. I waited and watched him to see if he would want me to carry on. He came back and knelt on the floor near me, so I gently tapped the tin, making a faint pinging noise. This time he leant right over me and thumped it as hard as he could! We really enjoyed that! The more content he was to stay near, the less distracted he became, spending more time with the same toy, allowing me to join in his game for a moment, indeed waiting for me to finish so that he could have his turn, and so it would develop. He began looking at new toys offered to him, started to respond to his name (or the sound of our voices) by looking straight at us, and initiated eye contact and physical contact for the sheer pleasure of it. We learnt so much about Gary like this, understood him better and really discovered his lovely personality. Obvious results like this didn't happen straight away, although the immense feeling of relief was apparent in all of us immediately.

What's so great about Intensive Interaction is that it legitimises how we, as parents, always felt we wanted to behave with our son. It feels the most natural thing in the world to be with Gary in this way, and the only thing preventing us from doing this was the rigid indoctrination of the accepted professional approach. This couldn't see inside Gary, and those who asserted that approach only looked at this huge 12-year-old and believed that if he was treated like a social 12-year-old he would become one.

The whole philosophy of Intensive Interaction means that one doesn't need specific equipment, or an allotted time schedule. If Gary is sitting at the top of our stairs, holding a favourite toy or just rattling the banisters, I can sit and join him, talk to him in my language and his. We relish the warmth of our physical closeness and share his delight when I show him a piece of his favourite tinsel found behind the settee. He gives me a kiss to say thank you and disappears off to his bedroom, all the time singing to himself. He says 'thank you' a lot these days, in his own way of course. Like the time I'd fixed the ceiling fan in his room. Once it was whirling round again, I called his name to come and look. Well, I didn't expect him to say 'Okay mum, I'm coming' or to find that he would drop what he was absorbed in and come running, but the fact that he wandered out of our bedroom and fixed me a look was wonderful enough. He went back into our bedroom so I had to go and retrieve him, but he willingly took my hand and plodded down the landing to his room with me. When he saw his fan spinning, he flapped his hands and did a funny shuffle dance around the floor, not taking his eyes off the fan and just squeaking and beaming with sheer delight. What I wasn't expecting was how he suddenly stopped doing all that, came over to me, put his arms around my neck, looked into my eyes, and gave me such a sweet gentle hug and kiss. He repeated this several times and, however you like to interpret that, he was truly sharing his enjoyment with me. WOW!

Gary's understanding of words is severely limited and he uses no words or signs to express his needs or feelings. Yet his face is a mass of expression, showing really very complex feelings. Through the tool of Intensive Interaction we have become close enough to Gary to be able to fully interpret those expressions. I believe that it has also enabled Gary to (at least) understand the feelings behind the words we use, albeit in a narrow context. If that is the extent of Gary's communication then it has exceeded our expectations. It's up to everyone else now to make the effort to get to know him, to know the wonderful and loving child he has shown himself to be.

Steve's commentary

I can remember very clearly returning home from a conference on autism. It was the first time I'd attended such a conference, where everyone present knew something about autism, worked in autism, and was committed to spreading what knowledge there was. I hadn't seen Gary for a week, it had been a very long drive home and, when I rushed up to where he was playing on the landing of our house, he simply glanced at me and walked away. I was absolutely heart broken.

In a way I wasn't surprised when we had a handicapped son, although I'm still unsure why this wasn't a surprise to me. It may be due to my having worked with children with severe learning difficulties for many years before Gary's birth, so perhaps it seemed little different from what I'd always known. I met my wife when we were both working in an SLD boarding school and some people say that it must help us as parents to have the knowledge of professionals. Well, there are different aspects to that! We know how little many 'professionals' actually know themselves. An empowered parent, one who is directed towards knowledge and with whom professionals willingly share their knowledge (or lack of), will in turn become far more proficient than the professionals. We have come to believe that the true definition of a 'professional' is a person who admits what they don't know and then finds out about it or passes you on to someone who does. All too often we have come up against professionals (particularly in the health services) who don't know, and don't want you to know that they don't know, and you end up being denied access to the support you require. Decent professionals do exist, and they are well worth seeking out (and then hanging on to!). We have found that getting a label of being 'difficult parents' has not hindered us. In fact, it has been an advantage as we don't get mucked about and poor professionals steer clear of us.

As a 'professional' dad, now the headteacher of an SLD school, I didn't understand my son's problems for many years. We didn't initially have sufficient understanding of autism to be able to recognise the problems of our child, and no one around us did. When Gary was a baby we thought he was okay, and that his delayed developmental milestones could be attributed to the repeated illnesses he had. His inconsolable screaming we put down to some sort of dietary colic, and the fact that the slightest sound would wake him and he wouldn't go to sleep again for hours we just said was because he was an ultra-sensitive baby. The health visitor, local doctor, and paediatrician gave us various preparations to help with the screaming sessions (they treated it as colic), and then it was 'Stop worrying and get on with it'.

We moved out of the city to a seaside town a few months before Gary's second birthday and then the illnesses stopped, but the developmental advances didn't come. Gary even started to lose some of the skills he had developed, and Beth (my wife) recognised there were real problems well before I did (she'd worked in nursery provision for mainstream children). Finally, the local clinic said there was something wrong, as by this time Gary had even stopped talking. It was a learning difficulty, no doubt of that, but they didn't know what it was or what the cause was. The then school doctor examined Gary, as did the consultant paediatrician, but all we got was shoulder shrugging and 'We don't know why you have a handicapped son – you'll just have to live with it'. Because of our professional connections and a sympathetic GP, we were referred to a specialist centre at a teaching hospital, and Gary was formally diagnosed as autistic with learning difficulties. To get this diagnosis was devastating, confirming beyond doubt that we had and would always have a handicapped child, but we were then able to use it as a beginning, a way forward, to seek some answers.

At this time little was known about autism. To many professionals it was the 'middle class excuse for handicap' and little more. We set about researching autism in detail and soon found that there were many different viewpoints, including those who argued that it didn't actually exist. As a professional dad I set about devising programmes for Gary and we used all of the behaviour modification techniques that were advocated at that time (such as EDY), with continual phased prompts and rewards. For Gary's first Statement of Special Educational Needs we submitted copies of the developmental stepped programmes we were working on (all the early literacy and numeracy discrimination exercises). These must have been torture to Gary, as he was put through activities he could see no reason for by parents who were making little connection with him, and inevitably he rebelled against this. It was no wonder that when he saw me after I'd been away at that conference he showed no interest in me. What did I offer him then? I was one of those people who expected him to do things which were totally meaningless to him, and I offered little in return. Looking back, these were very dark days as we struggled for the answers, and all of us suffered.

Now, ten years on, we have a different child (although some people may have difficulty in recognising this since Gary's academic development has been very limited). However, I know that when I get home from work Gary will run to greet me, will flap or clap with excitement, and will probably give me a sloppy toothy kiss (all his kisses are sloppy!). He wants to be with us, his parents, and shows it. In turn, we find it so much easier to be with him, and we absolutely enjoy being with him. It is a wonderful turn-around. Eighteen months ago we nearly lost him when he was critically ill, in a coma with viral encephalitis. When told at the hospital at 2am one morning that he was probably dying, I promised the earth to have him stay with us a bit longer, and I still feel that we won the lottery that night as, with brilliant medical intervention, he pulled through. In the time since then we have enjoyed every minute with Gary, and he clearly enjoys being with us.

It still isn't easy for us. Gary remains doubly incontinent, has to be fed, and owing to his epilepsy he has mobility problems and sleeps extremely badly, if at all. He never goes to sleep before midnight, wakes frequently in the night and can't go back to sleep until we settle him again, and then

221

is always awake before us in the morning. Then he crashes in and out of sleep throughout the day. His 'play' can be very destructive, and we have a house with plastic plants, plastic fronted pictures (he's broken all the glass frames), everything screwed or blu-tacked down or to the walls, and with his favourite 'toys' (shiny tinsel, Koosh balls, activity centres, and so on) available throughout the house. Beth turned Gary's bedroom into a multi-sensory room, and he also has a playroom full of the things that will interest him. Every room has something for Gary. We know that if we can't get out and about as much as we'd like, at least he can be busy and stimulated in his home, where he can explore things at his own rate and learn for himself control of his environment. We live the life of a handicapped family. Gary's disabilities severely restrict our family life, and society's attitude towards us handicaps our family also. We like to think that attitudes towards disability are becoming more positive, but in the meantime we make the best of it. We have another son, two years younger than Gary who, fortunately, is bright and very capable, and he keeps us in touch with life outside of the handicapped world.

In the 20 years or so I have been involved in the professional world around children with Severe Learning Difficulties, things have changed dramatically, and there is much room yet for further improvement. The approach we presented to Gary has also developed over the past 12 years in line with many of those developments, although we feel that many professionals have yet to come to understand the full philosophy and benefits of Intensive Interaction (or a 'non-directive' approach as we call it in the broader form). We started working with Gary at home when behaviourist programmes such as EDY were in full flood. At this time it was thought that everything could be taught through a regime of initially prompting (and rewarding) the child through the action and then fading out the prompts (and rewards) until the child was completing the action for the social response (praise) alone, and without allowing the child to be seen to fail. It undoubtedly worked (and still works) in some situations and with some children, but it didn't work for all and there were considerable problems with generalising learnt skills to different settings or with different adults present. I also remember the 'direct teaching' methods such as the 'Distar' reading and language schemes, where we read directly from the American manual to give the lesson prompts to the pupils and they responded mechanically, until the desired result was gained (Teacher: 'What is this?', pointing at a picture. Pupils: 'It is a hamburger'). As with

EDY, this had its successes, particularly with giving a consistency and an understanding of what was coming next to children who relied upon routine, but again it often failed to generalise beyond the immediate setting.

Portage, another long standing scheme where the teaching prompts are set out for the teacher, is still very much in use. It now tends to be used in pre-school and in early years intervention, but the good teacher will use it more as a developmental checklist rather than a prescriptive ladder to follow (and most Portage proponents will readily concur with this). Locally, Portage tends to be used particularly where volunteers are used, and with the parents of children who are newly diagnosed as having learning difficulties. As long as it continues to allow parents the opportunity to enjoy their child, as well as to gain satisfaction from helping their child make progress towards the next recognised milestone, then it is on the right track. What mustn't happen is that each Portage goal becomes the be-all and end-all reason for spending time with your child.

As time went on less directive teaching approaches began to come to the fore. We first heard of this from Sutherland House School (a school for autistic children run by the Nottingham Autistic Society), where the staff employed a play therapist and were developing communication through a form of music therapy (see Christie *et al.*, 1992). The music therapy wasn't the 'express your feelings through the mood of the music' stuff, but systematic, structured and above all enjoyable development of receptive and expressive language. At the same time clinical psychologist John Clements (see Zarkowska and Clements, 1988) was advocating an approach to children with difficult behaviour that was much more sympathetic to understanding their feelings, asking why their behaviour was seen as a challenge to us and why should we always be directing them in the way we thought best. Later, speech therapist Helen Cockerill developed her 'Special Time' approach, where the therapist shadows the child putting language to the child's actions, and the 'Gentle Teaching' methodology (McGee *et al.*, 1987) became better known in schools. There were and are undoubtedly others.

All of these approaches have a common thread, each with a strong 'non-directive' element. We were implementing this common thread with Gary, but were perhaps doing so in a disjointed manner. We didn't have the confidence to take it that step further, to let the non-directive approach become part of everything we did with Gary and the guiding factor in his education, and it was at this point that I first heard Dave Hewett speak on Intensive Interaction at a conference. What I like about Intensive Interaction is the way it challenges the professional, if they don't accept its rationale, to show why a more directive approach is more appropriate and what results it produces. Intensive Interaction isn't a technique, it's a philosophy. Given that the totally directive approach has clearly failed so many pupils, as is reflected in those pupils whose behaviour is still a challenge to us, the challenge to the professional is now to make the change. We had further training on the Intensive Interaction approach at my school, and Beth and I have continued to work and think with it. Intensive Interaction gave us the confidence to do what we as parents had always wanted to do but our professional roles had stifled, to be with Gary and to react to him in ways which gave him pleasure, and consequently gave pleasure to us. To put it frankly, to do the things that parents should do. Intensive Interaction not only freed us from the 'we must direct him' role, it also helped show us that this was the appropriate way to educate Gary. We won on both counts, as educators and as parents.

Gary is autistic, and I believe that it is entirely possible to link the theory of a non-directive approach to the present understanding of autism. Autism is recognised (diagnosed) through what is known as the 'triad of impairments'. These are an impairment of the development of language, an impairment of the development of social communication, and an impairment of imagination. It is the last of these, the impairment of imagination, with its ritualistic and obsessive behaviour patterns, that can so inhibit the child's possible progress in all other areas. Using a non-directive approach will not cure this, but it can help prevent these self stimulating behaviours becoming so ingrained that they become a blocking agent in themselves. As first explained to us at Sutherland House School, the child interacts with the object (or action) to shut out everything else, as the response the child gets is controlled by them, totally predictable, and therefore safe. The first thing the adult has to do is to become as unthreatening to the child as that object or action is, and this is what Intensive Interaction allows us to do. Once the child accepts you as something that isn't a threat, even something that can give them pleasure in itself, you can start to introduce new objects, actions and tasks. You have then reached the stage that the 'directive' teacher starts from, in that you can dictate more of the actions of the child, but the difference is that you have a child who gains the stability they need from your actions and is therefore much more accepting of the learning situation they are now in. They will then much more happily accept some of the essential skills based learning that they previously rejected, responding to you as opposed to being directed by you, and enabling you to guide them through tasks and activities that would have been completely alien to their understanding before. In terms of the 'triad of impairments', you have weakened the strength of the impairment of imagination, that area which can be so crippling to the child with autism.

Using a non-directive approach is now more widely understood in the field of education. However, many professionals whose understanding of it is as yet limited often feel threatened. It isn't easy to revise some of the learning we have had, but once you start down along the non-directive route it gets clearer all the time, and the results can speak for themselves. Although we still have problems with challenging behaviour at the school, as with Gary at home, these problems are very considerably lessened, both in frequency and severity. At my school some of the staff tried some non-directive sessions with some of the most able and socially interactive pupils and were staggered with the way these pupils felt truly empowered to make choices. We'd always believed we give them lots of opportunities to make choices, but all too clearly we now see that the range of choices was very artificially limited, and the real world offers far more scope and opportunities for choice than we were ever presenting to them.

Since we started fully on the non-directive route at home, Gary has developed dramatically. He still can't speak, can't feed or dress himself, and can't take himself to the toilet. On the other hand, we have a child who is happy to be with us (and even seeks us out to show this), who trusts and allows us to take him into new situations, and who lets us introduce him to new things. With all the horrendous problems that his epilepsy brings him, he now knows to trust us to comfort and care for him, he doesn't have to suffer in isolation (and suffer all the worse for this). It doesn't matter that it was nine months before he chose to set off the bubble tube in his bedroom by himself, or that he's only just decided to use the switch that operates the coloured light tube over his bed (in both cases after we'd repeatedly taken him to them and shown him how to operate them – which he allowed us to do), as he is making progress.

Where we go from here with Gary is clearer to us. We go on together, albeit with our lives built around his needs. We enjoy him as a person, and he enjoys us as his family and friends. He makes progress, and he undoubtedly copes with the trials and tribulations of life more effectively than he has ever done before. He's happy, therefore we're happy.

References

Christie, P., Newson, E., Newson, J. and Prevezer, W. (1992) 'An interactive approach to language and communication for non-speaking children'. In: Lane, D. and Miller, A. (1992) *Child and Adolescent Therapy: A Handbook.* Buckingham: Open University Press.

Cockerill, H. (1991) *Communication Through Play: Non-Directive Communication Therapy – 'Special times'.* London: The Cheyne Centre.

McGee, J.J., Menolascino, M.D., Hobbs, D.C. and Menousek, P.E. (1987) *Gentle Teaching. A Non-Aversive Approach to Helping Persons with Mental Retardation.* New York: Human Sciences Press.

Zarkowska, E. and Clements, J. (1988) *Problem Behaviour in People with Severe Learning Disabilities: A Practical Guide to a Constructional Approach.* London: Croom Helm.

Chapter 12

Francesca's Story: Facilitating the Earliest Developments

Ian Bruce, Antonella Bruce and Dave Hewett

Ian's commentary

Francesca is the third of our three children, born on 17 December 1992 at 11.15 am by Caesarean section. She weighed 6lb 12oz and looked like ET. We called her Francesca Guilia, after Antonella's grandmother, and after checking she had all the right bits and pieces we sighed with relief that our family was complete and that we could go on with our lives. It was only later that we realised that our life, as a family, would not be continuing but rather starting afresh as a new life, different from the old one, and much of it would be dedicated to Francesca and her needs. This is our story so far and it represents, as closely as we can make it, a true representation of how Francesca has grown and developed, our feelings and emotions and our activities to help those processes. We have also tried to give an idea of the effect the whole affair has had on our family and the way we see the future for us.

When Francesca was born she weighed much less than we expected. Our previous children had all been big babies and we had been led to assume that Francesca would be the same. However, instead of the 8 or 9lb baby that we had been expecting, she weighed much less. In fact, Antonella had lost weight during the last few weeks of the pregnancy and, although we attached no significance to this at the time, perhaps it had been Francesca rather than Antonella who had lost weight. To all intents and purposes, Francesca looked, and seemed to act, like a normal baby who was just a bit smaller than we had expected. The first issue that alerted Antonella to the fact that all might not be well was that Francesca did not suckle well and would not feed – or did so only with great difficulty. In fact, in the first few days after Francesca was born, Antonella tried breast feeding, expressing breast milk and then using a supplement baby milk to induce Francesca to feed. Rather than putting on weight and growing, Francesca actually lost weight, a fact which we were initially told was normal but which, as time progressed, became more and more obviously abnormal and worrying. Feeding Francesca became an enormous effort and took up tremendous periods of time. To get Francesca to drink as little as 50ml of milk would take up to two hours and most of Antonella's time was dedicated to trying to get her to take any form of food. Also it frequently happened that she would be violently sick immediately after feeding, effectively negating all of the previous effort.

The constant effort to get her to feed definitely started to create stress and tension. In the hospital, this difficulty of feeding was alternately described as either 'some babies are like this' or 'you are not breast feeding correctly', even though Antonella had previously breast fed our other two children. At the end of this period, the first two weeks, Antonella was discharged from hospital and sent home with Francesca and it was about that time that Antonella started to suggest there could be something abnormal with Francesca, although I put the difficulty with feeding down to just the normal variation that you might expect to find between children. It was only much later, when the problems with Francesca were much more apparent, that we learned that handicapped children were often difficult to feed as babies and that this could be an early indicator of problems with a child.

The other thing which was also apparent from about the second or third week was that Francesca did not engage in eye contact with, in particular, either Antonella or myself, nor our other children or other individuals involved with her. Once again it was Antonella who initially raised this as a possible concern although I did not then see it as a problem. At the time, I found every opportunity to suggest to Antonella that she was worrying about nothing and was concerned for no good reason.

Also, within the first month it became apparent that Francesca was not moving as much as we would have expected, given our experience with our other two children. She would lie immobile in her cot and not make the usual attempts to move, and this was also worrying.

All in all, by the end of the first or second month, Antonella was convinced that something was wrong with Francesca and that we ought to be seeking advice about her general condition from specialists who might be able to help. I did not want to admit to myself that something could be amiss with Francesca, but was equally happy to support Antonella in any way that could help to put her mind at ease or aid Francesca.

In terms of our family life, these first few months saw an almost exclusive devotion of Antonella to Francesca and this was particularly so because of her difficulty to feed. No sooner had one feeding session finished then another began because of the length of time it was taking to get her to take even a minimum level of milk. Additionally, Francesca slept very badly and suffered a great deal from colic – most nights we were up continually. I certainly felt, and feel, whether or not it was true, that we were neglecting our other children and that our family routines had become twisted to meet Francesca's needs. However, this was tempered by the memory that of our other two children, Caterina and Marco, one had been extremely demanding in a similar way with respect to sleepless nights.

During the first few months of Francesca's life she was also constantly unwell with either coughs or colds and was continually prescribed antibiotics from birth to the age of almost six months to combat one infection or another.

Frighteningly, we used to follow her progress on the charts used to monitor child development in terms of weight and height only to see her consistently falling below the fourth centile, obviously well below average. In fact, the developmental curve that she was following was increasingly divergent from what was desirable or expected.

The most worrying thing about this initial period was the feeling that maybe there was something wrong with Francesca and that we should have been doing something about it but were not, and that as a result she could be getting worse or would ultimately require more time and effort to recover from it; or, even worse, that she might never recover from it.

Luckily, our other children did not seem to mind that we were spending so much time with Francesca rather than with them and, since we never made an issue of our worries, they treated Francesca normally, just like any other baby or the 'normal' sister they had been expecting. Additionally, my parents, who live five miles away in the next village, were always on hand to keep Caterina and Marco busy if we felt that we needed a break or they felt we were neglecting them!

It was really when Francesca was about six months old that we started to be proactive in seeking advice and support for her lack of physical progress, interaction and communication development. At this point,

Francesca had not yet sat up unaided and had done hardly any of the things a 'normal' child would be doing by that age. I remember all our relatives and friends repeatedly doing their best to reassure us that nothing was wrong and that she was just a bit slow. All we felt, though, was an increasing panic and a growing unease that something was badly wrong.

The first proactive thing which we did in attempting to find out what might be wrong was to get an appointment with Francesca's paediatrician at the local general hospital. My first impression of the paediatrician was that he was pleasant and well meaning and I can clearly remember him saying that, although Francesca lacked muscle tone and did not respond as much as she ought to his attempts to interest her, she was just a bit slow and would be okay. I am not sure whether either of us felt reassured or more worried as a result of this verdict, and Antonella decided that she had to start to potentiate Francesca's physical development and abilities by dint of her/our own efforts.

Looking back now, four years on, watching Francesca running around our kitchen or the patio, interacting inquisitively with things and people, I wonder what would have happened if Antonella had not been so persistent, single minded and clear about what she wanted to do, and motivated to make it happen, on Francesca's behalf. Through the paediatrician at the local hospital, Antonella got access to physiotherapy and started to take Francesca, once a week, for a session with one of the hospital's physiotherapists. At the very beginning, when Francesca was very small, the physiotherapist came to our home. Antonella would spend hours with Francesca repeating the exercises which she had been shown by the physiotherapist who was trained in the 'Bobath' technique which, we learnt, was especially useful in aiding child development.

Antonella contacted the local Special Needs School and got access to the pool for Francesca to go swimming and she also started using the other school facilities to try and bring along Francesca's development. These included the games room, the dark room and a room where sounds and colours and moving shapes could be made. Although she was still less than a year old, we had already made the assumption that something was wrong and that we should try to do something about it. I suppose we were not, and still are not, the sort of people to sit back and let things happen on their own, but rather tend to reach out and make an extra effort to sort things out. In retrospect, I imagine that this has been good for Francesca and has helped rather than hindered her development. I also remember that when Antonella was at the Special Needs School pool she would help the teachers and assistants with the other handicapped children and this also got us and Francesca accepted more quickly within the community of which we are now a part.

One instance of this period stands out in my mind. Care for Francesca was passing from one paediatrician to another at the local hospital and, at her first meeting with the new paediatrician, when Antonella was questioning what we could do 'extra' to support Francesca, she was told to concentrate on our other children since Francesca would never even be likely to sit up unaided and why should we 'waste' the time on her.

Effectively at this point, Antonella's day was to take the children to school (and at that time this was five miles from where we lived, through heavy traffic, a journey of 45 minutes in rush hour) then go straight on with Francesca to one activity or another. She would not usually get home until after collecting the children from school and would often be out for eight or nine hours a day. It was tremendously exhausting and stressful and I remember that this, coupled with the problem of feeding and not sleeping – and a sort of primeval fear of the unknown, that something was wrong – left us both exhausted. We argued frequently and often for the most trivial of reasons. I do not know what effect, if any, this had on the other kids, but whenever possible we would do things with them and be with them – maybe almost in a compensatory way – to try and make them realise that we were all still a family and that they did belong as well. My parents helped tremendously in this respect because they would have Francesca for a few hours to give us such opportunities.

I do not think Caterina or Marco had any appreciation or understanding of what was going on and we certainly never intimated to them that Francesca was in any way different from other children. In fact, both Caterina and Marco accepted Francesca as their baby sister without any problem and it was not until much later that either of them became aware that she was different. When that awareness did come it was more a sort of 'why can't Francesca do what Simone (Francesca's cousin of approximately the same age) can' or 'why doesn't Francesca . . .' etc.

To return to the story of Francesca's physical development, one thing I vividly remember is being with Antonella playing with Francesca on the bed. Invariably Francesca would be immobile and non-interactive, although she would kick her legs and throw her arms about.

Over a period of months we worked on getting Francesca to roll over, taking her time and time again through the motions, leading her, a bit like two conductors, through what we had been shown by the physiotherapist. Slowly, almost imperceptibly, she started herself to follow the movements that we made with her limbs, but it was a long, long time before she managed to roll over. When she did we had the most incredible feeling of something being achieved. This confirmed our belief that she was capable, and that ultimately what she might achieve would depend in good part upon what we could, or were prepared to, do to help her.

By this point, at approximately nine months old, although Francesca was not interactive with people, or mobile, she would handle and examine objects with intense interest and considerable dexterity. She still could not sit up unaided or vocalise, in fact she hardly used to make any sound other than crying and screaming.

We decided that we needed a second opinion as to Francesca's condition and what we could expect for her future, and asked her paediatrician at the local general hospital to refer us to another consultant. It so happened that our local hospital had links with Guy's Hospital and the Newcowen Centre, which is the unit at Guy's linked with child development.

Every so often, one of the consultants from the Newcowen Centre would visit the hospital and assess the condition of certain children with special needs or other problems and it was suggested that we might like Francesca to be assessed. We agreed instantly and an appointment was set for several months in the future. In the meantime, we continued with the usual activities, trying to help Francesca's development. By this time, we were also involved with Portage, who were supposed – at least in principle – to help organise support for us for Francesca. I think at the beginning Portage was good and helpful, but maybe as our expectation for Francesca grew, as we saw her improve, their usefulness and ability to help decreased in our eyes.

Antonella was also involved with occupational therapy by this time and we had made contact with our local Autistic Society since the idea had already been planted in our minds that there was the possibility that Francesca could be autistic. We had no knowledge of what this could mean as neither of us had any experience of autism. We had a rather vague idea that being autistic meant that you were just a bit strange, that you could get fixed on certain things or were very good at certain activities such as painting or music. It sounds stupid in retrospect, but the idea that

232

Francesca might be autistic did not set any enormous alarm bells ringing in my mind; but I do remember clearly at about this time, approximately nine to 12 months, thinking, 'Why us?' 'Why me?' 'Why Francesca?'.

Living in the same road as us at the time were some friends of ours, Peter and Ruth. By coincidence, Peter was the headmaster of a local Special Needs School who had a severely handicapped son, and I used to think 'there but for the grace of God' and actually feel grateful that I could not understand or appreciate their problems. I used to feel this way most clearly when we were walking past their house. The reality of the situation we were finding ourselves in was that we had become like them, and one of our worst nightmares was coming true.

The time eventually arrived for our appointment with Richard Robinson from Guy's Hospital Newcowen Centre for Francesca's assessment at our local hospital. I cannot really relate how I actually felt but both Antonella and I were extremely nervous. Professor Richard Robinson turned out to be an extremely pleasant individual who exuded reassurance and confidence mainly because he did not try to console us with platitudes or say that there was nothing wrong. He examined Francesca thoroughly and I remember him holding Francesca and her playing with his glasses. At the end of the examination we both wanted to know what his views were and if he had a prognosis. At this point, the nurse who had been present throughout Francesca's assessment took her from Antonella and left us alone with Richard. Although I do not remember all he said I clearly recall him saying that Francesca had a learning disability and that it was quite severe. I also remember thinking, well that's okay then, if all she is going to have is a problem with learning then we have no worries. How simplistic – only later did I realise that learning disability is the current phraseology for handicapped. I remember Antonella crying but was still thinking that it was not that bad really, and that my worst fears had probably been unfounded. Antonella was so upset, though, that I too became worried and disturbed and I did not really know what to think or do.

On our way home we did not speak much, but when Antonella did it was to remark that we would really have to work and that we would make it right and that she (Francesca) was going to be okay.

Antonella's commentary

In the first year, I felt that Ian and I were vainly attempting to find out what was wrong with Francesca and that it was a problem to even get people to agree that there was something wrong! It is difficult now to remember exactly what happened during Francesca's first year mainly because life has been so full since and maybe because I do try and forget the experience. However, I feel quite certain that I knew that there was something wrong with Francesca from almost the moment she was born, she just didn't feel right. She didn't feed, wasn't looking, she didn't respond like the other two children did – and that was from day one. What may have made me feel worse was that I felt that I was having to convince everybody, including Ian, that this was the case.

My main feelings about, and memories of, the first year apart from the feeding problems are illness, worry and searching for an answer and a direction. I can't say that I really remember playing with Francesca much as such because of everything else that was going on but I was spending an enormous amount of time with her. I know I was talking to her a lot and that Marco, in particular, our second child who was two and a half at the time, was particularly close to her. I especially remember that he would frequently climb into her cot and lie in it with her.

I do have particular glimpses of specific memories. For example, I would be waiting outside Caterina and Marco's school and I would be playing with her and the other mums used to join in. I can't say that it was the same sort of play interaction that I'd had with the other two at that age, it was more a sort of attention giving and I'm sure that her response was not very pronounced.

One thing that helped a lot in the first year was that at about six months I went home with Francesca to Italy, at the beginning of June. I'm sure that in one sense I was thinking, I'll go home to mum and be 'safe', and I took the other two children as well. It did help me tremendously, and probably, as a result, Francesca too.

In the first year, as well as all the other activities, I started trying to develop Francesca's communication skills. To begin with, I had help from Portage, as the person assigned to Francesca would help me.

One of the first things we tried was offering her things like particular toys that she would be preferentially playing with, or a rattle, or keys, and not give them to her until she looked at them. I would hold these things between her head and mine, in my line of sight so that she not only had to look at the object to get it but also at me and my face. Something that she didn't do very much was to look at people, even though she would spend ages looking at, and playing with, inanimate objects.

Another thing that I started doing, this time with the speech therapist, was to sit alongside Francesca in front of a large mirror and try to get her to copy my actions. I would hold her hands and move them so that she could see herself moving in the mirror. Another thing was to try and get her to reach for her reflection. All these activities were attempts to get her interested and, through that, get her copying.

As well as the above I used to try clapping and tapping to get her to copy what was going on. To begin with there wasn't very much response from her and I suppose even now there's not a great deal, although it's much more than before! If she ever did respond by copying what I was doing then I would try and 'take turns' with her so that when she stopped whatever it was I would start again – and so on.

I also started to learn Makaton – the sign language – because I was told by the speech therapist that some children find this a facilitator for communicating. To begin with I tried to get her to make the sign for 'more'. I'm still trying to do this four years later even though she can now very easily and ably let you know when she wants something by screaming!

The speech therapist also gave me a few flash cards. Flash cards are like playing cards but with a picture. The ones I used were of a red ball, rattle, keys and a red beaker – Francesca has always liked and seems to respond to the colour red. I would hold the flash cards up and when she responded to them would reward her with the real object. Once again to begin with there wasn't much specific response – she just used to try and eat them!

Finally, I tried to start to introduce her to the idea of choices – biscuits, drinks and toys etc. I would hold the objects up in front of my face in her line of vision so that when she reached for whatever it was she was not only looking at the object but also my face.

Later, during her second year when I felt that Francesca was beginning to respond more and interact with me, I remember talking with the speech therapist and wanting her confirmation that what I was seeing was real. I wanted to repeat the exercises and interactions that I was doing alone with Francesca with the speech therapist so that she could tell me if I was imagining things or not. For a while I was really concerned that I was making things up about Francesca's responses because I wanted to see her doing things so much. In the end, I think I reached the position where I felt that if I believed there was 'something there' and if I believed that she was 'answering me', responding, understanding, it did not really matter what anybody else might think. I strongly believed that if I did whatever it was with Francesca often enough and with enough strength then ultimately something would happen.

I suppose I fundamentally believe that if you want things to happen badly enough, then they do. I'm like that. With respect to Francesca, I have always believed that the only reason why she may not be able to finally achieve something is because I can't control everything she is and does. Fairly radical I suppose!

I can't remember exactly when Francesca really started being what I would call interactive. It was certainly the case that for much of the first two years Francesca was 'switched off' much of the time. For example, on most occasions you could move your hand in front of her eyes and she would not respond, but suddenly, very occasionally, you would get a response when her eyes would follow your hand that seemed to say 'hey I'm here I'm awake', suggesting there was something there waiting, maybe wanting to be drawn out! A friend of ours also commented that Francesca was 'with it' sometimes more than others. I was encouraged by the fact that somebody else could see what I did since usually others were not with her as much as I was and they missed the few moments when something positive happened.

Slowly, the time when she is 'switched on' has increased and I have learnt to recognise it better and better. Now, I think, at the age of four and a half, she's 'switched on' mostly and 'not there' sometimes.

Ian's commentary continues

Shortly after Francesca's assessment we went on holiday to Italy for a month. Antonella's parents and all of her family live in Italy. Although we had been explaining to Antonella's relatives what had been happening with respect to Francesca, they did not and could not have properly understood what that meant practically, in terms of her condition or the way she appeared. I think I was dreading the holiday because of this. By now, at home, we were surrounded by people used to the fact that

Francesca had problems and needed help and I wondered what it was going to be like in Italy.

Needless to say, it was a month of people and relatives looking at, and in their own way assessing, Francesca. I remember comments such as 'There's nothing ever happened like this in our family' and 'I've read that in England people who live near nuclear power plants can have these sorts of problems'.

This is not meant to suggest that Antonella's parents were not supportive or understanding, it is just that what we really needed was a holiday and I certainly did not get one! To be fair, though, I think it was good for Antonella and that she felt better just by being with her family for a while. It was when we returned to England that things began again in earnest.

The next thing that we did was to get a second opinion about Francesca's condition. We went to the Great Ormond Street Hospital for Sick Children and basically had Richard Robinson's judgement confirmed. Francesca was handicapped and possibly autistic, but no definitive diagnosis nor a clear prognosis could be given.

Meanwhile, Richard Robinson had arranged for Francesca to be admitted to Guy's Hospital for a full medical assessment including a MRI scan, lumbar puncture and EEG as well as genetic testing for hereditary disorders. After all this testing, it was reported to us that everything seemed normal, that is, nothing could be found that was obviously wrong! For the first time, we realised just how little is known about the brain and brain function and how crude the methods are for gathering information about such matters. As we left the hospital, I remember Richard saying that there was not much more that he could do for us but keep in touch! We both felt very alone but every so often we still see him and his colleagues to check on Francesca.

At this time, when Francesca was about 18 months old, we started to think about the benefit of what an 'intensive therapy regime' could offer her. We had seen a programme on the television about a centre close to Chester, the BIRD Centre, which helped in the rehabilitation of children with brain injury, both accidental and congenital. I contacted the Centre and was sent some literature. We also bought the book authored by the Centre founder – David McGlown – discussing his philosophies and the work of the institute.

In discussions, the Centre staff said that the television programme had generated so much interest that there was no way that they could see Francesca for at least two years. They also said that they would need to assess her prior to accepting her. Cynically, even then, at the outset of our finding out about these things, we thought, well, they'll only take her if they can make her better otherwise we will not be a very good advertisement for their activities. Also, it was not cheap! Our other children were at private school and we did not have any spare cash. But, one way or another, if we had thought that it was a good idea we would have found the money, so we registered our interest. That was three years ago and we still have not heard from them.

At about this time, Antonella raised the issue of intensive therapy with the physiotherapist assigned to Francesca. Immediately she said that the Local Health Authority was totally opposed to such an approach to child development and that if we did take up any sort of programme of that type then they, 'the Authority', would almost certainly withdraw the limited provision of physiotherapy that Francesca was in receipt of. The justification on behalf of the Authority, we were told, was that we would have 'opted out' by not taking their advice not to follow such a course of action. I do not think this annoyed us but it did desperately disappoint us and for the first time we saw how rigid and how narrow minded (i.e. do this and you lose everything) 'the system' could be.

At this time, Francesca was getting at least two hours a week of physiotherapy, most of it paid for privately, and was going to occupational and speech therapy, the latter also paid for by us. Slowly Francesca was becoming easier to feed. She still did not feed herself but it was becoming easier to get her to eat, and although she was still sick very often after, or during, feeding this too was becoming less of a problem.

By this time, we had started to put Francesca in a sitting position and would see how long she could balance and remain upright. This was from about the age of 18 months. We would prop her upright with cushions all around her or 'jam' her into her high chair. Slowly we moved the cushions further and further away and finally at about two years old she was able to sit on her own relatively unsupported.

Very slowly, we took her through the motions of pushing herself up into the sitting position by lying her on her side, putting her weight on one arm and pushing herself up. We also slowly taught her how she could put one arm down to support herself in the sitting position to help her balance. I remember her doing the latter first. We would sit watching her to see how long she could remain sitting. I cannot remember when she actually did start to support and balance herself in the sitting position using her arms but it was much later that she actually started to sit herself up, and when she did she did not use her arms at all. She would pull herself up using her stomach muscles, something that I thought must have been an enormous effort, but she did it and I remember thinking, so much for 'She'll never sit up!' Like all other moments, when she had finally managed to do something we felt a great sense of achievement not only for her but also for us.

It is true to say that with children like Francesca it is not the big things you look for but the little ones and that you actually get as much satisfaction from a new type of facial expression or movement of hand or arm as you would from a much greater achievement from a 'normal' child.

Francesca had started going to the mothers and toddlers play group with Antonella at the local Special Needs School from the age of 10 months and at the age of two moved into the school's nursery department, initially for two days a week. We were told that we were extremely lucky to have been given a place at the school, and particularly so early, but since we had been involved in the system from such an early point it did not feel anything special. That sounds ungrateful and it is not meant to, but it just seemed a logical next step in her development. Most of the days that Francesca went to school Antonella would go with her because of her continuing need for physio-, speech therapy etc. Antonella wanted to learn what was going on so that she could repeat and expand on the exercises at home.

Shortly before Francesca reached the age of two we contacted the Local Authority about getting Francesca statemented. Neither Antonella nor I knew what was involved in this process, nor had we any experience of what would be needed. However, we both felt that a process which was designed to identify Francesca's special needs, devise a programme to deliver them, identify the resources required and make them available, could only be a good thing. Additionally, we truly believed that the Authority would be honest and truthful about Francesca's condition and be as supportive of us as parents as possible in making sure that her needs would be met.

Little did we know at the time how long the statementing process would take, nor the heartache, trouble and effort that would be involved. Frankly, neither did we know that it would leave us completely disillusioned with the Local Authority and to a certain extent the Headmaster of the Special Needs School that Francesca had started to attend.

At the time Francesca started at the Special Needs School, we made the point to its Headmaster that we felt it was important that she was also integrated into a mainstream educational environment so that she could be stimulated by 'normal' children within her peer group. Through a contact at Portage we were put in touch with the Headmistress of a local mainstream nursery. Antonella and I visited the school to meet the Headmistress and 'check out' their facilities. The school seemed well organised and offered what appeared to be a pleasant, well supported environment. It was agreed that Francesca could start at the school and that she would begin by attending two mornings per week, which she did aged two years and four months.

We enquired whether the Authority would be prepared to contribute towards the cost of her place at the mainstream nursery and were told no! However, we were told that certain of the pupils at the Special Needs School, who were deemed by the Governors to be worthy, were integrated into mainstream schools for limited periods during the week at the expense of the school and, in time, Francesca would be assessed to see if such an arrangement might be possible for her.

Although Francesca still couldn't move around, by now she could sit up and balance herself and play with objects that were placed within her reach.

I clearly remember the tremendous contrast between the two school environments. On the one hand Francesca was in a class of immobile, non-communicating children and, on the other, surrounded by active, noisy 'normal' children. We felt that by sharing her time between the two schools she would hopefully get the best of both environments. From the Special Needs School she would get the specialist support and services from which she could benefit such as physio-, speech- and hydrotherapy and intensive one-to-one interaction, whilst at the mainstream nursery she would get the stimulation that the environment and other children could provide. It seemed an ideal arrangement.

During the first four months of Francesca's attendance at the Special Needs School, the statementing process had been started and was going ahead. The first part of this process involved an assessment of Francesca by a Local Education Authority Educational Psychologist. This person visited our home and interviewed us and observed Francesca for about an hour. I think that she agreed with every point we made and Antonella and I both felt very positive about the eventual outcome of the statementing process if all of it was going to be that simple. I suppose that we had been concerned that whoever was involved in assessing Francesca from the Authority would not have agreed with our views as to what represented Francesca's needs or what was in her best interest.

We had made the point to the psychologist that we felt that Francesca could ideally benefit from a lot of intensive support, i.e. one to one, and that she needed integration into the mainstream school environment. We felt that we were already beginning to see the benefits of Antonella's involvement with her in that she was developing, albeit slowly, and that she was beginning to interact with other children in the mainstream nursery environment. We felt that the statement ought to reflect this. At this time we also made a parental contribution to the statementing process, in writing, making the above points. This was not solicited from the Authority but offered by us.

In our parental contribution, we stressed that since Francesca needed support in the mainstream nursery an ideal arrangement would be that either the same person was responsible for her in both environments or, if this was not possible, that there was very close liaison between the different individuals concerned so that her development could be closely monitored, her personal development programme implemented efficiently and for the sake of continuity.

We had read from the DfEE Code of Practice on the *Identification and Assessment of Special Educational Needs* that the parents of children being assessed are entitled also to receive copies of all advices received by the Authority to aid in its assessment of the child. It states 'Assessment can be stressful for parents. The value of early information and support to parents cannot be over emphasized. The better informed and better supported parents are the better they are able to contribute as parents to the assessment of the child'. This greatly heartened us as we wanted so much to be a part of the process. We honestly expected to be continuously involved at every stage of Francesca's statementing. In fact, quite the reverse proved to be the case.

Having read that the statementing process should normally be completed in no more than six months, we also had a clear view that having started in November the whole thing would be over by June of the next year. This too proved a mistaken impression and in the end we were to wait 15 months before the Authority issued a statement and 20 months until the final form was agreed – the latter was only after we had taken the

Authority to a Special Educational Needs Tribunal. I can fairly say that the whole affair ruined for good any positive relationship that we might otherwise have had with the Local Authority.

In the end we waited for about two months after our initial contact with the Educational Psychologist to receive something by way of advices concerning Francesca's condition. When we finally did it was only because I had written again requesting them. In fact, it came to the point where we could not understand why we had not seen anything and I wrote again asking if any advices had been issued. We knew that in the interim the physio- and speech therapists had both been consulted concerning Francesca, as well as her Paediatrician at the local hospital. We finally received their advices from the Authority, and they were broadly in line with what we expected and thought ourselves. However, the fact that they were only passed to us after we had 'chased' the Authority certainly left us feeling that they had neither been thinking of us nor proactively involving us.

When the copies of advices they had received arrived they were accompanied by a letter stating that the Authority's lack of contact with us was because of changes in the statementing process to which it was still adjusting and which were making workloads heavier than normal. All of this made us feel a little uneasy.

We had already made up our minds that we should seek independent advice about Francesca's condition and her needs but the above helped to settle any remaining uncertainty that we might have had over the issue. Through friends and contacts, we were put in touch with an Educational Psychologist, Dr Billy Conn. Billy was someone that we saw as an expert, not only in psychology but also in 'the system' and therefore somebody who could not only give us his professional opinion and advice on Francesca but who could also lead us through the process of statementing so that ultimately we could get the best for Francesca.

In a way he was our named person, an individual that is there to help and support you through statementing. We went to independent physio- and speech therapists to get their views on Francesca as well as SENSE – the organisation for the deaf-blind – and child developmentalists of Guy's Hospital. At the latter, we found Gillian Baird who, along with Richard Robinson, proved to be a font of wisdom, common-sense and hope, not so much in what they promised for Francesca but in their pragmatism in explaining her current and future developmental possibilities to us. Also, for their letters of support concerning our parental contribution to the statementing process.

All in all, we were amazed that we managed to amass so much evidence in such a short time and that there was so much consensus about what Francesca represented and needed, and that it exactly supported our position and the parental contribution we had already submitted to the Authority.

During this period – and about four or five months had passed since the start of statementing – we had been in close touch with the Special Needs School Headmaster. We liked and trusted him, and felt and hoped that he would be an ally in our case for Francesca. We therefore kept him continually informed of what was going on and he was, in turn, continually supportive. On numerous occasions, in discussions with him, I remember him saying that he was in complete agreement with our wishes and that what we were requesting was right and necessary for Francesca. He firmly believed in integration and in fact he was already looking at the school budget to make some money available for Francesca to receive classroom support at the mainstream nursery.

To permit us time to receive our advices and information, we had to request an extension to the time deadline for completion of the statement and were now in about the seventh month. However, as we submitted the final supporting piece of evidence Antonella and I both felt that it was over and that we could now look forward to seeing the statement represent what we wanted.

Time passed, one month, two months, three months and we heard nothing. In the interim we moved and I wrote informing the Authority of our new address. By now, Francesca was spending a day per week at the mainstream nursery and two days a week at the Special School, she was still involved in all her usual activities and Antonella was intensively supporting all of the experts' efforts when Francesca was at home.

At this point, we began to ask ourselves 'Why have we not heard anything' and 'Should we contact them (the Authority) to find out what was going on?'. Neither of us really wanted to do the latter, call it cowardice!

Francesca was now about two years old and able to push herself around on her back with her legs, as well as sitting and balancing herself. She did not walk or crawl but was making solid – albeit slow – progress in all aspects physical. Intellectually and socially she was progressing more slowly and still did not interact a great deal with other individuals. Antonella was continually trying to develop any or all aspects of Francesca's physical, social and intellectual abilities in any and every way possible. She still went to the Special School to work with her, did exercises with her at home in physio- and speech therapy and we were still paying privately for extra therapy of various kinds.

Dave Hewett's commentary

I met Francesca for the first time when she was two years and a few months old. On a fine, warm day I sat on the lawn with the family. I watched them all play with and take delight in Francesca, and to some extent marvelled at their ability to play with her.

Francesca was a beautiful little girl, quite small, though well-formed and just starting to stand and take steps with some assistance. It was easy to be attracted to playing with this pretty, appealing little person, but her large eyes didn't focus on me during my attempts to gain her attention and it became clear that it was going to be very difficult indeed to engage her socially – I wasn't sure that she had become at all aware of my voice and the proximity of my face. She gave her attention more easily to objects, in particular concentrating for a full minute on some toys floating in a bowl of water. She was mostly very quiet, gazing into the distance, occasionally making little murmuring noises.

However, the marvel was to watch the family play with her. Antonella's style was wonderful, all the more impressive when I considered the reality of how much feedback she, Francesca's mother, was receiving. The very small amounts of positive reassurance Francesca gave her did not daunt her one bit. Antonella laughed gently but with enormous genuine pleasure, she jiggled and rocked, she kept her face available to Francesca, she used pause and burst-pause, she waited with expectation at sensitive moments for the slightest behaviour from Francesca which she could interpret. Her performance in no way seemed to be determined or forced, she was genuinely effervescing as if Francesca was giving her the most detailed signals in return. She also stopped completely in response to some signal from Francesca I could not identify. I did see that Francesca was showing some small responses. There were a few episodes of direct eye contact, she smiled and giggled a few times, snuggled in and waved her legs a little.

Ian has a powerful personal presence and devotes formidable energy and concentration to conversation. However, I watched him stop abruptly in the middle of a serious, strident conversation to take a much softer and interactive tone as Francesca was passed to him, launching into a similarly sensitive and skilled play style, similarly marvellous considering the seeming lack of feedback he was receiving to sustain it.

I discussed their performance with Antonella and Ian. They recognised the issue, that they were somehow able to promote and sustain their own motivation to carry out regular, consistent, social play routines, even without receiving the rewards that parents would normally need to keep them going. They said that it was mostly an intuitive type of determination to carry on, and that somehow they had always enjoyed the play no matter what, though they had discussed and planned the need to keep the sessions brief but frequent.

Also, they both made the point that there were many tiny items of feedback from Francesca through physical contact that they had learnt to identify and respond to. Even more impressive was that Antonella and Ian felt that it was only during the last nine months or so that Francesca had started to respond at all, though they had maintained their play with her throughout the period prior to that. Episodes of eye contact from Francesca had been a very recent development, though Antonella felt that Francesca's eyes did not yet seem to give much meaning in the sense that they did not carry a particular message. Antonella also said that for some time she had been doing good turn-taking exchanges based on Francesca's noises, often whilst in the car.

Ian's commentary continues

In the end, I telephoned the Authority to find out was happening about the statementing. By that point approximately nine months had passed since the process had been initiated. Once again our Named Officer had changed and I remember that nobody could tell me anything about Francesca, so I wrote requesting a comment on what was going on. We received a reply – sent via our old address about two weeks later – asking us to attend a 'Statutory Meeting' with a representative of the Local Authority. In fact, this turned out to be with two people and the outcome of this was that they would put our views to a panel of headteachers from schools in the region to judge whether Francesca should have the sort of support that we had requested. It seemed as if nothing had happened or been decided with respect to Francesca's case.

We waited another three months – nothing happened. Finally, Antonella and I both lost our tempers. The whole thing had descended into a farce. It was as if the whole Local Authority organisation was either incompetent, ignorant or taking the mickey. I telephoned the Education Officer for the County and after providing him with the relevant information, name, etc. he promised he would find out what was going on. I told him that if the Authority did not resolve the issue immediately we would take them to the Local Government Ombudsman on the basis of failing to meet their legal requirements with respect to the time allowed for Francesca's statementing. Basically, I was saying that if we did not get satisfaction then we would try and get them in any way we could! Pretty antagonistic I suppose.

He phoned back almost immediately. I remember my heart beating. He said that a draft statement had been issued and that it would be with us within a few days.

Antonella and I were on tenterhooks for the next couple of days waiting for it to arrive. When it did arrive, we could not believe what it said. It did not recommend integration into the mainstream environment or one-to-one intensive support for Francesca and in fact all it did say was that her needs, which were stated in a highly ambiguous and unquantified manner, could all be met from a place in the Special Needs School. Neither of us could believe it. Nor was there any explanation in the letter accompanying the statement as to why it had taken so long, almost 13 months from the original starting date to get it to us.

We could not understand how, if the Education Officer had asked anyone involved with Francesca or anyone who had submitted an advice, such a draft statement could have been issued.

I telephoned the Education Officer to enquire as to how the draft statement had been formulated and confirm whom he had contacted for advice and why the statement had not been issued previously. He responded by saying that it was based on advice from the Headteacher of the Special Needs School and that there had been problems in the department within the Authority dealing with responsibility for children with Special Educational Needs that had 'held it up'. I could not believe it. I contacted the Headteacher and asked him point blank why he had not supported us and Francesca since he had always told us his position was identical to ours.

He claimed that we must have misunderstood his previous position and that I, or we, had made a mistake somewhere. I was amazed, disappointed, shocked all in one go. Antonella and I are thinking, caring human beings and it was unbelievable that anybody could have, as we saw it, so obviously misled us. I remember him ending the conversation by adding 'Well, you will get what you want in the end anyway' – Thanks!

We felt completely alone and demoralised. From a position of positive intention and hope but probably some naivety, we had passed to disbelief, complete lack of faith and confidence and, in fact, distrust of all concerned with the Local Authority.

We realised that the Authority was definitely not voluntarily going to give Francesca what we, and it appeared all parties, had indicated was in her best interests. They were only prepared to give her the baseline provision, in our view, of a place in the Special Needs School. We both realised that to get the best for Francesca we had a fight on our hands.

We wrote saying that we were unhappy with the draft statement and cited our independent advices, and the Authority responded by re-issuing the draft statement as the final statement 15 months after statementing had begun. We felt that we and Francesca were being kicked in the face and that all the evidence collected by us was being wilfully ignored. We also felt as if we were being totally ignored and that Francesca was being palmed off with a minimum that would not involve the Authority in any extra expenditure. It did not require any time for us to decide that we were going to take the Authority to a Special Educational Needs Tribunal to see if we could overturn their decision and get the statement amended.

Antonella's commentary continues

I suppose I like challenges and I've always readily taken on those that Francesca has presented us with. I've always believed that she is going to go a long, long way even when people have been saying 'Oh, she's not going to sit' or 'She's not going to move'. The physiotherapist would say, 'Don't waste time on her', 'Rest yourself in the evening', 'She gets enough during the day' and 'She's never going to walk'. Of course, I could not stand that. I never say never, that would just make something more of a challenge. Early on Francesca had a lot of input, Portage, swimming, physio- and speech therapy and I used to take her to the occupational therapist as well as the dietician. It was a continuous procession of people we had inserted into Francesca's life, one after the other, and the total input was tremendous and of course good for her in different ways. However, I think that the best time for Francesca was in the evenings when everybody had gone. Francesca functions really well at night and I could always get a lot more out of her then. I don't know if it was because it was quieter, maybe more relaxed or just that I work better at night. I used to get great things out of her at night.

Many of the exercises, especially physiotherapy, were very intense and although I knew they had to be done and were good for her I did, and do, feel that the exercises worked because I also repeated them at home. In my opinion, this ultimately made more of a difference than the half an hour a week spent with the specialists concerned. It was the continuation of the activities away from the hospital, school etc. that was particularly beneficial for Francesca.

These days Francesca has free range of the garden and house and will come into and out of the kitchen on her own. It's marvellous to see her walking about doing what she wants. Sometimes she will come into the kitchen and just stand there in a way that suggests something, but nothing definite! Sometimes she'll stand in a way that I know means she wants something. She just can't tell me what. I usually try things to find out. 'Do you want a cuddle?' I'll give her a cuddle but she'll still stand there. 'A kiss?' Still standing, same look. 'A drink?' I'll give her the drink and she'll wander back into the garden or wherever she came from. We go through everything until she gets what she wants and then she's off. I have to do it that way because she can't say what it is that's needed. Sometimes I even think that although she wants something, she doesn't actually know what it is until she gets it! I certainly believe that she wants things and she is thinking much more than we can understand from the way she presents herself to us.

I don't know quite how I read her, I can't explain it. I suppose you could say it's a body language thing and familiarity. I've learned to 'read' little bits of the way she moves and holds her head and if you can catch those things and respond to them it can make something happen, but I never consciously think about it in any detail and it's difficult to explain how I do it.

Now that she is mobile she is much more relaxed and it is easier to work with her. On the other hand, because she is mobile she will walk away when she has had enough. I don't like to make her do things she obviously does not want to do but we keep going. It is difficult to know about how far to insist with something or when to stop because she is signalling 'enough'. Like with the physio- exercises, I just try to make it a game as much as possible, it is easier to keep going longer that way.

The other two, Caterina and Marco, have always been really good with her. Marco says that she even fibs. He doesn't like it when she goes in his room and messes up his Lego. He says that when he asks her, Francesca, if she has been playing with his Lego and she says no, she is fibbing. I don't know what he is seeing as the 'no' signal, but he somehow is able to see Francesca's answer and the fact that it's a no.

I believe she will learn to talk. I can't think that she won't. I feel that there's enough time still available for that to happen and we are encouraged that we have achieved things that all the professionals said either would not or could not happen. I work and play with her with the belief that she will learn to talk.

Ian's commentary continues

By now, Francesca was just over three years old. She had just begun to be able to take her weight on her feet. Initially, we would put her in a standing position and she would balance herself by hanging on to any objects close enough to be useful. She could not move about when standing and she could not pull herself up into a standing position or sit from standing unaided. However, just to see her on her feet gave us a tremendous thrill. When she was standing, we would move her legs to give her a lead as to the movements she needed to make to be walking. You could see her trying, from her facial expressions, to make the same movements but, as with all new activities, to begin with she just was not able. Then I remember that she started to slide her feet forward one at a time and shuffle along as we were holding her – she was walking!

Over the next three months or so we were more or less continuously taking her through the movements of lifting her legs – i.e. bending her knees and placing one foot in front of the other – to get her to walk. At around three years old, she was actually walking, albeit slowly and hesitantly, and you could hold her hand and she would come with you. She would also, unaided, hold onto the worktop in the kitchen or the back of the sofa and move from side to side. All of these things were, we were informed by the physiotherapist, excellent activities for her to be involved in and would help her tremendously in learning to walk.

It was during the three or so months that this was going on that we were also waiting for the date set for Francesca's Tribunal hearing to arrive. We went backwards and forwards over the arguments trying to prepare for the meeting and trying to think of any and every case that the Authority might have been able to make to refute our claims on Francesca's behalf. Also, during this period, Francesca had increased the amount of time that she was spending at the mainstream nursery from one to one and a half days per week. She was also still attending the Special Needs Nursery for two days per week and so in total she was now spending the majority of a week at nursery school.

As Francesca began to become more mobile, to walk, it seemed as if all kinds of other abilities were being potentiated as well. It was only afterwards that Richard Robinson from Guy's eventually confirmed what we had already guessed at, that is, that a trigger in a specific area of a child's developmental pattern could have all sorts of knock-on effects in terms of benefiting other areas of development. This was certainly the case with Francesca. As she was becoming more mobile, she was becoming increasingly inquisitive and interactive. She was all over the ground floor of our home investigating rooms, drawers and cupboards and was starting to come to the table for food and the kitchen sink for a drink. The same sorts of things were also being seen at her mainstream nursery where, as she was becoming more mobile, she was going up to other children to investigate what they were doing, trying to take toys away from them, etc. In fact, she was beginning, in a limited way, to develop her social interaction and behavioural skills.

It frightened us that all of this development would almost certainly not have taken place unless she had been at the mainstream nursery, since at the Special Needs Nursery she was in a class of largely immobile, uncommunicating children, and that the Authority was against her integration into the former environment. This made us even more convinced that what we were doing was right and that we had to, as we saw it, fight and win to get Francesca what she really needed and would benefit from.

Through all this time, we were also reminding the Headmaster of the Special Needs School of his promise that the Governors would be considering support for Francesca for the time that she was spending in the mainstream nursery. By now, being completely mobile, Francesca needed a classroom assistant to more or less make sure that she was okay. The mainstream nursery school did not have any spare staff to do this. We were afraid that as a result the school would not be able to continue to offer Francesca a place and were continually asking the Special Needs School Headmaster what was happening. I have to say that I was unable, as a result of what had happened previously, to go back and speak to him and it was Antonella who tried to get some movement on the issue. In fact, nothing ever happened and it was only after the amended statement, as a consequence of the Tribunal hearing, was issued that the support was forthcoming and then the Authority did not have any choice in the matter anyway!

By now we were also well known to Social Services as, a while back, Antonella had started asking about the availability or possibility of respite care to give us and our other children a break, so that we could spend some time together without the immediate pressure of Francesca. Not least to enable us to do the things that were just impossible with Francesca around. I remember that we were interviewed and all sorts of advice regarding Francesca was offered. We made it clear that we were really after only one thing, and that was help with respite care. Maybe it is unfair but I got the distinct feeling that we did not figure particularly high on their list of priorities. Probably the image we present was as a well off, reasonably stable, middle class family living in a big house in the country, and I can sympathise with the fact that they must have thought that there were plenty of other cases more needy than us. Perhaps this was especially so because we had made it clear that if we needed to contribute financially to any arrangement then we would be happy to do so.

Also, I am not sure that we ever really hit it off with our social workers, but we certainly tried! Maybe it was because we were so disillusioned with everything to do with the Authority, or that their backgrounds – we had three different social workers over a period of 18 months – were so different from ours. The reason that we went to the Authority over respite care, rather than making a private arrangement, was so that Francesca would become known to 'the system' in a care context, so that if anything happened to us and ultimately the state had to look after her she might be treated better, or the process of assimilating her would be less complicated.

We had respite care for a while, then it stopped. We have not had any for a year and I do not know if we ever will again, despite pleading for it. We are not alone in experiencing this. Many people we know with handicapped children who are cared for at home in our part of the country do not get much help. The general feeling is – you are on your own! However, the few times that we have had respite care, especially overnight, it gave us an unimaginable sense of freedom; no one who has not experienced a situation such as ours can possibly appreciate the value of time given by respite care.

When the day finally arrived for the Tribunal hearing, we journeyed to London, Victoria, to present our case. I had learnt that amongst those representing the Authority against us was the Headmaster of the Special Needs School!

We took with us some of the best photographs of Francesca that we could find for those present to have an idea of what she was like, and as much of the correspondence and advices that we felt might be necessary to support our case. Billy was to be there too and we met him beforehand at Victoria Station and had a cup of coffee. I was so nervous that I was shaking – I had never been so nervous before, not for my degree finals, or job interviews. It seemed that my whole life was make or break on that day, based on the judgement of the Tribunal. The worst thing was that we had no idea of what to expect.

When we arrived at the building in which the Tribunal was to be held, we and the Authority's representatives were asked to wait in separate antechambers. At the appropriate moment we were called into a room to meet the three Tribunal members – the Chairwoman and another man and woman. The atmosphere was formal and introductions were made with titles being used. Each side was then asked to make their cases for and against amendment of the statement and questions were asked by the Tribunal panel members.

What amazed me most was how unprepared the Authority's representatives were. They could not even say how much time Francesca was at school for – not in the Special Needs School nor mainstream. Neither could they say how much physio- or speech therapy she got. They had to admit that they had not enquired about her progress at the mainstream nursery and had no idea what effect this could have had on her development even though they had copies of the Headmistress's advice from that school which clearly stated that she believed it had been beneficial. Frankly, we were disgusted, as were the Tribunal panel members, that they, the Authority, could have been so poorly informed. I particularly remember one of the panel members raising and lowering his eyebrows in what I hoped at the time was disbelief at their ineptness. I felt that could only have increased our chances of carrying the day. The Special Needs School Headmaster was particularly silent as the meeting went on and I still do not know whether this was from shame or embarrassment.

Somehow at the end I did not feel bad any more – at least we had finally had our say to an audience which was not the Authority, and which possessed the ability to tell the Authority what to do. I even remember shaking the Headmaster's hand. We left feeling tired and drained. It had been about 18 months since the start of statementing, 18 months of highs and lows, fear and elation, tears and joy. We were both physically and emotionally finished. We went home.

I cannot remember exactly what happened next but the Tribunal was due to deliver its verdict within a particular time-frame and it did. The letter they sent arrived after I had left for work and Antonella and I opened it together when I returned home in the evening. I read it slowly. It said 'Francesca should be integrated into the mainstream environment for at least the time that she was currently getting and that it would be the responsibility of the Authority to meet the costs involved'. It meant that not only was the Authority liable to provide an ancillary for Francesca but also that the placement itself had to be paid for by the Authority – we had won! I am not sure I could believe it, we had won! Nineteen months had passed, we had been ignored, lied to and finally forced to justify ourselves to an independent Tribunal and we had won.

In a way it was a bit of an anti-climax, in some ways we rather felt 'Why had it taken so much effort to get and do what was so obvious from the very beginning?' I do not remember gloating the next time that I spoke to the Headmaster at the Special Needs School about arranging a meeting to implement the views of the Tribunal but maybe there was a feeling of moral superiority.

The Authority arranged a meeting and suddenly we had everything we wanted – all at the expense of the Authority. However, one thing I clearly recall is that at the meeting we were accused of taking away resources from other children by having won our case for Francesca and by the Authority being liable for the extra costs. We both thought that this was particularly sick and I said that I hoped that other parents would be able to use the same mechanism that we had to get more for their children and that I would help them do so in any way I could.

In the interim, I had been appointed a Governor at a large local Community College and had assumed the responsibility for Special Needs within the Governing Body – a legal requirement. I began to understand how the Local Authority disburses its revenue for supporting Special Needs children and how this could work against the individual. Through my work in this area, I discovered that rather than being part of a small, antagonistic, minority of parents fighting against the Authority for their children's needs, we were one set amongst a large number of vociferous parents contesting the Authority's position with respect to their children and, what is more, they frequently won their cases.

It is now almost a year later. Francesca is four and a half. To look at her is sometimes to see a child that is four and a half and apparently normal, other times it is to see a child that is severely handicapped. She is a happy, easy going child with no special requirements in terms of medication or physical care other than attention so that she does not harm herself. She interacts with our other children but does not speak. As a family, we still hope and are working towards developing her social interaction and communication skills and our other two children are now actively involved in that.

Dave Hewett's commentary continues

September 1997 and I visit the family for the third time. Francesca is sitting on the floor in the living room and as I enter the room and she hears my voice there is something clear in her body language and her sudden stillness that she is aware of me. She is so much bigger and clearly more physically assertive than when I had last seen her a year before. I place myself on the floor beside her and Francesca's body language seems to be all about awareness of my presence. Her face turns toward me and though her look does not contain many facial signals and her eyes do not quite meet mine, I feel powerfully aware that she is regarding me. I start speaking and she listens, her head moves more toward me and I feel confident to lie down so that she can look downward into my face. Something in the movement of her shoulder and arm seems like an invitation and I reach out. She takes hold of my forefinger and holds it hard, moving my hand from side to side, her face turning toward me again. I realise that things have really moved on and I am finding it so much easier to read signals and responses from her. I keep going so much more easily than previously with my side of the conversation, because she is doing active things to keep me performing.

Later, I am in the garden with Caterina and Marco and Francesca walks out of the door to join us, followed by Antonella. Caterina and Marco in a seemingly effortless way position themselves to put their faces available to her and both start a conversation with Francesca, laughing, pausing, using gentle physical movements to emphasise what they are saying. Francesca is clearly responsive to them, moving hands and arms in delight, then pushing past them to take a walk across the lawn.

Ian and Antonella's commentary continues

We love our daughter Francesca. There is still a feeling of 'Why us?' and 'How did it happen?' and sometimes a sadness with respect to what might have been and, almost certainly in the way we expected, never will be. However, after four years we have largely come to terms with, but still perhaps cannot fully accept, what happened to Francesca.

One thing you realise is that for an individual such as Francesca the fight never ends over her best interests. As Francesca approaches five she will transfer from nursery to junior departments at school. The Authority is already making it clear that the Tribunal directed her integration into a mainstream nursery not a junior school and as a result is likely to take away Francesca's time in the non-special educational needs setting. What will we do? I am not sure, probably fight if we have to, we have come too far to go back, but it wears you down and I am sure they (the Authority) know this. Two years' effort for one year's educational provision, in terms of our previous fight, does not sound or feel fair, especially as she is making such good progress. Since we could not live with knowing that we had not done all we could to give her the best chance possible, I know we will fight if we have to.

We firmly believe that since Francesca is now so physically able, in fact 'virtually normal', her future quality of life will be governed principally by her ability to interact socially, be aware and, hopefully, communicate. This is what we concentrate on all the time now and what we feel should be supported through school and the other agencies involved with her. Whilst it's a simplification, we see that integration into the mainstream education environment, given the right sort of support, provides her with a route to achieve these things that would not otherwise be available if she was solely at the Special Needs School. Antonella wants and believes that Francesca will speak. In a sense I'm not too worried. Speaking is just one way of communicating. I want her to be aware. If she's aware then I think she'll communicate in one way or another and, at least at the moment, that would be enough for me.

We'd like to add that we are very lucky because our other children are so supportive of Francesca. They have never made a special issue of her disability nor the fact that, at times, we have either not spent as much time with them as maybe we should have or not done as many things together as might have been possible. They are great kids.

Ian's commentary concludes

Finally, on a personal note, I do not know what I, Caterina or Marco would do, or have done, without Antonella. She is the force that drives our family forward and is ultimately the guardian of Francesca's and our futures.

Chapter 13

Commentary Three: Learners with Autism. Parents Doing Intensive Interaction

Melanie Nind and Dave Hewett

Learners with autism

In *Access to Communication* (Nind and Hewett, 1994) we made some mention of autism, but we did not pursue this disabling condition as a separate or specific issue in terms of Intensive Interaction. Since writing at that time, an associate research fellowship with the Centre for Autism Studies at the University of Hertfordshire (MN) provided the stimulus for more in-depth reading and collaboration with colleagues in the field of autism. Some conceptions of autism hold that personal relatedness with others is the central impairment and that this is biologically based (Hobson, 1993). The focus on innate inabilities, particularly in the realm of social communication, carries an implication that individuals with autism are unable to learn from natural interactive processes. Increasing familiarity with this literature triggered a theoretical interest in whether this is so. It is our subjective understanding that people whose learning disabilities are compounded by autism *do* learn from Intensive Interaction and we have some empirical evidence of this from our work at Harperbury Hospital School. We also have the impression, however, that there is less take-up of Intensive Interaction amongst providers for people with autism, where more specialised approaches dominate. It is in the light of this thinking that the two accounts in this book of using Intensive Interaction with children with autism are of particular interest to us.

There is no doubt that the autistic triad of impairments in the areas of social interaction, communication, and rigidity of thought and behaviour, pose a massive challenge. The need for developing relationships and fundamental social and communication abilities in people with autism is paramount, yet may seem unattainable. Many specific interventions have achieved some successes in these areas. Ogletree (1992), for example, describes a communication intervention which employs a natural, interactive format and which was found to be associated with the development of a range of functional communication abilities. The essence of being social and communicative, however, has often eluded the learner/practitioner. Howlin (1986), for example, notes that while some approaches have led to people with autism showing a higher degree of social competence 'difficulties remain in the coordination of social skills, and in their use of language and play, and most important, they continue to show very little initiation of social contact' (p. 124). Similarly, Koegel and Koegel (1995) comment that many of the earlier interventions only addressed 'a small facet of the overall social difficulty, resulting in negligible changes in the child's social networks or quality of social involvement' (p. 57). Jordan and Powell (1995) highlight that the problem areas in terms of social learning arise because 'there may be some things that can be learnt (developmentally) but which cannot be taught' (p. 13). The two accounts in this volume are exciting because they tell of the development of elusive yet essential qualities, of the child's motivation to interact with others and of the emerging pleasure in this.

The literature on autism leads us to expect at least some of the following difficulties, additional to, or more extreme than, difficulties faced by those with severe learning difficulties[1]:

- early lack of interest in social contact and in the human voice
- failure to anticipate by reaching out when they are about to be picked up
- 'abnormal' eye contact
- abnormal imitation
- abnormal comprehension and use of facial expressions
- abnormal development and comprehension of gestures including pointing
- lack of exploratory behaviour
- abnormal and extreme sensitivity to environmental stimuli
- abnormal play dominated by objects and their sensory features rather than play with cultural or symbolic meaning
- failure to give positive feedback to others

---

[1]Many of these features are regularly cited and therefore unreferenced; references are given for more particular points associated with specific researchers.

258

- tendency for signals to be idiosyncratic rather than share universal features observed in normally developing infants (Ricks, 1979)
- inability to respond differentially to subtle changes in others' behaviours
- severely deficient abilities to learn through identifying and co-operating with other people
- severely deficient natural interest in what other people experience, feel and intend
- specific failure in comprehension of how to reciprocate with other people
- problems with recognition of the interpersonal functions of language (Lyons, 1977)
- frequent failure to engage in shared activities
- failure to initiate 'sharing of attention' (Sigman *et al.*, 1986)

Trevarthen *et al.* (1996) use the terminology problems with 'availability' when they talk about the effects of these specific difficulties on teaching and relating to people with autism. Many of these autistic or 'availability' problems are evident in the accounts of Gary's parents and Ben's teacher. Beth comments on the odd way Gary had of playing with toys and that 'he never came to me to show me things, or pointed at things that should have interested him' (p. 210). Ben rarely sought human contact and shrank away from the approaches of his peers.

Jordan and Powell (1995) have commented on a dichotomy in the options for intervening with individuals with autism in terms of compensation or remediation. Some approaches, like computer assisted learning for example, are far more compensatory. They take into account autistic difficulties with learning in social contexts and provide instead a less social, more cognitive context. Other approaches, like holding therapy for example, seek a more direct approach, attempting to 'make better' the autistic difficulties. In reality, of course, many interventions combine both compensatory and remedial elements. Intensive Interaction has at its core an intention to facilitate sociability and communication. When used with individuals with autism, with all the social and communication difficulties that go with the condition, it clearly belongs in the remedial camp. Ben's teacher, in her re-evaluation of Ben's needs and her response to them, chooses aims that go to the heart of his difficulties: 'give sustained attention to other people, learn more about enjoying giving the attention, take part in turn-taking routines with other people, learn how to have fun, be less socially remote, use and understand eye

259

contact, use and understand facial expression, use and understand physical contact, give Ben the knowledge that any noises he makes are important, and to use all these abilities in learning all kinds of things' (p. 190–91).

We can recognise the list of difficulties above in the descriptions of Gary and Ben, but we can also note significant progress in relation to them. Beth and Steve Taylor and Lynne Knott reflect with delight on the changes they saw in Gary and Ben. These changes include developments in the interpersonal behaviours of eye contact, facial expression and touch. Beth is keen to communicate 'the complete joy on Gary's face as he looks deep into the eyes of his companion'. Lynne Knott notes early fleeting eye contact for Ben and tolerance of their presence in his personal zone. The changes are also in the nature of interpersonal interaction and developments in shared emotion and shared attention are particularly significant. The shared space and contact, and enjoyment in this, seems to have emerged quite soon after beginning with Intensive Interaction. Beth notes that Gary soon became content to have her near and that he found pleasure in her as another human being. Closeness also developed with an intimate emotional relationship communicated with kisses and cuddles. We were intrigued by Beth's realisation that Gary was aware of her joining in with his play and that he wanted this. Typically, his signals of this were imperceptible at first, but Beth watched and waited during a pause and picked up on his fleeting look, interpreting his interest. We know from the literature (such as Goldberg, 1977) the importance of responding and sharing attention for feelings of well-being and efficacy for the parent, and Beth illustrates this when she tells of 'the immense feeling of relief' at Gary's responsiveness.

We were impressed with the unrushed interactive work of Ben's teachers. They clearly recognised the importance of early side by side play with only occasional sharing and did not push for too much too soon. Although they placed paramount importance on Ben feeling safe and unthreatened, they were made to feel effective by progress they recognised in his tolerance and enjoyment of them and his allowing a (probably much 'scaffolded') turn: 'this felt like turn-taking, a conversation; it felt good' (p. 193).

All the contributors in this section write of getting to know the person and really liking the person they found them to be. Intensive Interaction does work partly by changing the attitudes of those who use it, to be more accepting and positive. There must also be a sense, however, in which these children with autism became more 'available'. We have often written about the way in which, in Intensive Interaction, the interactions gain their own momentum, and that, as with good caregiver-infant interaction, the process sustains itself (Nind and Hewett, 1988, p. 56; Nind and Hewett, 1994, p. 138). We see evidence of this here: 'to see Ben responding to us and wanting to actually be involved with us – and we felt reaching out to us – gave all the staff motivation to get to know Ben even more' (p. 197). This is not to say that everything in the garden is automatically rosy. Ben's teacher writes honestly about the problems they faced and Gary's parents' reflections on the setbacks are very moving. The establishment of the relationship, however, and the increased comfortableness with one another, was clearly helpful in working through difficult times.

One of the features of working with people with autism is that we may never really know what their actual abilities are. We can be frustrated by the imbalance in the pattern of (in)abilities in that a lack of even basic abilities in someone's social interaction is so much harder to fathom when that same someone is so able in many other ways. A bonus can be, however, that if we do succeed in reaching that individual and in making them more 'available' we can discover skills which were previously blocked by behaviours or by fear and anxiety. We get a sense of this in Ben's story. We can also see development happen quite quickly. Ben makes a fascinating case study because of the language he develops. He began using language in a functional way, showing he understood some of the purposes of communication, that he could ask help of people. He also, perhaps more remarkably, began using words and sounds in a conversational way, as a vehicle for taking turns and sharing interactive play.

Parents interacting with children with autism

Intensive Interaction is based on the interactive style of caregivers with infants which is optimal for their development in general and for language learning in particular. An understanding of this optimal style has been generated primarily from studies of the interactions between caregivers and their normally developing infants. Studies of interactions between disabled caregivers and infants and more frequently caregivers and (learning) disabled infants has enhanced this understanding.

261

The literature on interactions between parents and their infants with autism illuminates some interesting issues when we consider Gary's and Ben's stories. Most modern texts on autism disassociate themselves from the old notions of 'cold parenting' contributing to autism (Wing, 1977). When a different, less facilitative interactive style is recognised in a parent–infant with autism dyad, the factors within the child with autism are cited as the most influential factors in the difference. Trevarthen *et al.* (1996) summarise this thinking:

> The orienting and expressive responses of autistic children tend to cut them off from emotional and communicative transactions with those around them . . . This evidently is related to (and may produce, rather than reflect) mis-timing of expressive behaviours of autistic individuals and break-down of the patterns that normally sustain efficient reciprocity or turn-taking in communication. (p. 92)

There are notable examples in the accounts here when the opposite of this happens, such as when Ben gave brief, but well-timed and good, direct eye contact which made his interactive partner feel 'allowed in' and 'good'. The transactional element is crucial – the interactive style was altered, which perhaps altered the child's behaviours (or allowed the practitioner to see them differently), which in turn reinforced the facilitative interactive style.

There is agreement in the literature that interactions between infants with autism and their caregivers are not typically reciprocal and synchronised, and various studies make specific contributions to the picture of what happens instead. Massie (1978) found that mothers responded to the strange behaviour of their infants by holding them less (than mothers of normally developing babies), with lower ratings for touching and mutual eye-to-eye gaze. The infants' lack of eye contact or other signals of interest inevitably disrupts any sense of communicative flow and de-motivates mothers from talking to and playing with them.

Papoudi (1993, cited by Trevarthen *et al.*, 1996) found that parents may respond to their autistic child's lack of attention-sharing by physically holding them on task and being more directive, a strategy which he maintains is often counter-productive. (Interestingly, this increased physicality and directiveness is also found with mothers of infants with visual impairments who have problems with joint focus (Behl *et al.*, 1996) and with parents of infants with language delays (Housman, 1996).) Dunst and Trivette (1988) remind us that the style of interaction is determined not just by characteristics within the infant and parent. Using a social systems model they identify multiple determinants including family climate, local support, styles modelled by others whom they esteem, and child diagnosis and developmental status. (Holroyd and MacArthur, 1976, cited by Hodapp, 1988, found mothers of children with autism experience more stress than mothers of children with Down's syndrome.) Beth and Steve Taylor imply that they were influenced by how others saw their son, their family and their role.

We can see examples of Beth adopting the controlling style when she tells how she used to try to show Gary how to build a tower, and hand over hand how to scribble with crayon on paper, although she acknowledges that 'the more I tried to direct, the more he withdrew' (p. 212). Later she recognises that although things were improving they still were not quite right because 'we were still playing the director's role and leading him for much too much of the time' (p. 215). Ben's teachers tackled this issue of the need to *make* people attend and Lynne Knott describes how one of the staff developed a new skill in 'allowing himself not to succeed in fully getting Ben's attention', learning not to be too 'pushy' and resisting the 'temptation to dominate Ben to get his attention' (p. 192).

The issue of not being in full control all of the time can be more difficult for teachers perhaps than for parents, though the culture that learning should be painful to be beneficial can be popular in our society. Beth and Steve Taylor are clearly enamoured with the non-directiveness of Intensive Interaction (and other also non-directive approaches), but even without the accountability professionals face, feel the pressure of 'what's he being *made* to do?'. Jordan and Powell (1995) are eclectic in their recommendations for practice, seeing a place for structured teaching as well as facilitative work. When it comes to the area of joint attention though, they are quite clear:

> In our experience the most productive way to begin to teach joint attention is to start as in normal development by noticing where the individual is looking, or what the individual is doing, and commenting or interacting with that so that joint attention is ensured. The important point is not to try to impose one's own agenda but rather to follow the lead of the child; he or she has to learn what an interaction is as well as what a particular interaction means. This means that time spent letting the child establish his or her own starting point is not time wasted if it

263

brings that child closer to understanding that they do have a starting point and that it is something that can mean something to someone else.

Trevarthen *et al.* (1996) conclude that 'it seems that mothers behave as they do in response to the puzzling ways their autistic children behave. They may behave automatically in ways that do not give the child the specially responsive and directed kind of response that is needed to help development'.

It is noteworthy that there seems to be some discrepancy between the advice of those interested in early intervention with children with autism and much of the general culture of advice for intervention. Many writers concerned with autism advocate very specialist interventions which do not mirror normal development (for example Lovaas, 1987: behavioural approaches; Waldon, 1983: asocial activities). In contrast, many writers (for example Trevarthen *et al.*, 1996; Davies, 1997) concerned with early interaction maintain the view that the interactive style in normal interactions is the most facilitative style and one which should be aimed for. The implication is that the parent has to adapt her/his style so that the adult behaviours and interactive processes that would be elicited by the infant in the ideal scenario are somehow produced when the autistic infant does not elicit them. This we have described as practitioners of Intensive Interaction needing to have an 'inner switch' (Nind and Hewett, 1994, p. 96–7), and is what the parents (and teachers) here clearly do.

An interesting tension emerges from this which provides a real challenge to the interactive partner of the individual with autism. The tension is between overriding the negative signals of the autistic person in order to do instead things which are not elicited by them but which are part of a nurturing interactive style, and continuing to be responsive to that person. Ben's teacher actually states 'we had to have a more responsive role and follow Ben's lead' (p. 191), and yet on one level this would mean leaving Ben to his preferred social isolation. The way through this tension is clearly complex. There is something quite skilled about the way a practitioner of Intensive Interaction maintains a responsive style, and does indeed respond to some very idiosyncratic behaviours and signals, whilst simultaneously overriding some automatic or intuitive responses which would not be helpful. We see examples of Gary's parents and Ben's teachers learning not to be offput by what are ostensibly the discouraging behaviours, and learning to look for and interpret the encouraging ones.

Beth comments on how they came to be close enough to Gary to be able fully to interpret his expressions.

Intensive Interaction is not alone as an approach which makes use of normal developmental principles and interactive processes with children with autism. We often read recommendations like that of Jordan and Powell above that we need to attend to how things are learnt in normal development. The usual recommendation, however, is that this is used in conjunction with some kind of structured, directive work. An obvious example of this is Duchan's (1983) analysis of a continuum of interactive styles. She describes a 'nurturing' style characterised by semantic contingency, motherese and 'acceptance of whatever the child says or does as legitimate and important' (p. 53) and a contrasting 'teaching' style characterised by adult-initiated activities and an application of adult standards of correctness. Duchan uses observational evidence of various interactive styles used with one autistic child (coincidentally also a Gary) to conclude that a nurturing style alone is ineffective and that one needs to use a combination of the best features of each style. Duchan comments:

> In order to be semantically contingent, one must wait for initiations from the child. Gary did not readily initiate. This suggests that mutual referencing, which starts with what is on the child's mind, is rarely feasible with Gary. Such semantic contingency on the part of the adult requires that the child be engaged in something that can be talked about in ordinary language ... Observing Gary in his 'self-stimulatory' states, one gets the sense that he is tuned out on the world. In other words, unless strongly encouraged, Gary does not do enough to offer his interactants a potential source for them to comment on easily or comfortably. Snow's description of mothers imputing intentionality and content to the infants' actions and vocalizations (Snow, 1977) does not work for interactants such as Gary, who fail to pay attention to what is going on around them.

Duchan makes some important points here, but there is a danger in her interpretation that the difficult parts of mutual referencing and imputing intentionality are impossible or that the usual adult strategies are inappropriate. We would argue instead that this kind of analysis highlights the challenge for the adult (sophisticated) interactive partner. Erring towards a reversion to the structured and the directive, we suggest, arises from not being able to imagine or see the nurturing style being used in the highly skilled ways that practitioners of Intensive Interaction have managed. Perhaps Duchan and others would draw different conclusion from observing interactions between our Gary and his parents.

Similarly, Olley (1985) recognises the importance of reciprocity and playful interactions in teaching people with autism, but holds back from fully embracing a natural interactive model. Garfin and Lord (1986) acknowledge the need for remediation efforts to take into account the link between social interaction and communication, and thus point to the need for mutuality, but still propose educational approaches with an emphasis on teacher-directiveness and skills training. Christie and Wimpory (1986) come very close to going whole-heartedly with the interactive, using musical interactions which 'parallel the mother-infant relationship' to 'give the child exaggerated and repeated experiences of pre-verbal communication' (p. 6). They combine this, however, with behavioural approaches to teaching gesture. We are excited by the communication work of Davies (1997) with young children with autism. Davies (p. 138) argues that:

> If a realistic understanding of how communication usually develops can be combined with an understanding of the disturbances which arise from autism, it is possible to develop strategies for keeping the process on track, introduce techniques to minimise the disturbance, and give this group of children access to the necessary learning experiences. These interactive processes of communication must underpin early speech development if the children are to learn meaningful communication skills.

In practice, this relates into Davies's approach in which the nursery staff attempt to get the interactions with the children into a pattern which is reciprocal and synchronous. As we discussed above, the adults' inherent skills are utilised, but 'it is also necessary to be aware of the impact of the child's disturbed signals and responses, thus limiting the disruption to the flow of communication' (p. 141). Again, the approach differs from Intensive Interaction in the way in which some artificial structure and directiveness is incorporated. In this case, the children are taught, through teacher-directed tasks, to behave in ways which trigger good adult responsiveness (to give eye contact and maintain good proximity, for example), rather than beginning with the adults adapting their styles.

Intensive Interaction does seem to go further down the non-directive line than other approaches. It does this practically as well as philosophically. This may be because of its strong practice-base – the way Intensive Interaction developed through exploratory work and critical reflection by very skilled, involved and supported teachers. In this way we were able actually to gain a knowledge of what imputing intentionality and establishing joint attention – with people who are very difficult to reach – looked and felt like. This is illuminated further in this volume. One might expect contributors here to have reached some degree of being comfortable with non-directive work; what is exciting for us is that they describe this in practice and that parents like Beth and Steve Taylor have found the approach to be so liberating.

Conclusion

We have found that taking a specific focus on autism has prompted us to think in some new ways and with some greater depth about the approach we advocate. The reflections of the parents and professionals in this book who use Intensive Interaction on a daily basis with individuals with autism are invaluable for clarifying how some of the ideas transcend into practice. There are complex theoretical ideas about why and how a naturalistic, interactive approach like Intensive Interaction may be relevant for people with autism (see Nind and Powell, pending; Nind, 1997). There is empirical evidence that the approach is effective with individuals with autism (Nind, 1996; Nind and Williams, under review), but this is sparse. The narrative accounts here enrich our understanding of the issues and inform any evaluation of the worth of the approach.

Parents using Intensive Interaction

In this commentary we have included some discussion of issues related to parents interacting with children with autism. We go on now to respond to the contributions by Beth and Steve Taylor and Ian and Antonella Bruce in a discussion of parents doing Intensive Interaction. The issue of what parents think about Intensive Interaction is an important one in the minds of teachers and we are often asked about it. We have heard from Val Stothard about how the approach was welcomed by the parents of students at her school. This positive response is often reported to us, but we need to remember that parents are likely to be just as varied in their outlooks as practitioners. They too may need time to adjust to the ideas and practices of interactive approaches, especially if they have been recipients of professional advice to interact more like teachers! We hope that the reflections by the parents writing in this book will be helpful to readers approaching Intensive Interaction from a parental perspective.

In this section we see parents reflecting on their struggles to meet their children's needs at all kinds of levels. Beth and Steve Taylor relate a sense of ultimately looking for an approach which would enable them as parents to be able to relate to their son and to improve his quality of life. In contrast, Ian and Antonella Bruce relate much more to an external struggle to have appropriate provision for their daughter, whilst spending less conscious energy debating how they should be with her. We see the Taylors feeling liberated by using an interactive approach which prioritises communication and social interaction. We see the Bruces using a powerful interactive style in an intuitive way. None of the professionals working with these parents seem to have advocated or encouraged this, what we would regard as fundamentally important, establishment of the underpinnings for communication development.

There is a whole body of psychological literature which analyses the style of interaction between infants, both normally developing and disabled, and their parents/caregivers. Much of this is based on observational studies, some with greater empirical sophistication (such as Behl *et al.*, 1996). Dunst and Trivette (1988) note the influence on interactive style of support networks because, according to a social systems perspective, support networks have an accumulative affect on parental well-being, family functioning and ultimately interactive style. For the parents writing here, social support networks tend to be informal rather than formal or professional. While intrafamily support is important, one might expect this to be insufficient to maintain a relaxed, nurturing interactive style. Hodapp (1988) adds to the picture of a complex medley of influences by arguing that interactive behaviours also reflect how both participants feel about each other and how they perceive each other. The parental accounts here give us insights into the parent–infant interaction process from the parents' perspective. We can see how Beth Taylor becomes painfully aware of how directive she was being in her interactions and how she increasingly begins to think and act in accordance with a more responsive style of interaction. We also gain insights into a pattern in which Francesca's parents channel their desire to make things happen for her in such a way that their style of interaction with her remains an effective one.

Several themes emerge for us from these parental accounts: the importance of reading and giving signals; the importance of imputing intentionality; the concept of good interactive match or 'fit'; and the importance of a sense of efficacy. We have mentioned already, in our discussion of Gary as a child with autism, the challenge for his parents of reading his signals and giving back signals which are meaningful and unthreatening. On this theme of signalling, Antonella Bruce conveys how, on reflection, she was trying quite early on to give Francesca the message that she was there with her and attending to her. She also describes how she was picking up on responses from Francesca which were barely perceptible to her, and quite probably not noticeable to others: 'I don't know quite how I read her . . . I've learned to sort of read little bits of the way she moves and holds her head' (p. 248). She describes her faith that wanting things to happen with Francesca's development would ultimately help them to happen. Without knowing that she was doing so, Antonella was doing what we technically describe as 'imputing intentionality'. She was picking up on the tiniest of behaviours or responses and giving them significance and meaning.

We can learn from the literature on caregiver–infant interaction that a feature of an optimum interactive style is there being a good 'fit' between the caregiver's input and the infant's need. This good fit incorporates a good match with the infant's developmental level and interests and also a good match in timing, with interaction which blends with the infant's tempo and with initiations made during times of optimum states of arousal. This last aspect is one which Antonella Bruce is conscious of in her play with Francesca. She writes about the evenings being good times for both of them and that she became 'better and better' at recognising when her baby was receptive and 'switched on'. The research of Guess *et al.*, (1997) emphasises the importance of maximising the states of 'alertness' and 'responsiveness' in young children with multiple and severe learning disabilities as this maximises learning opportunities. They are looking to identify or develop interventions which bring this about and observations of Antonella Bruce indicate that parents can create quality time, using interactional behaviour, which does just this.

This links in with the importance of parents' feelings of efficacy.

269

Goldberg (1977) argued that just as infants need to learn that they can be effective in making something happen in their caregiver's behaviour, so parents need to learn that they can have an effect – elicit a response – in their infant. This mutual efficacy is vital to the maintenance of interactive episodes. Antonella Bruce makes several references to this sense of efficacy being vital for her. She describes 'wanting to confirm the responses I thought I was getting'; she enthuses 'like all other moments, when she had finally managed to do something we felt a great sense of achievement not only for her, but also for us', and she reflects on how it felt when Francesca started to turn to her father's voice 'naturally this has made him feel very good'. Similarly, Beth Taylor conveys the importance of a sense of efficacy in that once she had found an interactive approach which enabled her to elicit a positive response from Gary she never looked back.

The sense of efficacy arising from these communicative interactions contrasts starkly with the low levels of positive responding thought to be a disincentive to staff in Clegg, Standen and Cromby's (1991) analysis of talk sessions between staff and adults with profound intellectual disabilities. These authors conclude that staff 'may need to become more responsive to client state and discover ways to fine-tune their attempts at interaction' (p. 399).

Finally, a complex and central issue requires consideration before we leave the issue of parents doing Intensive Interaction: is it helpful for parents to engage in intellectual reflection on their interactive style? In *Access to Communication* (Nind and Hewett, 1994) we described in great detail an interactive episode between Sue and Thomas, mother and infant. We reflected on the intuitive style of interaction which Sue used and argued that as teachers we need to do two things: one, allow ourselves to be intuitive in interacting with our learners; and two, intellectualise about this process in order to use the intuitions in a clever way and to maximum effect. We also wrote about the need to combine these in a 'judicious blend', switching between using natural, intuitive behaviours and a considered deployment of the principles of Intensive Interaction (p. 96). The question arises in terms of parents doing Intensive Interaction of whether they also should, or do, combine these two elements.

Part of what we are acknowledging in our commitment to Intensive Interaction is that 'parents know best'; that intuitions or instincts are good. We are emphasising the potency of the optimum parent (caregiver)–infant interaction style for teaching sociability and communication. We are advocating that we need to learn from parents' intuitive processes rather than seek to teach parents how to behave more like teachers. We are not, however, saying that knowing how best to interact with an infant with disabilities is easy or automatic. Again we would refer readers back to *Access to Communication* (chapter 2) for a discussion of the literature about how the positive interactive spiral may break down when an infant does not respond or develop as we would anticipate, based on our intuitions and experience. Some of the more recent literature (such as Beveridge, 1989; Behl *et al.*, 1996) shows how complex this issue can be. Parents may be using their intuitive style regardless of a lack of responsiveness from their infant, they may be responding intuitively to the lack of responsiveness by being more directive or by filling the turn-taking gaps themselves, they may be adjusting very sensitively to the mixed messages they receive from their infant, or they may be doing a mixture of all three.

Behl *et al.* (1996), in common with a trend in interpretations of interactions with infants with disabilities, postulate that the modified style they found in mothers of infants with visual impairments was matched with the infants' needs. Here the increased parental initiation of interactions, and the greater dominance of the children's activities, was seen alongside appropriate responsivity and effect. Interestingly, the authors also postulate whether these more positive findings, compared to studies of 10–20 years ago, may be related to the quality and quantity of early intervention and support services. This is an optimistic hypothesis. We perceive both potential dangers and benefits in family based early interventions with regard to these complex issues. There is a danger that exhausted and desperate parents, for example, may well welcome being told what to do and how to be with their infant, even if this detracts from them responding in some of the best natural ways. There is also potential for early interventions to help parents to see where they are already being effective and support them in continuing to use important interactive processes despite slow progress and limited feedback. Intensive Interaction as an early intervention may offer the best of both worlds in that it can give parents something very practical and tangible which they can be doing, but which builds on, rather than replaces, their natural, intuitive nurturing. This, in common with language interventions based on a conversational model (Girolametto, 1988), can empower parents as facilitators of development, which Hodapp (1988) prioritises. This is preferential to parents relying on an 'expert', an unhelpful position which Housman (1996) warns of. Similarly, McConkey (1994) argues that interactive games are more easily 'owned' by parents and more likely to be used and adopted by them.

The potential benefits and the dangers of Intensive Interaction used in this way, however, seem to rest on this notion of intellectualising the process. We have emphasised that, unlike teachers (and some other practitioners), parents do not have objectives, tasks, checklists and timetables – the power of the parenting interactive style is its tasklessness, relaxed atmosphere, open structure and responsiveness. Teachers doing Intensive Interaction have the challenge of thinking in terms of learning opportunities rather than tasks, of creating an atmosphere which is at once both relaxed and purposeful, of having a structure to their day which supports use of the approach. There is a need for teachers to monitor the effectiveness of their work, to reflect on what constitutes good strategy and powerful interaction for each individual, to share this with colleagues, and to learn principles which can be employed with other individuals. Parents perhaps need only to know what works with their individual infant. How much knowing this requires reflection will vary. There is again perhaps a delicate balancing act to be achieved between standing back enough to think about how operating a set of principles might help one across a difficult patch, and not standing back so much that one loses that rich, subjective involvement which allows one to operate at an instinctive level.

Parents doing Intensive Interaction will need to make decisions about this tension in the process, and professionals supporting parents have a duty here also. Housman (1996) argues that changing parents' interactive behaviour involves both learning new skills and enhanced levels of awareness. She also makes the point that intervening with verbal explanations and written instructions 'can be a way of compounding parental tendencies towards directive interactional styles' when they need to 'understand the positive processes which provide the framework for subsequent language development' (p. 9). Reflecting in any way on how we interact, however, can have the effect of making us self-conscious, it can even stultify our natural processes, at least in the first instance. For a while Antonella Bruce is, on the whole, not consciously aware of what she does in her interactions with Francesca which is so effective. To us it looks like Intensive Interaction because all the powerful interactive principles are in use. It is not Intensive Interaction however (at least not Intensive Interaction with capital letters!) because she does not think about it in these terms and because she is not using that element of careful reflection on the process. It may empower parents like Antonella and Ian Bruce and others to see what it is they do so well. Giving a name to the process may help them to discuss it more, and even to do it more often and with even greater skill. This would be our hope. We would certainly not want to disempower parents by not involving them in the abstract conceptualisation of their processes. Any formalisation of what they do into an 'approach', though, and any prompts for them to reflect on their processes, would need to proceed with caution if we are to retain the strengths of their intuitive interactions.

References

Behl, D.D., Akers J.F., Boyce, G.C. and Taylor, M.J. (1996) 'Do mothers interact differently with children who are visually impaired?', *Journal of Visual Impairment and Blindness*, Nov–Dec 1996, 501–511.

Beveridge, S. (1989) 'Parents as teachers of children with special educational needs'. In: Sugden, D. (ed.) *Cognitive Approaches in Special Education*. London: Falmer Press.

Christie, P. and Wimpory, D. (1986) 'Recent research into the development of communicative competence and its implications for the teaching of autistic children', *Communication*, **20**, 4–7.

Clegg, J.A., Standen, P.J. and Cromby, J.J. (1991) 'The analysis of talk sessions between staff and adults with profound intellectual disability', *Australia and New Zealand Journal of Developmental Disabilities*, **17**, 4, 391–400.

Davies, G. (1997) 'Communication'. In: Powell, S. and Jordan, R. (eds) *Autism and Learning: A Guide to Good Practice*. London: David Fulton.

Duchan, J.F. (1983) 'Autistic children are noninteractive: Or so we say', *Seminars in Speech and Language*, **4**, 1, 53–61.

Dunst, C.J. and Trivette, C.M. (1988) 'Determinants of Parent and Child Interactive Behaviour'. In: Marfo, K. (ed.) *Parent-Child Interaction and Developmental Disabilities: Theory, Research and Intervention*. New York: Praeger.

Garfin, D.G. and Lord, C. (1986) 'Communication as a social problem in autism'. In: Schopler, E. and Mesibov, G.B. (eds) *Social Behaviour in Autism*. New York: Plenum Press.

Girolametto, L.E. (1988) 'Developing dialogue skills: The effects of a conversational model of language intervention'. In: Marfo, K. (ed.) *Parent-Child Interaction and Developmental Disabilities: Theory, Research and Intervention.* New York: Praeger.

Goldberg, S. (1977) Social competence in infancy: a model of parent-infant interaction', *Merrill-Palmer Quarterly*, **23**, 163–77.

Guess, D., Roberts, S. and Holvoet, J. (1997) 'Observing Alertness and Responsiveness Among Infants with Multiple and Severe Disabilities', *TASH Newsletter*, May 1997, 24–25.

Hobson, R.P. (1993) *Autism and the Development of Mind.* Hillsdale: Lawrence Erlbaum.

Hodapp, R.M. (1988) 'The role of maternal emotions and perceptions in interactions with young handicapped children'. In: Marfo, K. (ed.) *Parent-Child Interaction and Developmental Disabilities: Theory, Research and Intervention.* New York: Praeger.

Housman, L. (1996) 'Helping parents to communicate', *Human Communication*, Nov–Dec 1996, 9–11.

Howlin, P. (1986) 'An overview of social behaviour in autism'. In: Schopler, E. and Mesibov, G.B. (eds) *Social Behaviour in Autism.* New York: Plenum Press.

Jordan, R. and Powell, S. (1995) *Understanding and Teaching Children with Autism.* Chichester: Wiley.

Koegel, R.L. and Koegel, L.K. (1995) *Teaching Children with Autism: Strategies for Initiating Positive Interactions and Improving Learning Opportunities.* Baltimore: Paul H. Brookes.

Lovaas, O.I. (1987) 'Behavioural treatment and normal educational and intellectual functioning in young autistic children', *Journal of Consulting and Clinical Psychology*, **55**, 1, 3–9.

Lyons, J. (1977) *Semantics Volume Two.* London: Cambridge: University Press.

Massie, H.N. (1978) 'Blind ratings of mother-infant interaction in home movies of pre-psychotic and normal infants', *American Journal of Psychiatry*, **135**, 1371–74.

McConkey, R. (1994) 'Families at play: Interventions for children with developmental handicaps'. In: Hellendoorn, J., van der Koij, R. and Sutton-Smith, B. (eds) *Play and Intervention.* New York: State University of New York Press.

Nind, M. and Hewett, D. (1988) 'Interaction as curriculum: a process method in school for pupils with severe learning difficulties', *British Journal of Special Education*, **15**, 55–57.

Nind, M. and Hewett, D. (1994) *Access to Communication: Developing the Basics of Communication with People with Severe Learning Difficulties through Intensive Interaction.* London: David Fulton.

Nind, M. (1996) 'Efficacy of Intensive Interaction: Developing Sociability and Communication in People with Severe and Complex Learning Difficulties Using an Approach Based on Caregiver–Infant Interaction', *European Journal of Special Needs Education*, **11**, 1, 48–66.

Nind, M. (1997) 'Is Intensive Interaction a useful and appropriate approach when learning disabilities are compounded by autism?', Conference paper, BILD International Conference, Manchester, 14–17 September 1997.

Nind, M. and Powell, S.D. (pending) 'Intensive Interaction and Autism: Some Theoretical Concerns'.

Nind, M. and Williams, L. (under review) 'Using Intensive Interaction with an adult with autism: A case study of Kris'.

Ogletree, B.Y. (1992) 'Communication Intervention for a preverbal child with autism: A case study', *Focus on Autistic Behaviour*, 7, 1, 1–12.

Olley, J.G. (1985) 'Social aspects of communication in children with autism'. In: Schopler, E. and Mesibov, G.B. (eds) *Communication Problems in Autism*. New York: Plenum Press.

Ricks, D.M. (1979) 'Making sense of experience to make sensible sounds: experimental investigations of early vocal communication in pre-verbal autistic and normal children'. In: Bullowa, M. (ed.) *Before Speech: The Beginnings of Interpersonal Communication*. Cambridge: Cambridge University Press.

Sigman, M., Mundy, P., Sherman, T. and Ungerer, J. (1986) 'Social interactions of autistic, mentally retarded and normal children and their caregivers', *Journal of Child Psychology and Psychiatry*, 27, 647–656.

Snow, C.E. (1997) 'The development of conversation between mothers and babies', *Journal of Child Language*, 4, 1–22.

Trevarthen, C., Aitken, K., Papondi, D. and Roberts, J. (1996) *Children with Autism: Diagnosis and Intervention to Meet their Need*. London: Jessica Kingsley.

Waldon, J. (1983) 'Understanding understanding'. Prviately published and circulated paper. One of occasional series of such papers on 'Functional Learning'.

Wing, L. (1997) 'The history of ideas on autism: legends, myths and reality', *Autism: The International Journal of Research and Practice*, 1, 1, 13–23.

275

Chapter 14

Future Developments

Dave Hewett and Melanie Nind

Introduction

In this final chapter we look to the future and bring together some thoughts on what might happen with the continuing development of interactive approaches. In our opening chapter we addressed some of the recent literature to put this work on Intensive Interaction into some kind of recent historical context. We now to some extent sum up where we are at – the state of the art of teaching communication. We highlight some of the obstacles to the ongoing development of interactive approaches and the quality teaching of communication. The first stage in responding to the challenge presented lies perhaps in delineating the problems, in setting some kind of agenda of issues to be resolved. The second stage may be in looking for allies, for others 'who speak our language', and for developments which fit with our own perspectives. We do some of this here, but we fully acknowledge that we do not have all the answers.

Intensive Interaction developed and continues to develop (not least by colleagues writing in this book), however, because of creative responding to students'/clients' needs, rather than reacting or responding to a poorly informed government agenda. In this spirit of being proactive, reflective and responsive in an appropriate way, this chapter goes on to explore opportunities for developing our practice and thinking. We share some ideas about how the teaching of communication, using an interactive/process approach, might be fruitfully understood. This will hopefully be a catalyst for the dialogue, the exchange of ideas and the sorts of experiences characterised by this book, to continue and to blossom.

Improving the teaching of communication

Teaching people who are still at early stages of development to communicate is difficult. We have stated in chapter 1 that the good but limited number of publications in this area is probably an appropriate reflection of the state of our arts. In education at least, it is only since 1971 that the education service has been fully involved in teaching people with learning difficulties, and a detailed focus on early, pre-verbal communication abilities has been a recent development within that.

We anticipate that practitioners in many places and disciplines will continue to study and evaluate Intensive Interaction and other such approaches. We judge that the signs of this happening are already there and hope that the examples of work that we offer in this book will contribute to the motivation of other practitioners. We hope too that the work that has so far appeared on Intensive Interaction has illustrated much of what we already know about the potential of the approach to enhance the lifestyles of the people we are caring for or teaching. However, we suggest also that there are pointers as to how much more may be achieved for individual service users everywhere, as the use of such techniques becomes more prevalent and staff ability with them is increasingly refined.

One already visible ramification of this work is that the absolute priority of work on communication is becoming manifestly more visible in service delivery as knowledge about how to work on communication becomes more available. There seems to be what might be termed a 'feedback cycle' between the increasing concerns of practitioners to deliver and the increase in publications describing the nuts and bolts of that delivery in terms of teaching communication.

Issues affecting communication teaching in special schools

In special schools, one of the immediate concerns remains that of resolving the priority of work on communication with the demand for broad and balanced curriculum delivery and ensuring for pupils a visible access to the National Curriculum. For many teachers it still seems that these two priorities can be in conflict with each other in terms of demands on time committed to the various priorities. The recent publication from

277

the School Curriculum and Assessment Authority: *Planning the Curriculum for Pupils with Profound and Multiple Learning Difficulties* (SCAA, 1996) is helpful, stressing such matters as:

- The whole curriculum is broader than the National Curriculum and religious education and must reflect priorities for pupils with profound and multiple learning difficulties. (p. 8)
- The priorities identified for a pupil with profound and multiple learning difficulties will often relate to the skills of communication, information technology or to personal or social development. (p. 15)
- The manner in which pupils are addressed and handled communicates messages about their personal worth and dignity which can contribute to their self-esteem. Hence, daily routines should be recognised positively and incorporated into planning rather than being regarded as an interruption. (p. 16)
- It is important to avoid anxiety over allocation of specific hours and minutes to each subject: schools will wish to aim for balance and breadth in the time available over the year or key stage, utilising the time most profitably and ensuring a productive atmosphere is established. (p. 17)

Anecdotal experience of special schools visited at the time of writing indicates that there is still significant 'National Curriculum stress' amongst teachers who are teaching pupils at very early stages of learning. One of the sources of this stress may well be the void in understanding between the authors of the SCAA document and the practice of many, not all, OFSTED inspectors in SLD schools. Signals from both bodies give reason to hope that this situation is being addressed. Indeed, there is also anecdotal evidence of SLD schools experiencing positive inspections from realistic and informed OFSTED teams. Perhaps even by the time this book goes to press, the comments we make here will be less relevant and school inspections will reflect the sentiments expressed in *Planning the Curriculum for Pupils with Profound and Multiple Learning Difficulties*.

The positive shift from SCAA can be traced back to the 1993 National Curriculum Council document, *Special Needs and the National Curriculum: Opportunity and Challenge*. Since the publication of this document, a number of publications have appeared that are helpful or important in various ways concerning planning the curriculum generally for pupils with severe learning difficulties, and the way in which National Curriculum access can be made available to such pupils (for example see Sebba *et al.*, 1993; Byers and Rose, 1996; SCAA, 1996). These publications stress that the National Curriculum programmes of study will comprise only part of the curriculum for pupils with the more severe learning difficulties. They also cite the centrality of work on such things as communication for these pupils, giving guidance particularly on the manner in which communication should be viewed and taught as a cross-curricular element to everything which takes place.

Issues affecting communication teaching in other services

In services other than education, barriers to take up of approaches such as Intensive Interaction are different, but there are similarities also. Some services in some areas seem to have heartbreakingly high staff turnover, with working conditions and rates of pay a major factor in the transitory nature of any staff group. A semblance of stability in a staff group is of course essential for any coherent, progressive work to be carried out. There remains a major imbalance in the responsibilities given to and technical expertise expected of staff in some services and the status accorded to them.

There are also difficulties with staff selection and staff training. Recognising and teaching good communication skills is not straightforward. Just as teachers have tended to do with their learners, there may be a tendency for managers to avoid facing the difficult areas and to focus on what is more directly observable instead. Failure to address the communication abilities of staff is a barrier to doing interactive work.

Another barrier to such work, particularly in adult services, may well be the otherwise totally laudable emphasis on issues such as community presence and ordinary life. We have explored these themes in detail elsewhere, but many workplaces we have seen have such an emphasis on the learning of skills, particularly 'life skills', and on training for what looks like normal behaviour, that the time available for matters such as communicating and simply relating seems devoured. Staff who absolutely dedicate themselves to matters of task and instrumental achievement may also find it culturally and technically daunting to involve themselves in the more discursive nature of communication-learning activities.

There are issues for service-managers here. Quite often we perceive that there is a gulf between the expectation of the managers of an organisation providing services and the desires of the face-to-face workers to explore ways of meeting individual need. One reason may be that many of the current middle-managers were the staff who were sent on courses such as 'Social Role Valorization' (Wolfensburger, 1983) during the 1980s. This may remain their guiding vision, whilst the outlook of the people they manage, though not rejecting those values, nonetheless has moved on into something more eclectic and sophisticated. Staff have begun, at the very least, to ask the question posed by Jenny Corbett (1991): 'What's so great about being normal?' (and others who critique normalisation such as Brown, 1994; Chappell, 1992; Emerson, 1992) . Whilst the Wolfensburger-style normalisation principles have led to practice which serves as an obstacle to the kind of practice we advocate, there is growing recognition that learning to communicate is essential to any concept of an 'ordinary life'.

We want to make sure that this section finishes unequivocally on the positive note intended. There are potential barriers to staff in all services giving the proper sense of priority to work on communication. Such barriers may well be barriers to innovative work and any change in working style and emphasis in various areas of our work, not just communication. Nonetheless, the interest displayed and the eagerness that many practitioners show to take on and develop work on communication with the individuals with whom they work is heartening and reassuring. There is a mature and growing debate around the setting of our various priorities for our service users in a manner which ensures they do not become priorities which are mutually exclusive. We have reason to expect that for the priority which is the focus of this book, communication, there will be increasingly available accounts of staff carrying out the practicalities of day-by-day work. We hope and expect that other practitioners will produce authoritative work on Intensive Interaction, or responsive environments, whatever they want to call it, which will push the boundaries of knowledge and aspiration.

Working with process, objective and structure

This section explores approaches to thinking about, conceptualising technically, work on communication and human relating within the structure of the daily provision of experiences in services. Inevitably, as educationalists we are approaching these issues primarily from the point of view of thinking about such things as 'curriculum'. However, we will make parallels throughout, either directly or by implication to what we identify as the similar issues for other services. Some of that which we set out here can be found in various places in our previous writing, some of it is thoughts we have been working with for some time but have not iterated previously. Part of our intention is deliberately to set out some thinking with a degree of incompleteness in many instances, with the intention that this points towards what we see as opportunities for further work.

The relationship between how something is taught and what is learnt

The title of this section suggests that we are about to venture into mysterious territory. We hope that proves not to be so, but we would be the first to admit that what we are to set out here needs to be the focus for a great deal of further thought. Our thinking on this topic commenced at the very earliest stages of our work on Intensive Interaction, indeed we went through a stage in the late 1980s of doing rather more reading and talking on curriculum theory, and the related practices of teaching within a particular curriculum framework, than we do now.

The issue arose for us because, as our work with Intensive Interaction reached the stage of coherence where we could talk and write about it and describe it (hopefully) to others in writing, the differences between what we were describing and other, then popular, approaches to teaching became obvious. The main differences are well documented, but briefly are concerned with: during teaching sessions the teacher is facilitative and interpretative rather than directive; the teacher looks for and encourages highly active participation from the learner in the session; the session virtually doesn't take place unless the teacher succeeds in gaining this participation; the teacher's activity – the teaching during the session – is a knowledgeable improvisation rather than following strict rules; it is

281

difficult and even unnecessary to describe a pre-determined objective for the session in terms of what the learner will achieve in that session; the learning attainments are measurable, but take place gradually over a period of time as a result of the learner's progressive involvements in the sessions.

Actually, that list of characteristics doesn't seem so daunting nor so radical now, more than ten years later, as it did when we first considered it. It seemed radical at the time because of the apparent departure from previous approaches. Much has moved on since then, owing to both work and thought taking place elsewhere at the time, and because of developments since. Indeed, recent publications mentioning interactive approaches (e.g. Collis and Lacey, 1996) are helping the use of thinking such as this to move into the mainstream of the conceptualisation of our work.

Prior to that time, behavioural approaches more or less ubiquitously held sway in our work and in most other people's. In many senses they still do, and the influence of behaviourist thinking is still general and we believe a limiting factor to many potential new developments – particularly, for instance, in many teachers being unable to think beyond the setting of strict session objectives and very directive work to achieve them. Indeed, this thinking can be identified in the OFSTED approach to accountability. However, as we shall assert, we are not arguing here against the use of the best aspects of behavioural approaches. We are easily able to point to both the professional benefits personally accrued from working with such approaches and the extent to which, for instance, a task analysis framework is a good tool for helping with the teaching of skills.

One of the main differences between behavioural and 'interactive/ process' approaches (a term used by Collis and Lacey, 1996, throughout) is the sense of what we might call 'linearity' endowed by behavioural approaches and not necessarily gained from interactive/process approaches. By this we mean the reassuring sensation that the teacher is attempting to set out the teaching in small, sequential, easily controlled steps, with one step logically following on from another. Each step has its own target and any teaching session is coherently related to the whole because of the presence of a session target. The learning attainments can be observed and measured similarly. The reassurance comes primarily from the sense of control over the learning that the teacher is able to observe and exert, from the sense of an accurate diagnosis of what still is to be learnt. This can give a (perhaps false) impression that involving the learner with the tasks is purposeful. Reassurance comes also from the ease with which assessment and record-keeping then demonstrate the overall sense of control to others, such as OFSTED inspectors.

Of course, there cannot be anything wrong with the state of affairs described above if working in that way fulfils all of the aspirations we have for the learning of our students and service users. Unfortunately it does not. There are many potential or actual drawbacks to allowing the behavioural framework for teaching described above to dominate expectations for all learning, or to dominate the nature of the learning environment. The debate and arguments on this theme continue if not rage, causing some potentially damaging splits into apparently opposing camps among psychologists and educationalists.

For us, the first and most obvious drawback to behavioural approaches, though not the only one meaningful to us, is that it never seemed possible to teach communicating and relating by use of them. These human attainments are just too complicated and multi-faceted to be set out in any degree of linearity without drastically limiting or damaging the nature of what we try to teach. This was one of our original starting points in our work on Intensive Interaction; we knew from the outset that whatever we did with our work, influenced by Ephraim's (1979) original thinking, what we ended up with would not be, could not be, a behavioural type approach.

Actually, this point, that communication cannot be taught by behavioural methods, is not even contested by most behaviourists. It is worth dwelling for a moment on an essential conundrum here. If it is accepted that highly teacher-controlled and directed teaching approaches do not work for teaching something so important, why is it so seemingly difficult to gain acceptance of approaches to helping people learn things which are not so teacher-controlled and directed, but structured and carried out differently? This is not a small matter. One of the problems may be that special education became so reliant on behavioural approaches that it has become difficult for some of those immersed in it to think differently. We have had various anecdotal reports from teachers criticised by OFSTED inspectors for failing to set a clear session target in terms of learner outcomes for an Intensive Interaction session. Their view seems to be that those teachers have then failed to plan and describe their teaching coherently. This is a major continuing area of concern and work for all of us in our field and it is another reason why the work by Collis and Lacey (1996) and Ware (1996) is particularly important. They contribute authoritatively and sensitively to the issue.

It is possible, of course, to set out communication attainments in some sort of linear, sequential fashion. Even in pre-verbal learning and pre-intentional communication development there is some sense of order to the learning, a developmental pathway which is, to some extent, generally similar among and across infants. What it is important to remember, however, is that developmental assessments provide a seemingly linear record of the attainments, not a sequential set of learning targets. If we try to teach strictly to the attainments as targets in a controlled and directed fashion, we will probably not be providing the type of dynamic learning experiences which commonly produce the attainments as part of a rolling, cumulative process.

Pre-verbal learning, the fundamentals of communication, seems to arise best when the learner is involved in progressive, highly dynamic social experiences all having their place in this rolling, cumulative process. These experiences lack a sense of being highly teacher-controlled, though the teacher's sensitive and thoughtful behaviour is essential to the structure of the learning experiences and to the attainments produced. Even though this type of process teaching and learning seems untidy, chaotic even by comparison to teaching in behavioural style, all of us have unquestioning faith in its efficacy for nearly all normally developing infants. Geraint Ephraim (personal communication) gave a pertinent warning in the early 1980s not to go off on a mad tangent and develop some highly artificially systemised approach to teaching communication, without looking first at the model of human learning which clearly is powerful and works well.

This brings us back to the differences between behavioural approaches and interactive process ones such as Intensive Interaction. Communication learning, certainly early communication, occurs because the learner is involved in a complex dynamic system of experiences with the teacher. We cannot describe this learning in behavioural terms nor break it down into small, sequential steps. We cannot even be consciously aware of all aspects of the workings of it.

Moreover, we know (from the social cognition literature and from experience) that much more is being learnt by immersion in the process than a set of visible, trainable behaviours. What is also being learnt is the

284

development of the learner's thinking processes, their concepts or schemata. We have speculated previously (Nind and Hewett, 1994) about the necessity in our teaching to generate the process of thinking about social cause and effect: 'I do something, and it makes her do something'. Experimentation with this involves the learner in turn-taking, due to the teacher's response to her/his experimentation. The impact of having an effect on someone else reinforces for the learner the usefulness of what has been tried. This makes it more likely that the learner will repeat, and vary, this behaviour. Thus the learner is progressively learning more and more about social exchanges by experimenting with her/his own behaviour and having these experiments responded to. This seems to explain why normally developing infants learn about social interaction so quickly and it also emphasises the importance of the adult responsive style in the process of this learning.

Fundamental also to the development of these, what we might term, schematic sub-structures are other issues such as physical and psychological security, motivation, enjoyment, self-esteem, general emotional well-being. Developments here also underpin the learner's likelihood to experiment, and the process of teaching by Intensive Interaction aims to progressively contribute to development in these terms also.

So, we can talk about communication learning in terms of an observable set of skills such as the ability to make eye contact. These are likely to be the sorts of things we write about in assessments in order to record attainments. However, the assessment is recording the observable only. In order for these skills to be observable, we must also assume that so much has been learnt which is not observable, but which underpins the production of the observable behaviours. Thus an important element of an approach such as Intensive Interaction is that the teaching method and the teacher acknowledge this state of affairs. We are knowingly setting out to teach schematic sub-structures and other sub-structures to the learner and it is these sub-structures which underpin the observable skills. The teaching process, which has an orientation towards process and a lack of orientation towards training visible behaviours, embodies this.

What we can also say, of course, is that there is naturally a great deal of reinforcement implicit within the process. The learner's experimentations are reinforced by the responsive behaviour of the teacher, making it more likely that the behaviour will arise again. However, this reinforcement remains embedded within a dynamic process. The reinforcement is maintained within 'untidy' activities of many possibilities. The reinforcement is not lifted out and isolated from the rest of the process so that the teacher can concentrate only on the reproduction of behaviours trained by reinforcement. Observable behaviours are not regarded as session targets separate from the activation of the dynamic process which produces them.

This is why we must accustom ourselves to the use of an interactive/process approach for this learning and, indeed, do what is necessary to document the work, plan it, describe the teaching methods and the process aims, and keep especially scrupulous records of the learner attainments. As an aside, having made that effort on behalf of the teaching of communication because it is so important and so difficult to teach any other way, we should then be in a position to think more imaginatively about the use of more dynamic approaches to the teaching of many things. Work with Intensive Interaction gives insights into elements of the teaching process which make teaching sessions definably 'interactive'. Figure 14.1 lists some of these elements and presents us with a challenge. In order to make many activities more interactive and process-based, can the elements of activity in figure 14.1 be designed in to the presentation of activities?

There is an inevitable relationship in the learning of communication between the nature of what is learnt and how it is taught. What is learnt, the knowledge about communicating and relating, is complex, subtle, multi-faceted, many-layered. The learning experiences are like this also, though in the earliest stages the more experienced person, the parent, the teacher, seems to be possessed of wonderful intuitive ability to offer progressively monitored but nonetheless dynamic and complex learning situations. Attempts to change this teaching style, to reduce it to something more linear, something therefore which seems more teacher-controlled, is likely to have a fundamental effect on the nature of what is being learnt. In communication terms, the effect of increased teacher directiveness in communication sequences, for instance, effectively reduces the opportunity for the learner to learn about communication. This kind of effect has been documented in the literature studying interactions between parents and their infants with disabilities or learning difficulties (see Nind and Hewett, 1994). This consideration can be seen too in the accounts by the contributors to this book.

- A sense of partnership between learner and teacher.

- An atmosphere of dialogue, with the teacher prepared to be influenced by learner behaviours moment-by-moment – overall teacher responsiveness.

- The teacher at all times 'tuning-in' and monitoring learner behaviour sensitively so that teacher behaviour can be influenced moment-by-moment by learner behaviour.

- The teacher is prepared to give regard to the learner's state, interpreting thoughts and feelings from feedback signals.

- The learner's cognitive and emotional engagement paramount as part of the process.

- The teacher is looking for the moment-by-moment cognitive and emotional engagement of the learner with the teacher and/or the task, by the process of 'tuning-in' and monitoring.

- The activity 'unfolds' as a result of the sense of dialogue generated.

- The teacher will use pauses in the flow of the activity influenced by feedback signals from the learner's behaviour.

- The personal power in the activity is shared between the learner and the teacher with the learner assuming power to lead in various degrees.

- In some learning, such as early communication, the 'content' of the activity is generated by the learner first and foremost or generated by the teacher's responses to learner behaviours.

- For other activities the content may be decided upon by the teacher, but the unfolding of the content is influenced by the teacher responses to feedback signals about the learner's state.

- The activity does not continue beyond a point where the learner is engaged by it.

- The activity does not commence until the learner's engagement is attained.

Figure 14.1 What is 'interactive' about interaction activities?

Thinking about teaching in these terms can bring a sense of unease, particularly for those of us involved in education. We do seem to work in an atmosphere at present where there is a continual striving for teaching with greater precision, greater detailed focus on predicting what is to be learnt and how and when it will be learnt. We would suggest that there is not necessarily anything about teaching through activation of process which is directly in contravention of this aspiration though we would predict the learning arising from processes rather than lessons. However, it does seem that for many of us, and perhaps for the whole culture of teaching and learning, more openness is needed with regard to what constitutes teaching, so that our teaching culture can embrace approaches which work in this way. This is important in order to continue to develop the teaching of, for instance, communication, but we would suggest it presently resides as a significant challenge generally to our ways of doing things.

Furthermore, there is still a need for more technical knowledge to be developed which will help us to manage, and indeed manipulate, learning through process. In terms of the learning of early communication abilities, we seem to be at a stage where we can see that the learning occurs through the continuous activation of a process. We can analyse and visualise much of what the process is, how it takes place and why, particularly with regard to teacher behaviour and its relationship to the learning. However, the process is highly complex and dynamic, it doesn't seem to lend itself to being interpreted in any simple, linear fashion and it does seem that we may not understand, nor even be aware of all the workings of it. Whilst this may not bother parents teaching their developing infants, in education and other services there is a constant striving for a rational analysis of what we are doing and why. Some work in the United States may be pointing in a profitable direction for helping us to visualise such systems.

Dynamic systems perspective

Doug Guess and Wayne Sailor at the Department of Special Education at the University of Kansas have been studying human behaviour (Guess and Sailor, 1993) with regard to the recently developed theories of chaos (e.g. Gleick, 1987) in the natural sciences. In studies on students with 'profound handicaps' they have been focusing on behaviour states, described by Wolff (Wolff, 1959) as behavioural and physiological conditions ranging from sleep, to awake and crying among infants. They have been investigating the transitions of students with profound handicaps between the various behaviour states, the environmental factors influencing state conditions, and the manner in which this will affect alertness and responsiveness (Guess et al., 1993). They further studied behaviour state changes among 'individuals with profound disabilities' (Guess and Siegel-Causey, 1995) in an attempt to demonstrate the 'nonlinearity' of state changes in the students with the existence rather of 'complex behavioural processes' which warrant further investigation. Guess et al. (1995) started to attempt to identify the complex relations between behaviour state and environmental variables, notably 'adult interactions', recommending further such research with a 'general system theory' perspective. These investigations seem to be still at a very early stage, centred really on suggesting the potential of the dynamic systems perspective or chaos theory as a fruitful tool for research in human development and attainment.

The term 'chaos theory' seems to imply something frighteningly chaotic or completely random. However, the theory really implies that many natural phenomena do occur within wide ranging and dynamic systems, with a great deal of interconnectedness and causality between many aspects of the system. They are only apparently chaotic because the system is so complex. The weather is often given as an example of such a system. There is increasing understanding that small weather changes in one part of the world might have large knock-on effects in another part. The sheer complexity and variety of possible interconnections in such systems makes it difficult to control or to use as a model for prediction. Nonetheless, increasing acceptance that this is the way a system works does seem to lead to better ability to understand aspects of it and use it for prediction, though there is also a present acceptance that 'total prediction for many phenomena can never be achieved, no matter how precise are the measurement systems used' (Guess and Sailor, 1993, p. 17).

Guess and Sailor see the use of chaos theory as providing a 'dynamic, macroanalytic approach to understanding interactive components of complex systems' (p. 16). They document the increasing interest of researchers in the behavioural and social sciences in chaos theory. Fogel and Thelan (1987) used a 'dynamic systems perspective' to provide a rationale for the development of the expressive and communicative actions of infants during the first year. They thus interpreted the expressive and communicative actions as part of an organised, complex, co-operative system with other elements of the infant's physiology, behaviour and social environment:

> Although this complexity and nonlinearity confounds experimental analysis and makes simple interactive models untenable, in real systems, it is the source of both stability and change. (Fogel and Thelan, 1987, p. 747)

Fogel and Thelan here are particularly highlighting the system which embraces connections between communicative developments and all other developments, with no sense of discreteness between any of them. However, we can also visualise the nature of communication learning as a dynamic system of its own, with a high degree of complex interconnectedness between the behaviour of the infant/student, the behaviour of the parent/teacher, the attainments of the infant, the behaviour of the infant, the behaviour of the parent/teacher and so on. This system operates over time in terms of the general cumulative nature of the processes of communication learning, but it is also identifiable as a complex system moment-by-moment within interactions. Hodapp (1988) offers a criticism of interactional and transactional models which over-emphasise behaviours:

> Much of this [transactional] research can only be described as a ping pong game. The child does A, the mother responds by doing B; the child does C, the mother responds by doing D. (Hoddap, 1988, p. 36)

Hodapp argues that the back-and-forth quality of interactions should not be over-simplified; it can become complicated by non-behavioural influences, by external pressures and internal emotions. He reminds us of the role of 'intersubjectivity' – the emotional and intellectual understanding of each other within the interactions.

We are attracted to a more complex dynamic model because it helps us to conceptualise aspects of working with Intensive Interaction. It helps us to visualise the rolling cumulative process of interactive experiences provided to the learner as a dynamic system in its own right. It thus helps us to visualise the increasing interconnectedness between these attainments and developments in other domains – expressed as the Intensive Interaction terms, 'spillover' and 'interactivity'. Having a model of such a dynamic system also reminds us to look harder for the interconnectedness with other attainments. There is a danger, of course, for us particularly, that our relentless interest in and focus on early communication attainments might prevent us from seeing the possibility of other concurrent developments for the learner – which might arise in part because of the communication experiences being provided.

We can then also better accept the sometimes enigmatic nature of the teaching act in Intensive Interaction. Our experiences and our work with other practitioners have led us to recognise that it is possible to be rationally, tactically aware of a seeming causal relationship between certain teacher behaviours and certain learner behaviours and attainments. Analysis of video of interactive episodes frequently leads to identification of examples of good tactical behaviour by the teacher. The major benefit of this for the teacher may well be to re-introduce such a behaviour into the process of interacting during the next session. On the other hand, it is also the case that learner attainments or exciting, profitable-seeming moments during interactions arise without an identifiable causal link to anything which was taking place in an interaction. An example of this is a young man whose visual disability was such that there was no real expectation that he would make eye contact; the teachers put much effort into identifying and responding to other body language signals from him. He nonetheless did start using eye contact, seemingly without overt efforts to promote it within the process of interacting, and the teachers were left without a rationale for why he had adopted this skill, other than that the process had caused him to find motivation. To put this briefly, it is as well to accept that we cannot fully understand all the workings of what we do in using Intensive Interaction teaching. The causal links between what the teacher does and the attainments of the learner may not be obvious nor predictable moment-by-moment. Visualising it as a highly complex dynamic system helps us to feel comfortable with this state of affairs.

A dynamic system perspective also helps us to understand the difference between teaching that is behaviourally orientated and that which is by process. It provides a potential theoretical backdrop for understanding why communication cannot be learnt through task analysis, and for accepting that it is learnt in a process which may not lend itself to being fully understood or having all aspects identified and rationalised. The danger with behavioural approaches is that the teacher behaviour is so organised and controlled that it is unlikely that the 'untidy', flexible

291

teacher behaviour necessary to a dynamic system approach will be present in the situation. We can nonetheless think about and look for a resolution to the differences between these two approaches to teaching, and one way is to search for better understandings of what is meant by 'structure' in learning situations. Firstly, however, it may be helpful to summarise our thinking on the potential for application of dynamic systems theory in communication learning:

- We can start knowingly to use teaching approaches which are identifiably dynamic systems, related to a new but growing theory on complex phenomena.
- We can be comforted by knowing that when we use such systems we may not achieve full predictability or control of the learning, but that learning takes place because of it.
- Knowingly activating the system, even without full knowledge of it, is a form of controlling it.
- Knowing that we are using such a system opens us up to strive for more understandings of the working of it.
- Knowingly using dynamic systems theory should enhance the occurrence of imaginative innovation in the teaching of communication.
- Dynamic systems may help us to conceptualise the bridge between communication developments and other developments.
- Dynamic systems help us to feel comfortable in formulating approaches to structuring activities which are not reliant on controlling and directing them.
- Knowing application of dynamic systems theory helps us properly to face up to how much we do not yet know.

Intensive Interaction sessions – unstructured activities?

One of the comments made to us from time to time is that Intensive Interaction sessions are unstructured or less structured by comparison to other experiences provided, particularly in schools. We understand the gist of what is being said here, but we would also suggest that such beliefs arise from a rather limited view of what constitutes structure in learning activities. Bluntly, there has been a tendency to equate structure with teacher directiveness and control of activities. Controlling or organising the activity so that the learner performs within given boundaries only, using teacher-predicted behaviours, is one way of structuring activities. This might well be a good procedure for certain types of learning. However, as we have suggested in the previous sections, the danger is that such practices will also limit the possible learning, especially when that kind of structuring is imposed on learning which cannot be carried out within such a structure.

The Penguin Dictionary of Psychology (Reber, 1985) gives us some helpful definitions of structure, and the several hundred words offered on structure actually don't contain the word 'control'. Here is a definition which should be usable for all of us in our work:

> Generally, the term is used whenever one wishes to convey the notion that the entity being characterized, taken as a whole, has intrinsic organization and that this organization is, in fact, one of its most salient aspects. (p. 739)

We would argue that Intensive Interaction activities conform to this definition, are highly structured, but that they have a structure which is different from structures which rely on teacher control or precise step-by-step organisation of what will happen. We suggest that what we are really looking for when we provide any type of activity is that the activity has a structure, a framework which can be identified both by the teacher and by the learner, which will provide a continuously available set of reference points to guide the activity of both. This may be especially important for people at the earlier stages of learning, who are still developing the most basic sense of structure for their own behaviour, and for people with autism, who have a great struggle to find structure in their lives. A set of sequential instructions might provide this framework, but there are other ways of constructing identifiable frameworks.

Intensive Interaction activities are structured in the first place by the behaviour of the participants. At the very earliest stages the structure is mostly provided by the organised behaviour of the teacher, which conforms to a set of principles. The principles for teacher behaviour in Intensive Interaction sessions have been set out in detail (e.g. Nind and Hewett, 1994). The principles do ask for, demand, a sense of flexible behaviour from the teacher within a sense of 'artistry' (Eisner, 1985) even – but within the workings of the principles. One of the aims of the process of providing the activities is that the sense of structuring provided by organised behaviour is increasingly shared with the learner. In early communication activities, the structure given by the adult behaviour also contains the knowledge elements of the learning – things like taking turns, making eye contacts and so on. Ultimately the aim is that this knowledge about communicating and relating, which goes with the structure provided by the participants' behaviour, is totally transferred to the learner. We have already referred to Bruner's (1983) concept of 'scaffolding' in early learning. This gives us the vivid image of the adult/teacher constructing a scaffold for the learner around the activities, then gradually dismantling the scaffold as the learning is seen to be taking place and the responsibility for it is increasingly shared with the learner. A scaffold is an organised framework, usually built so that something can be constructed within it.

Perhaps here we are also making some comments about what constitutes the nature of teacher control. Once underway, successful Intensive Interaction sequences are highly controlled by the structure which supports them. When an activity ceases to be controlled in this way it is the end of the activity. Thus there is a big element of teacher 'control' since the teacher in the early stages has the major responsibility for providing the structure and the knowledge elements. The more the activities are successful, the more they are controlled by and referenced to the structure. We must remember too, though, that one of the knowledge elements for the learner, and an increasingly obvious aspect of the structure, is that the learner leads the activity with the teacher responding.

The general point we are arguing towards here is that in planning activities in, for example, special schools, we lack a vocabulary of structure. We lack the ability to define what we mean a structure to be, to understand fully the purpose it will serve. We therefore lack the vocabulary to differentiate between and select from a range of various structures which will best serve different types of learning. We need the technical know-how which goes with thinking 'this person needs to learn "x", the teaching technique should probably be "y" and I will structure it by using "z"'. To illustrate further, we have mentioned two approaches to structuring activities. One could be called 'teacher directed', the other, 'teacher scaffolded'. The structures, thus named, also have implicit within them some concepts about what teacher technique will be within the named structures. These are just two examples offered as engines for further thought rather than as our definitive conceptualisations.

Conclusion

In *Access to Communication* we shared our thinking about Intensive Interaction, its rationale, its development and its potential, and we ended with a series of illustrative case studies. In this book the illustrative case studies have been our starting point. In transactional terms, our using, thinking and writing about Intensive Interaction led to others using, thinking and writing about Intensive Interaction, which has in turn furthered our own thinking. In terms of a dynamic systems perspective there have, of course, been all kinds of other more complex interactions and spin-offs in this process. In the commentaries we have engaged directly with the contributions the authors make to our practical and theoretical understanding of the interactive process. In this final chapter we have attempted to bring some coherence to a range of ideas inevitably influenced by the fruitful collaboration we have enjoyed with these and many other practitioners of Intensive Interaction. We very much welcome dialogue on these ideas .

References

Brown, H. (1994) '"An ordinary life?": a review of the normalisation principle as it applies to the sexual options of people with learning difficulties', *Disability and Society*, **9**, 123–44.

Bruner, J. (1983) *Child's Talk: Learning to Use Language*. New York: Oxford University Press.

Byers, R. and Rose, R. (1996) *Planning the Curriculum for Pupils with Special Educational Needs: A Practical Guide*. London: David Fulton.

Chappell, A.L. (1992) 'Towards a sociological critique of the normalisation principle', *Disability, Handicap & Society*, **7**, 1, 35–50.

Collis, M. and Lacey, P. (1996) *Interactive Approaches to Teaching: A Framework for INSET*. London: David Fulton.

Corbett, J. (1991) 'So, who wants to be normal?' *Disability, Handicap & Society*, **6**, 3, 259–260.

Eisner, E.W. (1985, 2nd edition) *The Educational Imagination on the Design and Evaluation of School Programs*. New York: Macmillan.

Emerson, G. (1992) 'What is normalization?'. In: Brown, H. and Smith, H. (eds) *Normalization: A reader for the nineties*. London: Tavistock/Routledge.

Ephraim, G.W.E. (1979) Developmental Process in Mental Handicap: A Generative Structure Approach. Unpublished Ph.D Thesis. Uxbridge: Brunel University Department of Psychology.

Fogel, A. and Thelan, E. (1987) 'Development of Early Expressive and Communicative Action: Re-Interpreting the Evidence from a Dynamic Systems Perspective', *Development Psychology*, **23** (6), 747–761.

Gleick, J. (1987) *Chaos: Making a New Science*. London: Sphere.

Guess, D. and Sailor, W. (1993) 'Chaos theory and the study of human behaviour: Implications for special education and developmental disabilities', *The Journal of Special Education*, **27**, 1, 16–34.

Guess, D., Siegel-Causey, E., Ault, M., Guy, B. and Thompson, B. (1993) 'Analysis of behaviour state conditions and associated environmental variables among students with profound handicaps', *American Journal on Mental Retardation*, **97** (6), 634–653.

Guess, D. and Siegel-Causey, E. (1995) 'Attractor dimensions of behaviour state changes among individuals with profound disabilies', *American Journal on Mental Retardation*, **99** (6), 642–663.

Guess, D., Roberts, S., Siegel-Causey, E. and Rues, J. (1995) 'Replication and extended analysis of behaviour state, environmental events, and related variables among individuals with profound disabilities', *American Journal on Mental Retardation*, **100** (1), 36–51.

Hodapp, R.M. (1988) 'The role of maternal emotions and perceptions in interactions with young handicapped children'. In: Marfo, K. (ed.) *Parent-Child Interaction and Developmental Disabilities: Theory, Research and Intervention*. New York: Praeger.

NCC (1993) *Special Needs and the National Curriculum: Opportunity and Challenge*. York: NCC.

Nind, M. and Hewett, D. (1994) *Access to Communication: Developing the Basics of Communication with People with Severe Learning Difficulties Through Intensive Interaction*. London: David Fulton.

Reber, A. (1985) *The Penguin Dictionary of Psychology*. Harmondsworth: Penguin.

SCAA (1996) *Planning the Curriculum for Pupils with Profound and Multiple Learning Difficulties*. London: SCAA.

Sebba, J., Byers, R. and Rose, R. (1993) *Redefining the Whole Curriculum for Pupils with Learning Difficulites*. London: David Fulton.

Ware, J. (1996) *Creating a Responsive Environment: For People with Profound and Multiple Learning Difficulties*. London: David Fulton.

Wolfensburger, W. (1983) 'Social role valorization: a proposed new term for the principle of normalization', *Mental Retardation*, **21**, 234–9.

Wolff, P.H. (1959) 'Observations on newborn infants'. In: Stone, L.J., Smith, H.T. and Murphy, L.B. (eds) *The Competent Infant*. New York: Basic Books.

Author Index

Subject Index

accessing 2, 30, 42–3, 44, 47, 49, 90–2, 111, 126–9, 131, 153–4, 161, 171, 191–3, 217–18
accountability of staff 6, 74, 141, 174, 263, 278, 282–3
adult learners vi, 25, 46–63, 58, 61, 82, 103–144, 279
age appropriateness 4, 6, 57, 72, 74, 118, 121, 122, 124, 127, 130, 137–8, 142, 150, 152, 169, 177–80, 218
aggression 30, 43, 47, 194
alone (preference for being) 30, 43, 46, 114, 130, 134, 194, 213, 217, 264
assessment 10, 15–16, 26–7, 29, 39, 46, 93–97, 138, 143, 188, 240–41, 283, 284, 285
atmosphere 54, 58, 60, 106, 157, 159, 170, 174, 196, 199, 272, 287
autism vii, 46, 111–12, 130–38, 152, 169, 186–208, 209–226, 232–3, 237, 257–93
availability 259, 261

baseline 26–7, 29, 96, 162
behaviour modification 29, 32–3, 221
behavioural approaches 6, 13, 19, 29, 32–5, 84, 87, 121, 140, 143, 150, 175–7,221, 264, 266, 282–4, 291–2
blind learners 37, 43, 129–30
body language 2, 28, 31, 32, 40, 51, 69, 131, 190, 248, 254

burst-pause 2, 77, 78, 80, 244

caregiver–infant interaction 1, 3, 4, 16, 18, 28, 31, 37, 42, 180, 261–6, 268–71, 286
cause and effect 51, 60, 68, 89, 285
challenging behaviour 25, 33, 37, 44, 46–7, 49, 59, 61, 65–6, 67, 116, 120, 124, 154, 177, 183, 186, 194, 208, 225
cognitive development 12, 60, 90–94, 180, 198, 243–4, 285
collaboration vii, 8, 62, 119
college environments vi, 46, 48, 57, 61, 62–3
combining approaches 6, 13, 15, 19, 33, 154, 175, 263, 265, 266
commentary 192, 216
communication audit 27–9, 39, 108, 115
communication development vii, 1, 3, 12, 13, 17, 18, 19, 28, 31, 37, 43, 57, 60, 65–6, 67, 82–3, 116, 120, 124, 154, 177, 183, 189–90, 193, 197–203, 234–6, 261, 266, 276–80, 283, 284, 290, 291
communicative competence 3, 9, 11, 16, 27–9, 62, 108, 258, 284
community living/participation 119–25, 138, 279
contingent environments 11, 14, 19,

300